Rematerializing Shakespeare

Also by the editors

Bryan Reynolds

TRANSVERSAL ENTERPRISES IN THE DRAMA OF SHAKESPEARE AND HIS CONTEMPORARIES: Fugitive Explorations (London: Palgrave Macmillan, forthcoming)

PERFORMING TRANSVERSALLY: Reimagining Shakespeare and the Critical Future (New York: Palgrave Macmillan, 2003)

BECOMING CRIMINAL: Transversal Performance and Cultural Dissidence in Early Modern England (Baltimore: John Hopkins University Press, 2002)

SHAKESPEARE WITHOUT CLASS: Misappropriations of Cultural Capital, *co-editor with Donald Hedrick* (New York: Palgrave Macmillan, 2000)

William N. West

THEATRES AND ENCYCLOPEDIAS IN EARLY MODERN EUROPE (Cambridge University Press, 2002)

Rematerializing Shakespeare

Authority and Representation on the Early Modern English Stage

Edited by

Bryan Reynolds

&

William N. West

Introduction, editorial matter and selection
© Bryan Reynolds & William N. West
All chapters © Palgrave Macmillan 2005

All rights reserved. No reproduction, copy or transmission of this publication may be made without written permission.

No paragraph of this publication may be reproduced, copied or transmitted save with written permission or in accordance with the provisions of the Copyright, Designs and Patents Act 1988, or under the terms of any licence permitting limited copying issued by the Copyright Licensing Agency, 90 Tottenham Court Road, London W1T 4LP.

Any person who does any unauthorised act in relation to this publication may be liable to criminal prosecution and civil claims for damages.

The authors have asserted their rights to be identified as the authors of this work in accordance with the Copyright, Designs and Patents Act 1988.

First published in 2005 by
PALGRAVE MACMILLAN
Houndmills, Basingstoke, Hampshire RG21 6XS and
175 Fifth Avenue, New York, N.Y. 10010
Companies and representatives throughout the world.

PALGRAVE MACMILLAN is the global academic imprint of the Palgrave Macmillan division of St. Martin's Press, LLC and of Palgrave Macmillan Ltd. Macmillan® is a registered trademark in the United States, United Kingdom and other countries. Palgrave is a registered trademark in the European Union and other countries.

ISBN-13: 978–1–4039–9120–1 hardback
ISBN-10: 1–4039–9120–0 hardback

This book is printed on paper suitable for recycling and made from fully managed and sustained forest sources.

A catalogue record for this book is available from the British Library.

Library of Congress Cataloging-in-Publication Data

    Rematerializing Shakespeare : authority and representation on the early modern English stage / edited by Bryan Reynolds and William N. West.
      p. cm.
    Includes bibliographical references and index.
    ISBN 1–4039–9120–0 (cloth)
      1. Shakespeare, William, 1564–1616 – Stage history – To 1625.
2. Shakespeare, William, 1564–1616 – Stage history – England. 3. Theater – England – History – 16th century. 4. Theater – England – History – 17th century. 5. Theater audiences in literature. I. Reynolds, Bryan (Bryan Randolph). II. West, William N.

PR3095.R46 2005
822.3'3—dc22   2005049195

10 9 8 7 6 5 4 3 2 1
14 13 12 11 10 09 08 07 06 05

Printed and bound in Great Britain by
Antony Rowe Ltd, Chippenham and Eastbourne

For
Robert Weimann

*Because of your courageous example,
your manifold inspiration,
and your well-deserved authority*

Thank you

Contents

List of Illustrations ix

Acknowledgments x

Notes on Contributors xi

Introduction
Shakespearean Emergences: Back from Materialisms to
Transversalisms and Beyond 1
Bryan Reynolds & William N. West

**Part I The Form and Pressure of the Time: Popular
and Unpopular Traditions** 17

1 'Strike All that Look Upon With Marvel': Theatrical and
   Theological Wonder in *The Winter's Tale* 19
   Huston Diehl

2 Performance and Urban Space in Shakespeare's Rome,
   or 'S.P.Q.L.' 35
   D. J. Hopkins

3 Shakespeare's Little Boys: Theatrical Apprenticeship and the
   Construction of Childhood 53
   Catherine Belsey

**Part II What's the Matter? Revisions and
Reversions in Pen and Voice** 73

4 Rematerializing Shakespeare's Intertheatricality:
   The Occidental/Oriental Halimpsest 75
   Jonathan Gil Harris

5 The Politics of Shakespeare's Prose 95
   Douglas Bruster

6 Mercutio's Bad Language 115
   William N. West

7 Nanti Everything 130
   Terence Hawkes

| 8 | Authority and the Early Modern Theatre: Representing Robert Weimann
John Drakakis | 139 |

Part III Creatures Sitting at a Play: The Authority and Representation of Audiences — 159

9	*Homo Clausus* at the Theatre *David Hillman*	161
10	Figuring the Consumer for Early Modern Drama *Kathleen McLuskie*	186
11	The Delusion of Critique: Subjunctive Space, Transversality, and the Conceit of Deceit in *Hamlet* *Anthony Kubiak & Bryan Reynolds*	207

Index — 226

List of Illustrations

1	Sanders Portrait. Digital Image © Art Gallery of Ontario.	2
2	Kevin Chadwick, 'Shakespeare Dude,' used by the World Shakespeare Congress, the Shakespeare Association of America, and the Folger Shakespeare Library. Reproduced by permission of Chadwick Design Inc.	3
3	'Tattoo Bill,' by Mathew McFarren. Poster from The Colorado Shakespeare Festival, 2003. Reproduced by courtesy of The Colorado Shakespeare Festival and Mathew McFarren.	4
4	'Flying Will,' by Mathew McFarren. Poster from The Colorado Shakespeare Festival, 2005. Reproduced by courtesy of The Colorado Shakespeare Festival and Mathew McFarren.	5
5	Jacket design by Julia Kushnirsky, with 'Shakespeare Dude' image by Kevin Chadwick for Bryan Reynolds, *Performing Transversally: Reimagining Shakespeare and the Critical Future* (New York: Palgrave Macmillan, 2003). Reproduced by permission of Palgrave Macmillan and Chadwick Design Inc.	14
6	Tomb of Jane, Lady Waller, 1630s, Bath Abbey (detail). Photo by Andrew Belsey.	64
7	Marcus Gheeraerts, Barbara, Lady Sidney and her Children, 1596. Reproduced by kind permission of Viscount De L'Isle, from his private collection at Penshurst Place.	65

Acknowledgments

Along with this book's dedicatee, Maja Weimann is an inspiration for her generosity, kindness, and wisdom.

Bryan Reynolds is grateful to Peter Eversmann, Amy Cook, Glenn Odom, Janna Segal, and especially Allison Crilly for their valuable feedback on his and Anthony Kubiak's contribution to this book. He is also happy to have been pampered along by Greg Ungar, Thomas Augst, Cipriana Petre, Ayanna Thompson, Henry Turner, Jonathan Gil Harris, Janelle Reinelt, Robert Cohen, and Cameron Harvey when trying to contend with way too many commitments. He was fortunate to be doing some pampering himself, since it was during the process of putting this book together that his lovely daughter Sky joined him and his wife Kris in this wacky world. It is Kris that makes it all so wonderful.

Will West also thanks his colleagues in early modern studies at the University of Colorado, Chris Braider, Katherine Eggert, and Valerie Forman, honorary Renaissance guy Mark Winokur for keeping the intellectual pressure, and administrative heroes Katherine Eggert (again), John Stevenson, and Doug Burger for taking the committee pressure off. But above all Will is grateful to Amy Ebert, who arrived almost at the beginning of this book and has stayed on despite late nights until its end.

Reynolds and West are both grateful to Mell McDonnell and Dick Devin of The Colorado Shakespeare Festival, who generously allowed us to use their posters. They are grateful to Allison Crilly for her tireless editorial wherewithal and persevering laughter. Finally, they would like to thank Paula Kennedy, their editor, and Helen Craine, Paula's assistant, for their unrelenting enthusiasm for this project and for their hard work in bringing it to fruition.

Notes on Contributors

Catherine Belsey is Professor of English and Chair of the Centre for Critical and Cultural Theory at Cardiff University, Wales. She is the author of *Critical Practice* (1980), *The Subject of Tragedy: Identity and Difference in Renaissance Drama* (1985), *Desire: Love Stories in Western Civilization* (1994) and *Shakespeare and the Loss of Eden* (1999).

Douglas Bruster teaches Renaissance literature, film, and modern drama at the University of Texas at Austin. He is the author of *Drama and the Market in the Age of Shakespeare* (1992), *Quoting Shakespeare: Form and Culture in Early Modern Drama* (2000), and most recently *Shakespeare and the Question of Culture: Early Modern Literature and the Cultural Turn* (2002).

Huston Diehl is Professor of English at the University of Iowa. Her most recent book is *Staging Reform, Reforming the Stage: Protestantism and Popular Theater in Early Modern England* (1997). She has published extensively on Shakespeare and Renaissance drama, Protestant art and aesthetics, and the English emblem book. She is currently writing a book on comedy and the reformation of early modern English culture.

John Drakakis is Professor of English Studies at the University of Stirling in Scotland. He is the editor of two editions of *Alternative Shakespeares* (1985, 2nd edn, 2002), of *Shakespearean Tragedy* (1992) and the Palgrave Macmillan New Casebook *Antony and Cleopatra*. He has written many articles on Shakespeare, Renaissance Drama, and critical theory, and is currently completing the Arden 3 edition of *The Merchant of Venice*.

Jonathan Gil Harris is Professor of English at The George Washington University, where he teaches Shakespeare and critical theory. He is the author of *Foreign Bodies and the Body Politic: Discourses of Social Pathology in Early Modern England* (1998), and *Sick Economies: Drama, Mercantilism and Disease in Shakespeare's England* (2004), as well as the co-editor (with Natasha Korda) of *Staged Properties in Early Modern English Drama*. He is currently at work on a new project, provisionally entitled *Unbecoming Shakespeare*.

Terence Hawkes is Emeritus Professor of English at Cardiff University. He is the author of a number of books on Shakespeare, including *That Shakespearian Rag* (1986), *Meaning by Shakespeare* (1992) and *Shakespeare in the Present* (2002). He is also General Editor of the *Accents on Shakespeare* series published by Routledge.

David Hillman is a Fellow of King's College Cambridge as well as a Lecturer in English at the University of Cambridge. He has trained as a child psychotherapist at the Tavistock. He is editor of Robert Weimann's *Authority and Representation in Early Modern Discourse* (1996) and co-editor (with Carla Mazzio) of *The Body in Parts: Fantasies of Corporeality in Early Modern Europe* (1997). He is completing a book entitled *Shakespeare's Entrails: Solitude, Scepticism, and the Interior of the Early Modern Body* and editing (with Adam Phillips) *The Book of Interruptions*.

D. J. Hopkins is Assistant professor at San Diego State University and before then was Mellon Post-Doctoral Fellow in Performing Arts and English at Washington University in St. Louis. His publications have appeared in *Modern Drama, Theatre Topics, Theatre Survey*, and in several collections including *Shakespeare After Mass Media*. Hopkins holds both a PhD and an MFA from the University of California, San Diego. His current book project theorizes the relationship between performance and representation in the urban spaces of postmedieval London.

Anthony Kubiak is Professor of Drama at the University of California, Irvine. He is the author of *Stages of Terror: Terrorism, Ideology, and Coercion as Theatre History* (1991) and *Agitated States: Performance in the American Theater of Cruelty* (2002). He has published articles in *Theatre Journal, TDR, Modern Drama, Performance Research*, and numerous other publications. He has contributed to numerous collections as well, including *Psychoanalysis and Performance* (2001), *Drama and the Classical Heritage* (1992), and *The World of Samuel Beckett* (1991).

Kathleen McLuskie is Director of the Shakespeare Institute in Startford-on-Avon. She is currently at work on a book to be entitled *Commercialization of Early Modern Theatre* and is the author of *Renaissance Dramatists* (1989) and *Shakespeare and Modern Theatre* (2001, with Michael Bristol). She has edited *Plays on Women* (1999) with David Bevington.

Bryan Reynolds is Professor and Head of Doctoral Studies in Drama at the University of California, Irvine. He is the author of *Transversal Enterprises in the Drama of Shakespeare and his Contemporaries: Fugitive Explorations* (Palgrave Macmillan, 2006), *Performing Transversally: Reimagining Shakespeare and the Critical Future* (Palgrave Macmillan, 2003), *Becoming Criminal: Transversal Performance and Cultural Dissidence in Early Modern England* (2002), and co-editor with Donald Hedrick of *Shakespeare Without Class: Misappropriations of Cultural Capital* (2000). Reynolds is also co-General Editor, with Elaine Aston, of a new book series in theatre and performance studies, *Performance Interventions*, from Palgrave Macmillan.

William N. West is Associate Professor of English at Northwestern University. He is the author of *Theatres and Encyclopedias in Early Modern Europe* (Cambridge University Press, 2003) and most recently of articles on early modern anatomy and poetry, significance in architecture, and on the groundlings in Shakespeare's theatre. He is writing a book called *Understanding and Confusion in the Elizabethan Theaters*.

Introduction
Shakespearean Emergences: Back from Materialisms to Transversalisms and Beyond

Bryan Reynolds & William N. West

In the last quarter-century, the study of Shakespeare has proliferated explosively and multifariously across disciplines, classes, cultures, and media. The Bard's plays now comprise most of the university and professional theater productions in the United States, and there have been over three hundred English-language film adaptations of them distributed worldwide, including one Academy-Award winning film about him, *Shakespeare in Love* (1998).[1] More books on Shakespeare are published than ever before, some becoming bestsellers, such as Harold Bloom's *Shakespeare: The Invention of the Human* (1999) and Stephen Greenblatt's *Will in the World: How Shakespeare Became Shakespeare* (2004). More students than ever before are enrolled in classes on Shakespeare. But what, or who, is this Shakespeare?

The recent fascination with the Sanders portrait, a painting that may be the only surviving likeness of Shakespeare done in his lifetime, reflects the mainstream interest in imagining Shakespeare the person as a cultural icon, while in comparison exploring his texts has become increasingly less important.[2] We reach the complexities and influences of his works, and they reach us, with greater difficulty – 'post-textually.' Most of the students who take Shakespeare in universities do so because they are required to for an English major, or as a token course in humanities, and they generally encounter only his best-known works and fewer by his contemporaries. So the subject of Shakespeare is in no danger, except of becoming an image or a motif that speaks for itself so fully that it stands in for culture like a snapshot.[3] One such snapshot of iconic Shakespeare is Kevin Chadwick's 'Shakespeare Dude,'[4] a large-format oil painting that has been used by such pillars of Shakespeare studies as the World Shakespeare Congress, the Shakespeare Association of America, and the Folger Shakespeare Library. For all its ostensible novelty, the Shakespeare Dude is assimilated to a concept of Shakespeare the person,

Illustration 1 Sanders Portrait. Digital Image © 2005 Art Gallery of Ontario.

another 'not-the-familiar Shakespeare' like the historically unfamiliar Shakespeare of the Sanders portrait, to which it is a counterpart. A postmodern joke bringing the iconic bald forehead and page-boy hair together with equally iconic SoCal coolness, this Dude invites interest but tells interpreters to fuck off.

Illustration 2 Kevin Chadwick, 'Shakespeare Dude,' used by the World Shakespeare Congress, the Shakespeare Association of America, and the Folger Shakespeare Library.

The Shakespeare Dude reflects the increasingly prevalent representation of Shakespeare as 'all image.' It is by no means alone in this. The Colorado Shakespeare Festival makes a practice of using incongruously contemporary Shakespeares by painter Mathew McFarren on its posters, the *New York Times* Book Review has featured various Shakespeares, from a vampire to a punk in Times Square, and Picasso remade Shakespeare in his signature styles as a cubist portrait and as a quick line drawing of bald head, beard, and hair. This interest in the immediacy and accessibility of the image mirrors a growing rift between popular conceptions of Shakespeare and the

Illustration 3 'Tattoo Bill,' by Mathew McFarren. Poster from The Colorado Shakespeare Festival, 2003.

Illustration 4 'Flying Will,' by Mathew McFarren. Poster from The Colorado Shakespeare Festival, 2005.

traditions of Shakespearean scholarship. But there are greater disjunctions within the academy, where Shakespeare criticism cleaves into a more varied assortment of approaches than ever before, including textual studies, print history, performance analysis, and historical, political, cultural, and/or ethical criticism. More importantly, where incommensurability is perceived, conversation among the varied disciplines and approaches becomes harder, leaving them looking (from the inside) a little too autonomous and (from the outside) a little too partial. In response, instead of an interdisciplinarity that tends to divide us into camps, we might start thinking of ways to forge both intradisciplinary and transdisciplinary studies of Shakespeare.

If there is a common thread in both popular and academic criticism of the final decades of the previous century and the first years of this one, it is a desire to find something real in Shakespeare, for Shakespeare to reflect reality, for a (or even *the*) real Shakespeare. In popular discourses, this real Shakespeare is usually personal, in love, in the world, inventing the human. For academics, the reality of Shakespeare might be visible in the original printed editions and their variants, the modes of performance with which those texts have been taken up, the cultures of events and objects within which those texts appear, or contemporary discourses on politics, education, and other fields that invoke Shakespeare's authority. This interest is historically specific as a symptom of capitalism's drive to instantiate social identities in material bases. When the ideologies associated with Ronald Reagan and Margaret Thatcher were seen as threats to liberal education, works like Robert Weimann's *Shakespeare and the Popular Tradition in Theater: Studies in the Social Dimension of Dramatic Form and Function* (1967; English translation 1978), Lisa Jardine's *Still Harping on Daughters: Women and Drama in the Age of Shakespeare* (1983), Jonathan Dollimore's *Radical Tragedy: Religion, Ideology, and Power in the Drama of Shakespeare and his Contemporaries* (1984), and Peter Stallybrass and Allon White's *The Politics and Poetics of Transgression* (1986) productively reintroduced the political and cultural vividness of ordinary life to the study of Shakespeare's plays. The cultural materialism of these works softened somewhat during the following years as criticism drifted away from focus on conflict within power structures and ideological frameworks to embrace more materialistic concerns and focus on sociohistorical details. The developing interest in particularity, defined as the irreducible uniqueness of material objects, can be seen in two important collections, *Subject and Object in Renaissance Culture* (eds Margreta de Grazia, Maureen Quilligan, and Peter Stallybrass, 1996) and *Staged Properties in Early Modern English Drama* (eds Jonathan Gil Harris and Natasha Korda, 2002). The Marxist aesthetics and ideology that defined the earlier scholarship transformed in the later scholarship so that whereas their ethos still emerges, albeit sometimes only between the lines, their outspokenly leftist concern with ideological structures through which things become significant has become less manifest.[5]

From our experience teaching criticism of both types to undergraduate and graduate students, the new emphasis on particularity seems to hold greater cogency for mindsets prevalent of today, which are more of the everything-is-genetically-encoded ('hard-wired') and less of the everything-is-socially-constructed varieties. This is not to say that students today are not aware of the beguiling powers of performance and representation, especially when mediated through electronic and digital technologies. They see, and parody, these all too clearly. Rather, it is precisely because of this growing awareness that they are more invested in the truth-telling qualities of objects – the nakedly observable and tangibly real – than they were during the 1980s to mid-1990s. (The prospect of United States presidents unreservedly lying to the public about both mundane and grave issues, from Bill Clinton's dubious relationship with Monica Lewinsky to George W. Bush's accounts of Saddam Hussein's nuclear weapons and links to Al Qaeda as justification for waging war on Iraq, may have also contributed to the amplified yearning for material substantiation.) The ever-increasing naturalization of human relations under capitalism and the assured positivism that attends it are at work here as well. But while materialist readings of Shakespeare can no longer claim in that regard to be resistant or even novel except in the matter that they investigate, it seems to us that they are undoubtedly on the rise.

The movements in Shakespeare criticism – perhaps, given the amorphous heterogeneity of the field, 'motion' would be a better term – and in the field of early modern English studies generally can be seen as ongoing gestures towards the remnants of an ever more detailed reality. The escalating localization of what counts as reality has promoted a corresponding parochialism and Balkanization of criticism, so that there no longer seems to be a way – though there may never have been a way – to relate things that scholars are finding in Shakespeare other than as and through what Bryan Reynolds and Donald Hedrick refer to as 'Shakespace': the specific 'articulatory space' that encompasses the multiple expressions, overlappings, and interconnections among all ideational-material formations of the Shakespeare industry (ideas, images, products, discourses), and the synchronic, diachronic, and even, as Jonathan Gil Harris suggests in his contribution to this anthology, 'anachronic' means by which these ideational-material formations palimpsestically move through places, cultures, and eras.[6] It is as if Shakespeare scholars have taken to heart Hamlet's protest, 'Seems, madam? Nay, it is. I know not "seems" ' (1.2.76), but have thereby inherited the problem of reality that plagues him throughout the play, as Anthony Kubiak and Bryan Reynolds discuss in their contribution to this anthology on the layers of deceit that play invents. If every way that Hamlet could conceivably manifest the truth of his grief is an action 'that a man might play' (1.2.84), for him there can be no encounter with the material that does not at the same time discredit its own truth: reality in one sense impeaches reality in another. For us, what is real in Shakespeare has proven as hard to grasp as Hamlet's elusive 'that within which passes show' (1.2.85) and for the same reasons. But the discovery of reality is not our goal, at least not of a reality that would speak for itself, as Hamlet and perhaps other readers of Shakespeare might want us to believe. Rather than remain committed to a totalizing reality, we believe that we are better served by pursuing the particularities of its mediations.

Within and passing through Shakespace are such mediations, notions of life, history, and culture as monolithic, deterministic, finite, or as unlimited, dialectical, flexible, plural, and so on. Guided by these notions, also within and passing through Shakespace, are various representations of Shakespeare by audiences, theater-makers, and critics from early modern England to today. Of these, the critics have given the most detailed attention to the conditions of production of the texts we read, to the theaters that staged them, and, often self-referentially, to the history of scholarship on them. For over thirty-five years, Robert Weimann has been a key proponent of these kinds of contextualization; a statement he made then in his groundbreaking work, *Shakespeare and the Popular Tradition in the Theater* (1967/1978), captures the reasoning behind the movement to simultaneously historicize points of inception and reception across time and space: 'We are all – the great dramatists of the past, the contemporary producers and critics, and ours – characters in history; our own points of reference are, like those of our predecessors, the results of history. In this, our present values emerge from the same historical process that is reflected in and accelerated by Shakespeare's contribution' (xiv). However, the reality of Shakespeare studies, then and now, is neither necessarily nor universally grounded in ideas of recovering histories, cultures, and meanings. As Terence Hawkes does in 'Nanti Everything,' his contribution to this anthology, scholars also engage with and learn from parodies and 'misappropriations,' with iconoclastic productions of Shakespeare from the 1960s BBC Radio program 'Round the Horne,' to Bertolt Brecht, to Robert Wilson, to Troma Films, to Richard Curtis's *The Skinhead Hamlet*. Typically, such works, and such criticism, both reaffirm and exploit the historical authority of the early modern stage. But they also provide the opportunity for scholars to reconsider the discourses that take Shakespeare as central for a diverse range of purposes.[7] We want to encourage the increasing 'investigative-expansiveness' of the field that has produced so much diverse and inspiring scholarship, pedagogy, and art.[8] And this means attentiveness to as many modes in which Shakespeare matters as possible. The actual and imaginary, inside and outside of Shakespace, are only important to us insofar as they are experienced and articulated by people.

The contributors to *Rematerializing Shakespeare: Authority and Representation on the Early Modern English Stage* examine many of the deductions and assertions made by critics who have tried to understand Shakespeare through information and ideas about the world in which he lived. Rather than offering a single theoretical stance on any of the various styles and expressions of critical materialism (Marxism, cultural materialism, new historicism, gender studies, performance criticism, transversal poetics), *Rematerializing Shakespeare* brings together twelve Shakespeare scholars to address the problem of Shakespearean materiality and its appearances in criticism, and attempts an ambidextrous criticism that offers detailed local readings of the particular instances of Shakespearean and related texts while simultaneously stepping back to survey the field and interrogate its procedures and assumptions. These instances – individual, irreproducible, yet joined together in the ambiguous currents of Shakespace – are what we call 'rematerializations.'

To rematerialize in the sense of *Rematerializing Shakespeare* is not to recover a lost material infrastructure, as Marx spoke of, nor is it to restore to some material existence its priority over the imaginary. Indeed, as the essays in this anthology variously demonstrate, the material is incomplete without the supplements of the imagination, the intended, and the desired. In only one example of how the semiotic exceeds the material, Catherine Belsey shows how in Shakespeare's theater discourses and conventions combined with mimesis and physical characteristics to render the early modern actor's body as that of a 'boy' onstage. Physical age was neither necessary nor sufficient to present a child; instead, the actor's body was rematerialized as a child's through a combination of strategies. Nothing material merely returns in the rematerializations analyzed and practiced in this anthology, unless it is a return in the sense of the repressed, which, when it comes back, comes back as something else. What is rematerialized through the essays generates, among other things, fresh readings and histories, products that may gesture toward causes, narratives, and materiality that are absent, but that also initiate new procedures as they interrogate, revive, and transform older ones in new environments.

In his 1996 book, *Authority and Representation in Early Modern Discourse*, Weimann notes with concern: 'As the distance between then [early modern England] and now increases, there emerges an ever widening gap between what these texts say and what actually, as we decipher them, they can be made to mean' (7). Against the representation of the material properties of Shakespeare's theater as self-presenting, the essays in this anthology offer that materialism as part of their own critical performance. Moreover, inasmuch as what Weimann refers to as a conflict between 'the authority of signs versus the signs of authority' (*Authority* 6) stubbornly remains across changes in horizons of expectation in various histories and cultures and subjective and official territories, we can only ever interpret, not resolve. Yet, as Huston Diehl suggests in her essay on Protestant rematerializations of the Catholic privileging of wonder, or as D.J. Hopkins does in his recovery of the imaginary *Senatus Populusque Londinensis*, the continuity of various forms of conflict ensures that the new addresses the old, the old continues to speak back to the new, and that there is always the opportunity to manufacture new material out of old. *Rematerializing Shakespeare* acknowledges and comprehends material as that which stands out or can be presented as real, evanescent, imaginary, contrafactual, and/or projective. Separately and together, the essays in this anthology seek to exemplify Shakespeare criticism that is simultaneously expansive and affective in relation to the possible future as well as a result of the materialist lenses through which they treat the present in light of the past and vice versa. With essays from several materialist perspectives, *Rematerializing Shakespeare* reaches outside of established critical discourses, sometimes fugitively, to give a varied account of related concerns and it understands the process of criticism as rematerialization.

When scholars analyze the elements of history in the interest of constructing a narrative by which to make sense of them, they rematerialize those elements. The elements transform into something other than what they were. The same goes for literary-cultural criticism. The critic rematerializes elements from a given text or set of texts, thereby authoring a new materialization, an object that is, in turn, subject to subsequent critique, engagement, representation, which is to say, to further rematerializations. Weimann describes how authority typically operates in this process: 'Representing the words and actions of another presupposes an arrangement in which "the actor acteth by authority": in other words, the business of delegation and authorization, in this particular economic and judicial frame of reified relations and references, constitutes the act of representation itself' (*Authority* 12). Building on this concept of representation as performance, we want to emphasize that as the words of one writer become the words of another, in the process the secondary voice also becomes a medium, and not just a presenter or adapter, of the words of the first. An intersubjective experience occurs, even if it is not acknowledged, anticipated, or recognized. In effect, to use the language of transversal poetics, 'becomings' and 'comings-to-be' of the writers transpire interactively, although to varying degrees, even if evidence for these identity negotiations can only be found textually or discursively; that is, if they can only be tracked in material form, as the objectified expressions of humans. To rematerialize, then, is to negotiate the active, willful processes of becomings and the passive, unintentional processes of comings-to-be of the ideational-material formations in question in relation to the governing attributes of the medium or the media through which they journey. The media could be a composite of the discursive characteristics of an articulatory space, like Shakespace, and/or idiosyncratically or officially informed by 'sociopolitical conductors,' such as individual authors and, by extension, familial, religious, educational, juridical, and ruling structures.[9]

In their new book, *Prologues to Shakespeare's Theatre: Performance and Liminality in Early Modern Drama* (2005), Douglas Bruster and Robert Weimann describe prologues in terms that reflect our understanding of sociopolitical conductors: 'They [prologues] thus helped conduct theatre-goers over the threshold of a fictional world that allowed new perspectives on a host of issues relating to these centres of power and their affect on playgoers' lives' (44). Bruster and Weimann rematerialize prologues of early modern English drama not only as dynamic participants in the framing of a particular performance, but also as transmitters and orchestrators of ideas and people, and as Kate McLuskie demonstrates in her contribution to this anthology, the identities of theater audiences took shape through the result of dialectical pressures exerted in part in the prologues. Bruster and Weimann's rematerialization of prologues endows them with a new value, opening new areas of relevance to the study and teaching of early modern English literature and culture. To rematerialize is to translate – to make stuff over, as qualitatively better, more valuable, more alarming, more present for a certain audience, although always conditionally. Places of knowledge, reception, and experience of the rematerialization are the vantage points from which value and coherence can be most effectively imbued, where the power to impact is strongest, depending on the stability of the places relative to the interpretive communities and official territories in which they operate and to which they are beholden.

An intervention like Bruster and Weimann's into any environment or system refreshes its existing parameters, tenets, structures. Such a challenge is also what we attempt here into the motion of Shakespace. Adapting the notion of emergent properties from physics, biology, and philosophy of science to make its qualities of dynamism and collectivity explicit,[10] we have coined the term 'emergent activity' to describe this kind of critical enterprise. Here, we are also recalling Raymond Williams's definition of 'emergent culture' as 'new meanings and values, new practices, new relationships' (123), and 'as distinct from both the dominant and the residual,' and 'never only a matter of immediate practice; indeed it depends crucially on finding new forms or adaptations of form' (126). Although interventions, like emergent activities, can be the result of either unconscious or intentional occurrences, or both, for an intervention to qualify as emergent activity, it must be expressed as novel or irreducible with respect to significant characteristics of the preexisting system. As Williams points out, a characteristic of an emergent culture is its resistance to articulation, because the operations of naming and identifying something tends to fix its structures of feeling into more codified and inflexible forms. The essays in this anthology, we think, likewise, resist both categorization and calculation. But while they do not seek to define the nature of the criticism that is underway, they can nonetheless serve, like twigs in its stream, as markers of its flows. The contributors to this anthology constitute an 'emergent community,' a group formed around an organizing principle in the interest of achieving 'affective presence' within an extant network or discourse, that is, to become a combined material, conceptual, and symbolic force with measurable importance.[11] In this case, affective presence is produced through rematerializations within Shakespace. Whereas this is a tall order for any body of academic work, much less a single essay, we believe that the essays in this anthology, taken together as an amalgamated rematerialization of existing knowledge-bases and methodologies, make a powerful effort.

To conceive of authority and representation as multifold, multivocal, and processual, we want to adapt Weimann's historically specific 'bifold' concept of 'author's pen and actor's voice,' brilliantly developed in his book by that name (2000), and complexly demonstrated by David Hillman's contribution to this anthology, into the phrase, 'playtexts in history, critics' pens, and so on,' as a way of applying Weimann's model investigative-expansively across Shakespace. In conjunction with 'bifold authority,' Weimann uses the concept of 'doubleness' to address the issue that, 'In the Elizabethan theatre, the imaginary play-world and the material world of Elizabethan playing constitute different, although of course partially overlapping registers of perception, enjoyment, and involvement,' and to discuss 'the sites of conjunction, interplay, and duplication where "in one line two crafts directly meet" [*Hamlet* 3.4.210]' (*Author's Pen* 10). When this doubleness 'assumes contestatory forms, that is, a deliberate, performance-inspired use of cultural disparity in question,' he applies the concept of 'contrariety,' which he specifically defines as: 'not simply the existence on sixteenth-century stages of cultural disparity, but the ways and means by which this disparity could stimulate some "contrary" impulse to playing, a "contrarious" impetus in the production and reception of the plays' (10; 79). Although Weimann's understanding of 'contrariety' is purposefully applied to the subject matter of his investigation, we would like to briefly critique this concept as a means by which to move beyond the interfaces of 'author's pen and actor's voice' in early modern England to further elucidate the enterprise of rematerialization in critical discourse.

There is a magical quality to rematerializing, just as there is to theater, as if a wizard were at work, waving his wand over an object, like a play-text, thereby transforming it into something else. But this wizardry exceeds the immediate act of transubstantiation, superseding in the process the tautology-inspiring open-ended ceaselessness of contrariety, what Derrida calls *différance*, that emerges for those who subscribe, as Weimann does, 'to the Saussurean maxim that difference is a condition of meaning; in other words, theatrical signs – verbal, corporeal, and props – signify only in relation to, and as distinct from, other signs' (13).[12] What we are getting at here, alternatively, is the underlying idea that definition *can* occur without negation, and without a metaphysical *deus ex machina*, through rematerialization. For instance, one need not comprehend either desire or subjectivity as predicated on lack. Gilles Deleuze and Félix Guattari argue, rematerializing arguments from David Hume, G.W.F. Hegel, Ralph Waldo Emerson, Friedrich Nietzsche, and others, one can simply desire any number of objects or experiences, including desire itself. Subjectivity can be defined through and as becomings.[13] And so can critical inquiry.

Rematerialization is not just position, or positing, but positive, and its force lies largely in this preemption of negation. It works with materials at hand, and thus requires neither an absent 'that within which passes show' (*Hamlet*, 1.2.85) nor a *meta* to its *physics*. In this spirit, we are interested in each rematerialization as positively differentiated from whatever materials are transformed and as situated within the articulatory spaces through which it now travels and may continue to travel. As Douglas Bruster argues in his contribution to this anthology, when Shakespeare's writing career began, the meanings of prose and verse onstage were defined as opposites; as time went on, Shakespeare recovered the use of prose for characters of all classes, so that it became less a marker of inborn status than of acquired proficiencies. Such a shift, whether represented onstage, described in criticism, or lived through, requires movement into what transversal theory refers to as 'subjunctive space,' thought and experience catalyzed by the hypothetical ventures of 'as if' and 'what if,' the first of which privileges the past and the latter the future for the fueling of emergent activity. It also requires assessing the presence of what has been rematerialized qualitatively, and in light of an understanding of quality as positive becomings. It was Shakespeare's own period that saw the rise of a differential, quantitative sense of the structures and laws of the world over the previous sense of the world as a complex of discrete qualities. The transformative effects of this conceptual power of negation and quantification have been widely documented and continue to be felt.[14] We contend that at this point an approach through quality says more about the real, the material, and the critical than an approach through quantity or mere difference. No longer can the critical terrain be mapped exclusively in terms of binaries, dialectics, pyramids, squares; critical intervention must offer itself as interconnected and vibrating in sympathy with other interventions, but fully reducible to no other unit or category.[15] The intervention is the emergent product of the forces and discourses of the community, but the properties uniquely associated with the community depend for their existence on the individuals who comprise the community but themselves lack the emergent properties, much as consciousness emerges from the ensemble of the discrete physical structures of the brain. Rather than seeking to define through negative differentiation, we define (and see these essays, multifariously, as defining) positively, by what is present. The presence of the Shakespeares we present here is not reduced to meaning, but carried back to the multiple experiences and affects to which Shakespeare can be linked.

This carries *us* back to the beginning of the introduction, to the Shakespeare Dude, and to what's the matter in rematerializing. We suggested that the contemporary attractiveness of topics like the authorship question, the nature of Shakespeare's person, and the Shakespeare Dude lies in how each of these authorizes itself in something real in Shakespeare, and in so

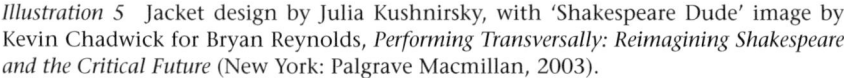

Illustration 5 Jacket design by Julia Kushnirsky, with 'Shakespeare Dude' image by Kevin Chadwick for Bryan Reynolds, *Performing Transversally: Reimagining Shakespeare and the Critical Future* (New York: Palgrave Macmillan, 2003).

doing makes that reality into an icon that needs no comment. From one position, or in one experience. But in and from others, the Shakespeare Dude is not a reflection of something real, but a rematerializing that captures one path within Shakespace – one that intersects and parallels a number of others, among them the Droeshout portrait, Baz Luhrmann's 1996 film *Romeo + Juliet*, now quaint-seeming anxieties about the new millennium, or collaborative transversal projects for the future of criticism. That is, what is real about the Shakespeare Dude is not something outside him that can be easily pointed to or thought in an icon. Nor is it really something in the image itself, something that talks to things in other images, texts, memories. It is the conversation, the translation, the rematerialization, that gives us reality here. The Shakespeare Dude brings together, uniquely and positively, these and other images and conversations. Saussure might observe that Shakespeare is defined as not-me, not-you, or not-Marlowe. Countering Saussure, this Dude is not not-the-real-Shakespeare, not not-the-only-Shakescene, not not-Marlowe. The Dude asserts, and we concur, positively: Shakespeare+. With its emphasis on affective presence, rematerialization speaks to those interested in the real even though it does not claim reality. Its acknowledgment of process as the means by which rematerializations can only ever occur privileges potential for the critical future.

Notes

1. In his book, *Author's Pen and Actor's Voice: Playing in Writing in Shakespeare's Theatre*, Robert Weimann astutely observes: 'For a significant, and significantly increasing, majority of people the encounter with Shakespeare is not through reading what he wrote but through watching certain electronically processed images of filmed performances. To acknowledge this major shift in the reception of the classic is to take cognizance not simply of deep-going changes in the media access; no less important, the shifting mode of the reception significantly affects the meaning of what is received' (2).
2. Stephanie Nolen, *Shakespeare's Face: Unraveling the Legend and History of Shakespeare's Mysterious Portrait* (New York: Free Press, 2004).
3. See Richard Burt, *Unspeakable ShaXXXpeares: Queer Theory and American Kiddie Culture* (New York: St. Martins, 1998), on why pornographic film adaptations of Shakespeare appeal less for thematic or semiotic reasons, and more because Shakespeare is recognizably ironized in a new context.
4. Consistent with the increasing capitalist commodification of Shakespeare, Chadwick Design Inc. charged us more than twice the amount that they previously charged Bryan Reynolds to use the image on the cover of *Performing Transversally: Reimagining Shakespeare and the Critical Future* (New York: Palgrave Macmillan, 2003).
5. See David Hawkes' review essay, 'Materialism and Reification in Renaissance Studies,' *JEMCS* 4 (2004): 114–29.
6. On Shakespace, see Hedrick and Reynolds, 'Shakespace and Transversal Power': 3–50; on the concept of articulatory spaces, see Bryan Reynolds, *Performing Transversally: Reimagining Shakespeare and the Critical Future* (New York: Palgrave Macmillan, 2003): 1–28.

7. For examples, see Hedrick and Reynolds eds, *Shakespeare Without Class* and Reynolds, *Performing Transversally*.
8. On the investigative–expansive mode of scholarship and pedagogy, see Bryan Reynolds, *Becoming Criminal: Transversal Performance and Cultural Dissidence in Early Modern England* (Baltimore: Johns Hopkins University Press, 2002): 1–22; Joseph Fitzpatrick and Bryan Reynolds, 'The Transversality of Michel de Certeau: Foucault's Panoptic Discourse and the Cartographic Impulse,' in *Diacritics* 29:3 (Fall 1999): 63–80; ZOOZ (James Intriligator and Bryan Reynolds), 'Transversal Poetics: I. E. Mode,' in *GESTOS: Teoría y Práctica del Teatro Hispánico* 18:35 (April 2003): 9–21, and Bryan Reynolds, 'Transversal Performance: Shakespace, the September 11 Attacks, and the Critical Future,' in his *Performing Transversally*: 1–28.
9. On sociopolitical conductors, see Reynolds, *Becoming Criminal*: 1–22 and *Performing Transversally*: 1–28.
10. 'Emergent properties' are properties or characteristics that do not appear at a lower level of organization but only at a higher one, as a population has a birth and death rate, but not any of the individuals that comprise that population, or as wave patterns do not appear at the molecular level. A whole, in other words, exhibits properties greater than the sum of its parts.
11. On affective presence, see Reynolds, *Becoming Criminal*: 1–22 and *Performing Transversally*: 1–28.
12. For further discussion of *différance* in relation to transversal theory's understanding of positive differentiation, see Bryan Reynolds, 'Transversal Poetics and Fugitive Explorations: Subject Performance, Early English Theatre, and *Macbeth*,' in *Early Theatre* 7.2 (2004): 110–22, and Reynolds and Janna Segal, 'The Reckoning of Moll Cutpurse: A Transversal Enterprise,' with Janna Segal, in Craig Dionne and Steve Mentz eds, *Rogues and Early Modern English Culture* (Ann Arbor: University of Michigan Press, 2004).
13. For more on Hegel's concept of becoming, see his *Phenomenology of Spirit*, trans. A.V. Miller (Oxford: Oxford University Press, 1997): 10–14. See Gilles Deleuze and Félix Guattari, *Anti-Oedipus: Capitalism and Schizophrenia*, trans. Robert Hurley, Mark Seem and Helen R. Lane (Minneapolis: University of Minnesota Press, 1983) and *A Thousand Plateaus: Capitalism and Schizophrenia*, trans. Brian Massumi (Minneapolis: University of Minnesota Press, 1987).
14. See, for example, Max Horkheimer and Theodor Adorno, *Dialectic of Enlightenment* (London: Continuum, 1976).
15. Christopher Braider, *Baroque Self-Invention and Historical Truth: Hercules at the Crossroads* (Burlington, VT: Ashgate, 2004).

Works cited

Bruster, Douglas and Robert Weimann. *Prologues to Shakespeare's Theatre: Performance and Liminality in Early Modern Drama*. New York: Routledge, 2005.
Weimann, Robert. *Authority and Representation in Early Modern England*. Ed. David Hillman. Baltimore: Johns Hopkins University Press, 1996.
——. *Author's Pen and Actor's Voice: Playing in Writing in Shakespeare's Theatre*. Ed. Helen Higbee and William West. Cambridge: Cambridge University Press, 2000.
——. *Shakespeare and the Popular Tradition in Theater: Studies in the Social Dimension of Dramatic Form and Function*. Ed. Robert Schwartz. Baltimore: Johns Hopkins University Press, 1978.
Williams, Raymond. *Marxism and Literature*. Oxford: Oxford University Press, 1977.

Part I
The Form and Pressure of the Time: Popular and Unpopular Traditions

1
'Strike All that Look Upon With Marvel': Theatrical and Theological Wonder in *The Winter's Tale*

Huston Diehl

'Nowhere,' Jonathan Bate writes of the final scene in *The Winter's Tale*, 'is there a creative coup more wonderful.'[1] Indeed, Paulina's carefully orchestrated unveiling of the marvelous statue astonishes, perplexes, and surprises, holding on-stage spectators and theater audiences alike rapt with wonder. But if Shakespeare seeks, with Paulina, to 'strike all that look upon' his spectacle 'with marvel,' he also self-reflexively explores the nature of theatrical wonder itself in this play.[2] Contrasting the admiration aroused by Paulina's wondrous statue with that elicited by Autolycus's dazzling but duplicitous theatrics, he raises compelling questions about the role of trickery, sense perception, and collective desire in the production of theatrical wonder. He asks, too, why verbal accounts reporting the 'admiration,' 'notable passion of wonder,' and 'deal of wonder' aroused when Perdita's true identity is discovered fail to produce the feelings of wonder they describe (5.2.10, 13–14, 21). And, by invoking the language of religious awe at the dramatic unveiling of the statue, he entertains a relation between theological and theatrical wonder.

A number of scholars, attentive to the way the language of the statue scene is theologically inflected, have recently associated the theatrical wonder aroused in *The Winter's Tale* with the theological wonder nurtured by the medieval church. Michael O'Connell finds an incarnational aesthetic operating in this and other early modern English plays, one he identifies with the visual and corporeal aspects of Roman Catholic rituals. He believes that *The Winter's Tale* 'fully associates theatricality with idolatry,' an association that Shakespeare 'embraces' by insisting on the primacy of the visual and nurturing 'a faith in what is seen.' The statue scene in *The Winter's Tale*, he argues, 'appears to construct visual wonder' – with its roots in medieval incarnational theology – 'as the truest image of what theater can be.'[3] In his book on wonder in Shakespearean theater, T. G. Bishop similarly links

Shakespearean drama with the incarnational theology of the medieval church. Although he distinguishes Shakespeare's 'poetics of incarnation' from the 'transcendentalizing use of wonder' in medieval drama, Bishop believes that Shakespeare's drama draws on the 'sacramental model' of the medieval church, has 'a kind of secular "real presence" as its dramatic ideal,' and invokes a 'therapeutic magic.'[4] Julia Reinhard Lupton develops a sustained analysis of the discourses of idolatry in *The Winter's Tale*, one which attends closely to the play's underlying dialectic between idolatry and iconoclasm, but she, too, sees Shakespeare drawing on 'the vestigial thaumaturgy' of the medieval church and its sacred images to produce theatrical wonder. Arguing that *'The Winter's Tale* smashes the Catholic idols in order to extract their fascinating power,' she believes 'the idolatrous ambience of the Church' in the statue scene 'serves to heighten the sense of mystery and magic; when this supernaturalism is finally naturalized, however, the play does not dissipate its energy so much as surreptitiously transport it onto the dramatic image itself.'[5] (Stanford University Press (1996) pp. 217, 207. See also Ruth Vanita, 'Mariological Memory in *The Winter's Tale* and *Henry VIII*', *Studies in English Literature* 40 (2000): 311–37.)

These scholars tend to assume that there is no place for wonder in the Protestant imaginary. Lupton, for instance, views the Reformation, with its pronounced iconoclastic impulses, as a secularizing movement, in league with the 'classicizing ... humanist, rationalist, and empiricist initiatives of the Renaissance.'[6] Thus implicating Protestantism in the disenchantment of the world, she shares with O'Connell and Bishop a predisposition to align theatrical wonder in Shakespearean drama with medieval Roman Catholicism – a religion of miracles, saints, relics, and efficacious images – and to see the secular Renaissance stage as a site of recuperation, where the 'remainders' of the old religion, 'emptied of their theological content,' are reanimated.[7] But in viewing Roman Catholicism as an ideology of an earlier epoch that was 'canceled out' in England by a demystifying and secularizing Protestantism, these scholars fail to take into account the role of wonder in reformed theology – or even to grant the reformed religion its underlying theological premises. And by looking back to the medieval church as the primary source for theatrical wonder, they tend to ignore the way wonder figures in contemporary controversies about images and representations.

My essay seeks to locate *The Winter's Tale* in those controversies. Shakespeare, I will argue, engages competing Protestant and Counter-Reformation theories of wonder in this play in order to address the legitimacy of his own theatrical representations, a legitimacy that was being vigorously contested by radical Protestants and moralists. In staging a statue that elicits awe, arouses desire, and miraculously appears to come to life, Shakespeare directly addresses the reformers' charge that the theater is idolatrous. But, I contend, he draws on Protestant theories of wonder to defend against those charges. Rather than appropriating Roman Catholic notions of wonder – notions that would make his theater particularly vulnerable to the enemies of the stage – he aligns the wonder his theater arouses with a kind of theological wonder endorsed by the Protestant English Church and thereby makes bold claims about the authority of his own representations. The statue scene raises the specter of idolatry, I am suggesting, in order to liberate theater from the charge it is idolatrous.

My work is informed by Robert Weimann's provocative reflections on the impact of the Reformation on early modern discourse, and in particular his sense of 'a previously unknown element of vulnerability in the assertion and appropriation of authority.' Arguing that in the aftermath of the English Reformation 'how to be "justified" – authorized – was the most "politizing" question of the time,' Weimann asserts that 'the act of representation was turned into a site on which authority could be negotiated, disputed, or reconstituted.' The Elizabethan and Jacobean theater, he points out, is an especially rich and complex site for such a negotiation, for players and playwrights had 'a special stake' in authorizing their representations and 'were in a special position … [to] negotiate the issue of authority' through performance, utilizing, for instance, dramatic conventions like the direct address, the social identities and material bodies of actors, and the responses of their audiences.[8] I want to suggest that Shakespeare exploits this new vulnerability of authority to appropriation in order to authorize his own wondrous, theatrical spectacles.

Especially relevant for my purposes is Weimann's observation that playwrights and players, among others, authorized their work through 'unlicensed appropriation of the word,' for I will show how Shakespeare uses the very Pauline texts that the anti-theatricalists cite in their attacks on the stage to legitimate the stage.[9] Naming Paulina after Paul, whom Protestants celebrate as a man of 'miracles … Signs, Wonders, and myghtie deeds,' he casts her in the roles of both preacher and playwright, and in doing so claims for the playwright the preacher's authority.[10] Furthermore, he invokes Pauline texts on theological wonder to counter anti-theatrical attacks that also draw on Paul, and specifically Paul's condemnation of idolatry and witchcraft, to denounce theatrical spectacle. In doing so, Shakespeare not only authorizes his theater, but achieves a new synthesis of art and nature and claims the reformative power of the preacher for the playwright.

Lupton finds an 'unconscious Christianity' operating in Renaissance texts like *The Winter's Tale*, 'one whose formulas, emptied out of their theological content, continue to operate all the more powerfully precisely because of their abstraction.'[11] But the anxious distinctions characters draw in the statue scene between lawful and unlawful images are highly self-conscious and seem calculated to call attention to, rather than empty out, contemporary, theological arguments about the power of images, arguments that turn on questions of wonder and representation. Perdita tries to distance her desire to 'kneel' before the statue and 'implore her blessing' from the 'superstition' associated with the veneration of images (5.3.43–4). Leontes expresses an intense desire that the wonder he experiences is a legitimate one, a desire that barely suppresses his fear that it is magical and thus, in a Protestant culture, illicit: 'O, she's warm!/ If this be magic, let it be an art/ Lawful as eating' (5.3.109–11). Throughout this scene Paulina alludes to the charges of witchcraft that iconoclasts level against artists whose sacred images were believed to have magical or supernatural power. Even as she intimates that she can make the statue move, however, she explicitly denies that she possesses 'wicked powers,' and she invites anyone who thinks her 'business' is 'unlawful' to 'depart.' Although she does not deny her power to elicit wonder – in fact, she triumphantly asserts it – she insists her 'spell is lawful' (5.3.91, 97–8, 105).

In their efforts to legitimize the statue and to justify their responses to it, all these characters seek to draw crucial distinctions between idolatrous and acceptable images, even as they express their attraction to the statue. The distinctions they make echo those made in Protestant tracts on images. William Perkins, for instance, carefully distinguishes between 'lawful' and 'unlawful' representations in a series of tracts written around the same time as *The Winter's Tale*. Maintaining that 'the arts of painting and graving are the ordinance of god and to be skillfull in them is the gift of God,' he nevertheless rejects art that seeks 'to represent the true God, or, to make an image of anything in way of religion, to worship God thereby,' and he urges his readers 'to suspect a doctrine taught for the wonders sake.' For him, Roman Catholic images and rituals are tainted with the 'sinne of Magick, sorcerie or witchcraft,'and he condemns them as 'unnatural.' Invoking Paul's question to the Galatians ('Who has bewitched thee?'), he cautions that the sacred images of the Roman Catholic Church are the products of a 'wicked art' and a 'devilish art' because they delude the 'the eye with some strange sleight done above the ordinarie course of nature' and make a man 'to thinke he sees that, which indeed he sees not.' Nevertheless, he deems all kinds of other images 'to be lawful,' including those that 'keepe themselves wholly within the powre and practice of nature,' those that are put to 'civil uses,' and those that 'are used for memory and representation.'[12]

Perkins's tracts fully engage and seek to refute the arguments of Jesuit writers like Orazio Torsellino who teach that Roman Catholic images are supernatural and efficacious. In *The History of our Lady of Loreto* (1608), a tract written in English and especially targeted for readers living in England (that 'distressed country'), Torsellino ardently seeks to persuade his readers that the famous shrine of Loreto far exceeds anything in nature. He celebrates 'the great miracles,' 'rare wonders,' and 'many thousands of supernaturall wonders, wholy surpassing the power of all naturall meanes' that have occurred at Loreto, and he urges his readers to believe that Loreto's 'sacred Reliques can worke any effect above nature,' including 'the reviving of dead men,' 'the curing of diseases,' and 'heavenly visions and revelations.' 'Who,' he asks rhetorically, 'would not be present at all the wonders Christ wrought' at Loreto?[13] The wonder that Torsellino endorses and seeks to arouse in his readers is thus grounded on a belief in the miraculous powers of sacred images. Many Counter-Reformation paintings attest to those powers, including some that depict ecstatic visions in which a sacred image appears to come to life before its adoring worshiper, sometimes even embracing its rapt spectator.[14] According to Victor I. Stoichita, the goal of such post-Tridentine paintings was to make ' "uncertain things" plausible, convincing even.' To that end, they position their viewers as empathetic witnesses, 'capable of testifying to the "actual reality" of the apparition.'[15] By arousing wonder, these paintings thus seek to verify the visionary experiences they represent.

For English Puritans like Perkins, however, the kind of wonder Torsellino and Counter-Reformation artists so wholeheartedly endorsed was deeply suspect. They vehemently sought to undermine the authority of miraculous, Counter-Reformation images, an authority so strictly controlled that 'only visions whose authenticity had been verified and whose holy interpretation had been accepted [by the Roman Catholic Church] were allowed to become a pictorial representation.'[16] Denouncing such images and visions as the unnatural products of witchcraft, they also accused the Catholic clergy of deliberately deluding the senses of unsuspecting worshipers. They thus condemned as fraudulent the very images that the Roman Catholic Church sanctioned and celebrated, arousing anxieties about the authority and validity of visual representations. Those anxieties pervade *The Winter's Tale*. In marked contrast to the visionary paintings of the Counter-Reformation that seek to make the miraculous plausible, Shakespeare's play repeatedly calls attention to the implausibility of its fictions and reminds its spectators of its own artifice. Rather than verifying the truth of the 'miracle' it represents, it explores the status of its own representations and interrogates its own capacity – as a fanciful 'winter's tale' – to evoke wonder.[17]

In the fourth act, Shakespeare uses the rogue Autolycus to expose as false and superficial a kind of theatrical wonder widely associated in the antitheatrical tracts with Roman Catholicism. A shape-shifter, con-artist, and profit-seeker, Autolycus traffics in the same kind of dazzling sensory tricks that the antitheatricalists, in their effort to discredit the common players, contemptuously attribute to Roman Catholic priests. Surprisingly, this rogue openly declares that his theatrics are idolatrous, thus acknowledging and embracing an accusation against the stage repeatedly made by Protestant moralists. Singing over his wares as if 'they were gods or goddesses,' he gloats that his customers 'throng who should buy first, as if my trinkets were hallowed, and brought a benediction to the buyer' (4.4.205–6, 588–90). He boasts, too, about how he manipulates the sense perceptions of his unsuspecting audiences, scornfully viewing their wonder as evidence of their failure to comprehend how they are being conned. Taken in by his 'trumpery' (the reformers' dismissive word for Roman Catholic spectacle) and performances, they have, he tells us, 'No hearing, no feeling but my sir's song, and admiring the nothing of it' (4.4.585–99). His words reinforce the idolatrous nature of his performances, for they echo Paul, who denounces idols as 'nothing' and cautions the Jews that, although they have ears and eyes, they have no true hearing, seeing, or feeling because they fail to 'understand with their heart' (1 Corinthians 8:4; Acts 28:26–7). By his own account, then, his theatrics arouse an idolatrous wonder, one which he exploits for financial gain, precisely what the antitheatricalists fear.

Yet the character of Autolycus is highly entertaining. His rogue antics, coming as they do after the tragic losses and bitter rebukes of the early acts, can't help but delight Shakespeare's own audiences, to whom the actor cast in this role shamelessly plays. The play thus alerts its audiences to their own propensity to be conned by dazzling theatrics even as it dazzles them, producing for their pleasure the very kind of wonder it exposes as superficial and meaningless. In this way, the authority of its representations is continually being negotiated in performance. This self-authorizing mode of representation is strikingly different from that used in the visionary paintings of the Counter Reformation that Stoichita analyzes. Whereas the Catholic paintings seek to persuade their spectators of some *a priori* truth, making the incredible convincing and positioning their spectators as witnesses who can attest to the validity of a supernatural wonder, Shakespeare's play engages its audiences in a dialectic of wonder and skepticism, one which demands that they examine the nature, power, and authority of theatrical spectacle, as well as their own responses to it, including ones that are potentially idolatrous.

Rather than insisting on the efficacy of its wondrous spectacles and celebrating them, as the Jesuit Torsellino does the spectacles of Loreto, *The Winter's Tale* raises unsettling questions about the spectacles it displays. How, it asks, does Perdita's 'admiring' response to the marvelous statue differ from the bamboozled gaze of the country folks who are conned by Autolycus's deceptive theatrics into 'admiring the nothing of it'? What distinguishes the entrancement of Autolycus's 'senseless' dupes so charmed by 'trumpery' they have 'No hearing, no feeling' from the 'madness' that Leontes feels when he gazes upon the statue, preferring its pleasure to any 'settled sense of the world' (5.3.72)? Why do Autolycus' theatrics leave his spectators with worthless trinkets and picked pockets, while Paulina's elicits an 'exultation' in which all its spectators are invited to 'partake' (5.3.131–2)?

Through his multiple appropriations of Paul, I want to suggest, Shakespeare critiques some forms of theatrical wonder – forms associated in English Protestant culture with Roman Catholicism – even as he lays claim to his own legitimate power to enchant. While he draws on Pauline texts to identify Autolycus' theatricality, and the admiration it elicits, with idolatry, thus distancing it from his own enterprise, Shakespeare also marshals Paul to authorize Paulina's wondrous spectacle – and, I would argue, his own Protestant theater. Although contemptuous of the false wonder aroused by the images of the pagan religions, Paul nurtures a profound sense of theological wonder in his writings, describing in his epistles the central mysteries of the Christian religion – the mystical body of Christ, the infinite grace of God, the marvel of revelation, the holy madness of faith – in terms of awe and wonder. It is this Pauline wonder, embraced by the Protestant reformers as an alternative to the discredited 'magic' of the Roman Church, that I suggest Shakespeare appropriates and deploys as a source of theatrical wonder in *The Winter's Tale*.

I will focus here on two aspects of theological wonder that Shakespeare appropriates from Paul in order to legitimate his stage. In the first, Paul fosters a wonder in the natural world, understood to be God's creation, while arousing suspicion of all human creations. In the second, Paul nurtures wonder in God's power to regenerate – to re-create – the fallen soul while addressing the role of the preacher in this regenerative process. In both he attributes wonder to a godhead whose creative powers dwarf those of men. The Protestant reformers routinely invoke both these Pauline notions of wonder in their critiques of Roman Catholic images and ritual practices.

In his tirades against the false wonders of pagan images, Paul advocates a turn from the carnal to the spiritual, but he also encourages a turn from the magical to the natural, urging his audiences to find in the wonders of the created world compelling evidence of God. Commenting on these passages, the reformers celebrate God as an artist, author, and 'Wonder Worker,' and they depict the natural world as both a 'most beautiful theater' and a 'goodly ... spectacle,' far more wonderful than any thing made by the hands of man, for 'by beholding' it man 'might be carried unto the author him-selfe.'[18] According to Calvin, Paul called 'this honorable stage of heaven and earth, furnished with innumerable miracles ... the wisdome of God' and taught that 'by beholding' it 'we ought wisely to have known God.'

The central actors in this theater of the world are human beings, understood to be the prime creation of God. Calvin encourages his readers to view man as 'a token of gods glory, replenished with infinite miracles.' Even the 'body of man,' he argues, is so cunningly made 'that for it the maker of it may worthily be judged wonderfull.'[19] Drawing a clear distinction between divinely-created humans and the man-made images of the Roman Church, the reformers thus seek to replace the veneration of images with a re-energized love of one's fellow human beings, who are, they emphasize, the very images of God. Because he is 'the living image of God, & made by the very hand of God,' man is, according to Martin Bucer, 'a thousand fold more excellent then all images made by the hand of man.' Working with this assumption, an English catechism for children urges its readers to turn away from worshiping 'dumme and dead images' and instead to focus on 'the praisynge and charitable lovynge of the lyvely images of god.' Similarly, one of the official homilies of the English Church advises that 'if you truly honour the image of God, you should by doing well to man, honour the true image of

God in him.'[20] The wonder these texts nurture thus has an important ethical dimension; it is never 'for wonder's sake,' the charge Perkins levels against the Jesuits' religion.

The Winter's Tale might be read as a sustained response to the challenge this Protestant view of creation poses to artists. If only God can create, how can they escape the charge that they are presumptiously rivaling God? If God is the sole wonder worker and man's own artistry is nothing, how can they avoid the accusation that the wonder their art arouses is fraudulent or unlawful? These questions inform the debate in Act Four in which Perdita objects to any human effort to improve on 'great creating nature' and Polixenes defends grafting as an art 'That nature makes' because the human creator is himself a product of nature (4.4.89–92).[21] They are central as well to the statue scene, where Paulina, suggesting she can bring a stone statue to life, orchestrates a wondrous theatrical spectacle that culminates in the revelation that the statue is no work of art at all, but a living woman, wrinkled by time.

Even though Paulina seems to encourage her spectators to marvel at the prodigious skills of the sculptor – 'that rare Italian master Giulio Romano,' an artist who 'would beguile nature of her custom, so perfectly he is her ape' (5.2.85–90) – Shakespeare problematizes that admiration by subtly introducing God's creation as an alternative source of wonder. Before she draws the curtain and reveals the statue of Hermione, silencing her spectators with 'wonder,' Paulina assures them its 'dead likeness. ... Excels what ever yet you looked upon,/ Or hand of man hath done' (5.3.22, 15–17). Her words, echoing as they do the reformers' warnings against 'dead ymages of wood or stone' carved by the hand of 'some man a folysshe counterfaiter of god,' don't just arouse anxiety that the statue is an idol. They also hint at the possibility that the statue is not, in fact, man-made and point to the final revelation when Paulina's spectators find themselves marveling at something no artist can make: a person who breathes, moves, and is warm and whose very presence attests to the mysterious workings of grace, love, and time.[22] For the on-stage spectators, as well as for Shakespeare's own spectators, the statue – initially described as a 'piece ... now newly performed' – poses all the fundamental questions that a *trompe l'oeil* painting like those for which Giulio Romano was famous conventionally raises. Like the viewers of such paintings, they experience 'a feeling of *astonishment*' when they realize how they have been tricked by the artist and must re-examine their own act of perception.[23] But, in contrast to such paintings, the astonishment this scene produces seems calculated to deflect attention away from the artist's wizardry in imitating nature and to focus it instead on what we might call a divine artistry, its 'fine chisel' capable even of 'cut[ting] breath' (5.3.78–9).

At a time when antitheatricalists accuse players of performing 'subtill sleights, as if in derision of nature to scoff theyr maker, they were more cunning than their Creator,' Shakespeare, I am suggesting, had something invested in differentiating his own art from that of a sixteenth-century Italian artist whose name links him to Rome and whose reputation was based on his daring ambition to rival God's own artistry.[24] De-coupling the magic of his own theatrical illusions from the 'wicked' and 'devilish' art of the reformers' Roman Catholic Church, he locates the source of true wonder in God's creations, not his own, and creates a theater that, in Perkins' words, is 'wholly within the powre and practice of nature.' In the process, Shakespeare differentiates his medium – the actor's body – from the sculptor's stone and naturalizes his own artifice by identifying his fictional characters with the actors who embody them. The statue scene succeeds in part because it focuses its spectators' gaze on the material body of the living actor who plays Hermione, an actor who, however skillfully she imitates a stone statue, cannot help but breathe, have 'motion' in her eye, and appear to the audience as if 'the very life' were 'warm upon her lip' (5.3.66–7). In performance, the statue is never entirely a stony object, never truly a dead image. Shakespeare exploits the actor's own aliveness, simultaneously creating the illusion that a statue is coming to life and calling attention to the fictitious nature of that illusion. Redirecting the wonder of his spectators from a 'piece' to the living Hermione, played by an actor who is herself a 'lively' image of God, Shakespeare corrects the Protestant predisposition to see theater as a product of magic or witchcraft, marks the crucial difference between sculpture and theater, and counters antitheatricalists who accuse playwrights of trafficking in dead and stony images. Making Pauline wonder the grounds for his own theatrical wonder, he claims as legitimate the spectacle of his stage.

Theatrical wonder in *The Winter's Tale* is thus not extracted from the remains of the medieval saints, with their mysterious, supernatural powers, as Lupton argues, nor is it marked off as a 'false wonder,' merely a 'trick, mystified by talk of magic,' as Gareth Roberts asserts.[25] Instead, it is identified with the natural world, understood to be a divinely-created world and thus for Protestant believers far truer than any wonder that human artifice is capable of eliciting. The revelation that Hermione is alive and has performed the statue naturalizes a work of art that initially appeared to be magical, but it is a mistake, I think, to equate that naturalization with demystification. As he does at the end of *The Tempest*, when Sebastian declares the sight of Miranda and Ferdinand playing chess 'a most high miracle' and Miranda pronounces the men of Milan and Florence a 'wonder' (5.1.180, 184), Shakespeare asks his spectators to look upon the natural world, and in particular upon the human creature, in a new way, one that intensifies, rather than dissipates, a sense of mystery. Startling them with the discovery of the marvelous in the human, he deflects his own power to enchant onto a divine creator, and he insists as well that they look on human beings with fresh eyes.

For it is 'dear life,' and not a moving statue, that 'redeems' Leontes. Although he has wronged her terribly, Hermione 'embraces him' and 'hangs about his neck.' In the wake of her miraculous return and in response to her warmth and breath, he asks her forgiveness, admitting that his own 'ill suspicion' caused all his losses, and not any betrayal on her part (5.3.11–12,103, 150). By locating the cause of the play's tragic events in Leontes' irrational suspicion that his beautiful wife was an adulteress, Shakespeare calls into question Protestant culture's propensity to suspect beauty and to associate it with magic, witchcraft, and idolatry. That suspicion also poisons Polixenes' response to the ravishing Perdita. Replicating Leontes' initial error, he denounces her as 'a fresh piece/ Of excellent witchcraft' because she tempts him to 'only live by gazing' (4.4.109, 410–11). But if Shakespeare refutes the reformers' tendency to suspect the beautiful and spectacular, perhaps even freeing his own theater from puritan charges that it is a seductive piece of witchcraft, he rejects as well the kind of idolatrous adoration that objectifies women, turning them into stone. His play celebrates instead the wonder of a natural world understood to be God's creation. Achieving what we might call a new, Protestant synthesis of art and nature, he not only defends his theater from the antitheatricalist accusation that dramatists appropriate for themselves magical powers that properly belong to God, but he also claims its superiority over the 'dead' images of the visual artist, including, even, those remarkable Renaissance sculptures that almost seem to breathe.

If Shakespeare deflects the wonder his theater elicits onto 'great creating nature,' he also makes compelling claims about its capacity to unsettle and transform its spectators. In marked contrast to Autolycus' theatrical spectacles, which dazzle and deceive, Paulina's statue shames and rebukes Leontes, 'conjur[ing]' his 'evils … to remembrance' and 'piercing' his 'soul' (5.3.32–77). Shakespeare draws here on another aspect of Pauline wonder: God's 'wonderful and secrete power' to soften the stony heart, regenerate the sinful soul, and restore 'the Image of God which was defaced by sinne.' Describing that power as 'a miracle of the grace of God, and not a woorke of humayne labour,' the reformers viewed it as the ultimate form of God's creative power, superior even to the original creation, and the basis of their assertion that 'wee bee Gods workmanship.'[26] Although they emphasized that this power belonged solely to God, Protestant theologians, drawing on Paul's description of his own ministry, taught that the minister played an important role in cultivating it. It is this role, I contend, that Shakespeare audaciously appropriates for the secular playwright as a way of authorizing his theater and refuting the charges of the antitheatricalists that the stage is idolatrous.

The historical Paul served as a model for the Protestant preacher, and Protestant commentaries devote considerable attention to analyzing his rhetorical strategies and explaining his persuasive power. They also take great pains to distinguish Paul's 'many and … great miracles and wonders' from 'papist' miracles, insisting that the apostle was not himself the author of the miracles he performed, but only the vehicle through which God worked. Paul's 'wonders & signs are shewed by the hande of men,' Luther writes, 'so that the praise thereof is ascribed to God alone as to the author: & man is only the minister.'[27] Citing Paul's statement 'I have planted, Apollos watered, but God gave the increase' (Corinthians 3:6) to reinforce the point that God is the source of all wonder and man is, in Paul's words, 'not anything,' they nevertheless emphasize 'how necessary the preaching of the word is.' Calvin likens the minister to a 'husbandman' and describes the way he serves as God's instrument, diligently cultivating the soil, so that the 'wonderfull ... springing and growing of putrifacted seed' – the product of God's grace – might occur.[28] Although he declares that Paul is a mere man with no creative power of his own, he and other reformers thus depict him as a powerful instrument through which God works wonders.

If Shakespeare casts Paulina in the role of the minister, dramatizing early in the play her diligent attempts to reform Leontes by means of the rebuke, a rhetorical genre closely associated with her namesake, he complicates that role by also casting her as a playwright whose wondrous statue silences all who gaze upon it. But Paulina's turn to spectacle and theater in the final act should not be understood as a turn away from her original goal of ministering to and reforming Leontes. Rather, it is a means of accomplishing that transformation, and thus a bold claim on Shakespeare's part for the affective power of the stage. Appropriating the role of the preacher for the playwright, Shakespeare authorizes his theatrical spectacle by showing how it, no less effectively than the Protestant sermon, can 'pearce with lively feeling into mans soules,' 'move all our inward senses,' and bring us 'to nothing.'[29] Like the disruptive spectacle that Ariel performs for the rulers of Milan and Naples in *The Tempest*, causing them to remember their sins and feel their guilt, Paulina's theatrical unveiling of the statue accomplishes the very goals outlined for preachers in Protestant manuals, arousing in Leontes 'shame,' eliciting 'compunction of heart,' awakening his 'conscience,' and inducing 'true repentant sorrow'[30] Shakespeare imagines here a theater that, although it is spectacular, penetrates the inmost part of its viewers. Suggesting a reciprocity between the gradual animation of the statue and the way Leontes is inwardly 'stirred' by gazing upon it, he deliberately counters the antitheatricalists who warn that those who 'so looke, so gaze, so gape upon plaies' will become like those 'men [that] stare on the head of Medusa [and] are turned to stones,' and will 'freeze unto yse [ice].'[31] Far from turning its spectators into stone, Paulina's theatrical spectacle appears to work on Leontes in much the same way as those 'lawful images' allowed by the English reformers do, by serving as 'stirrers of men's minds' and causing 'them to remember themselves, and to lament their sins.'[32] It cultivates the king's stony heart, helping to prepare him for the wonder of spiritual regeneration.

Shakespeare describes the wonder that Paulina has 'wrought' with her statue as a kind of madness that Leontes finds both pleasurable and entirely preferable to his quotidian experience of the world, the world he perceives with his outward senses. Identifying that 'madness' with the holy madness of Pauline theology, a madness he sees as 'redemptive,' Anthony Gash writes that Leontes has traveled 'from a destructive madness which he previously mistook for an empirically grounded reason to a liberating madness when the soul no longer identifies with the senses.'[33] I agree. But it is important to remember that, in appropriating Paul, Shakespeare is making an important claim here for the disciplinary power of the stage. Leontes' madness – like his shame, his awakened memory, and his regeneration – is provoked by Paulina's unsettling rhetorical strategies and marvelous theatrical spectacle. When Leontes gazes upon the statue – or, rather, Hermione's performance of the statue – he is 'transported.' The same might be said of Shakespeare's own spectators who, silently assenting to Paulina's command to 'awake your faith' by staying in their place when she asks any skeptics present to depart, participate in a collective enactment and share in the resulting 'exultation' (3.94–6, 132). What does this act of faith require? And why does Shakespeare give faith, a term charged with theological meaning, such a crucial role in the aesthetic experience of his secular stage?

Michael O'Connell believes that this scene requires the play's spectators to have faith in what they see. But such a reading ignores this play's narrative and thematic links to *Much Ado About Nothing* and *Othello*. Leontes' suspicion of Hermione connects him to Claudio, who erroneously puts his faith in the visible evidence of Hero's infidelity and as penance is required to marry a woman sight unseen, and to Othello, who fatally trusts in Iago's ocular proof instead of his wife's invisible virtue. It ignores as well the way the audience's experience of the statue is mediated by Paulina's words, which artfully shape what her spectators see. The unveiling of the statue is not a silent spectacle; it is a fully realized theatrical performance in which seeing cannot be divorced from hearing. However spectacular and marvelous the statue scene, it is surely an oversimplification to assume, as O'Connell does, that it demonstrates Shakespeare's 'confidence in what is seen' and thus 'constructs visual wonder as the truest image of what theater can be.'[34]

I suggest instead that Shakespeare, adapting to his stage Paul's distinction between the dead letter and the 'wondrous' spirit, invites his spectators to relinquish their trust in what they literally see (nothing but a mere boy on a bare stage, a commoner player pretending to be a Sicilian queen posing as a statue) and enter into the spirit of this scene by embracing its larger truths.[35] He invites them, in other words, to turn away from the literalism that imprisons the puritan Malvolio in the dark and instead to choose, with Sebastian, the 'wonder' that 'enwraps' them, even if that means they must 'distrust' their eyes and 'wrangle with' their 'reason' (*Twelfth Night* 4.3.1–21). Countering the anti-theatrical prejudices of the puritans by associating them with the literalism Paul attributed to the Hebrews, he depicts the stage as a place where the physical senses are disrupted so that a truer kind of seeing and hearing – one that involves 'the understanding of the heart' – can be attained. By merging the roles of preacher and playwright in the character of

Paulina and giving her wondrous spectacle the capacity both to reveal the divinity of the natural world and to pierce its spectator's soul, Shakespeare imagines a legitimate role for the stage in a Protestant England deeply suspicious of images and theater. When Paulina asserts that her magic is 'lawful' and invites everyone present to partake of its wonder, she reminds her spectators that, while the stage engages the eye and ear, their seeing and hearing need not result in their merely 'admiring the nothing of it.'

Notes

1. *Shakespeare and Ovid* (Oxford University Press, 1993), pp. 238–89.
2. 'The Winter's Tale' (5.3.100) in *The Norton Shakespeare*, ed. Stephen Greenblatt (New York: Norton, 1997). All citations to this and other Shakespeare plays are to this edition.
3. *The Idolatrous Eye: Iconoclasm and Theater in Early-Modern England* (Oxford: Oxford University Press, 2000), pp. 140, 141.
4. *Shakespeare and the Theatre of Wonder* (Cambridge: Cambridge University Press, 1996), pp. 15–16, 87.
5. *Afterlives of the Saints: Hagiography, Typology, and Renaissance Literature* (Stanford: Stanford University Press, 1996).
6. Lupton, *Afterlives of the Saints*, pp. xxxii.
7. Lupton, *Afterlives of the Saints*, p. xxvii. Lupton's position echoes here that of Stephen Greenblatt when he argues that the theater of early modern England appropriates, but fictionalizes, secularizes, and 'empties out,' the sacred rituals and images of the medieval church. See *Shakespearean Negotiations: The Circulation of Social Energy in Renaissance England* (Berkeley: University of California Press, 1988), pp. 127–8.
8. *Authority and Representation in Early Modern Discourse*, ed. David Hillman (Baltimore: Johns Hopkins University Press, 1996), pp. 5, 8, 67, and 21.
9. *Authority and Representation*, p. 67.
10. Calvin, *A commentarie upon S. Paules epistle to the Corinthians*, trans. Thomas Timme (London, 1577), fols. 299r–v.
11. *Afterlives of the Saints*, p. xxvii.
12. *A discourse of the damned art of witchcraft* (Cambridge, 1608), sig. B5r; *A warning against the idolatrie of the last times* (Cambridge, 1601), sig. B5r; *Witchcraft*, sig. C3r; *A reformed Catholike* (Cambridge, 1597), sigs. Y3v, A4v, K7v, L5r, L6v–L7v; M25; *Witchcraft*, sig. K8r; *A reformed Catholike*, sig. L5r.
13. (Saint Omer, 1608), sigs. 2v–7r; 4r–5r. Castigating England as the only nation 'of all nations under the sunne [that] doth not know, doth not honour and reverence this glorious paradise of the earth,' Torsellino condemns the Protestant teaching that the age of miracles is past, sigs. 2v–7r. In a direct attack on 'Turselline the Jesuit' and his 'five bookes of the Ladie of Lauretto,' William Perkins attacks the 'Ladie of Lauretto' as a prime example of Roman Catholic idolatry. He condemns 'her apparitions and miracles' because they 'tend all to erect, establish, and maintaine the worship of her self,' and he attributes the image's so-called 'miracles' to 'Satanicall operation,' *A warning against idolatrie*, sig. B6r.
14. See, for examples, Caravaggio's 'Madonna of Loreto' (c. 1603–06); Francisco Ribalta's 'St. Bernard Embracing the Crucified Christ' (c. 1621–25); and Gasper de Creyer's 'Saint Lutgard Embraced by the Crucified Christ' (1653).

15. *Visionary Experience in the Golden Age of Spanish Art* (London: Reakton Books, 1995), pp. 23, 198.
16. *Visionary Experience*, p. 25.
17. On this point, I agree with Peter Platt, who argues that 'Shakespeare does not repudiate art or wonder here, but shows us that only an art that admits its artifice ... is an art capable at once of teaching, delighting, and moving,' *Reason Diminished: Shakespeare and the Marvelous* (Lincoln: University of Nebraska Press, 1997), p. 167.
18. John Calvin, *Institutes of Christian Religion*, trans. Thomas Norton (London, 1562), 1.14.20; Calvin writes: 'let us not be ashamed to take pious delight in the works of God open and manifest in this most beautiful theater ... [and] to be mindful that wherever we cast our eyes, all things they meet are works of God'; Calvin, *The commentaries of M. John Calvin upon the Actes of the Apostles*, trans. Christopher Fetherstone (London, 1585), sig. Ee8r; Calvin, *A commentarie upon the Epistle of Saint Paul to the Romanes*, trans. Christopher Rosdell (London, 1583), sig. B5r.
19. *Institutes*, 1.5.2; 2.6.1.
20. Martin Bucer, *A treatise declaryng [and] shewing dyvers causes ... that pyctures [and] other ymages which were wont to be worshypped, ar i[n] no wise to be suffred in the temples and churches of Christen men* (London, 1535), sig. E4r; *A shorte Cathechisme: A briefe and godly bringing up of youth in knowledge and commandements of God* (London, 1550), sig. B7r.; 'An Homily Against perill of Idolatrie and superfluous decking of Churches in the time of Queen Elizabeth,' *Certain Sermons or Homilies appointed to be read in Churches in the Time of Queen Elizabeth I* (London, 1623), p. 74.
21. Working with the premise that 'only God can create,' the reformers engage in essentially the same debate. Explicating Paul, Luther articulates a position very similar to Polixenes: 'Creation is attributed onely to the Divinity of Christ: for the humanitie doth not create, and yet notwithstanding it is truly sayd, man created, because the Divinitie, which only createth, is incarnate with the humanity,' *A commentarie of M. Doctor Martin Luther upon the Epistle of S. Paul to the Galathians* (London, 1602), fol. 130r.
22. *A shorte Cathechisme*, sig. B7r. Arguing that 'Christians themselves are the images of Christians,' William Perkins writes that 'the meaneste man that can be, is a more excellent image of God, then all the images of God or of Saints that are devised by men,' *A reformed Catholike*, sigs. L6v, M2r; *A warning against idolatrie*, sig. C7r.
23. Sybille Ebert-Schifferer describes the *trompe l'oeil* painting as 'highly self-reflexive' and notes that it is 'created to elicit a feeling of *astonishment*.' Noting that it ' "contain[s] directions for the viewers," ' she argues that its goal 'is not the continuous deception of the viewer' but rather 'the pleasure one derives from seeing through the trick,' '*Trompe l'Oeil*: The Underestimated Trick,' in *Deceptions and Illusions*, ed. Sybille Ebert-Schifferer (Washington, DC: National Gallery of Art, 2002), pp. 24, 31.
24. William Rankins, *A Mirrour of Monsters* (London, 1587), sig. C3r. Leonard Barkan speculates that Shakespeare may have known of Giulio Romano through Vasari, who wrote in an often quoted epitaph that the artist rivaled Jupiter in his skill. 'To a reader of Vasari,' Barkan writes, 'Giulio Romano would appear as a great and godlike creator, master of many arts and worthy opponent of Nature herself as creator,' ' "Living Sculptures": Ovid, Michelangelo, and *The Winter's Tale*,' *ELH* 48 (1981): 657.
25. Lupton, *Afterlives of the Saints*, p. 207 ; ' "An art lawful as eating"? Magic in *The Tempest* and *The Winter's Tale*,' in *Shakespeare's Late Plays: New Readings*, ed. Jennifer Richards and James Knowles (Edinburgh: Edinburgh University Press, 1999), p. 140.

26. Calvin, *A commentarie upon ... Corinthians*, E1v; see also, William Perkins, who writes in his *A warning against idolatrie* that 'To create is a proper and immediate work of the godhead: to regenerate is to create: and man in that he is regenerated is created again. ... Nothing therefore can actively regenerate but God.' sig. C1r; Calvin, *The sermons of M. J. Calvin upon the Epistle of S. Paule too the Ephesians*, trans. Arthur Golding (London, 1577), sig. 77r.
27. Luther, *A commentarie upon Galathians*, fol. 100r. See also, William Perkins who explains that the 'napkin of Paul,' in contrast to Roman Catholic relics, 'did not cure the sick, but [was a sign of] the power of God onely, dispensed by the hands of Paul,' *Witchcraft*, sig. 7r.
28. *A commentarie on ... Corinthians*, fol. 33v, fol. 34r.
29. John Calvin, *Comentarie upon ... Corinthians*, sig. 225v; John Calvin, *A commentarie on the whole Epistle to the Herbrewes* (London, 1605), sig. F7r.
30. Richard Bernard, *The Faithfull Shepheard, amended and enlarged: with the Shepheards practise of preqching annexed thereunto* (London, 1609), sigs. K3r–v, L1r; note that Thomas Heywood makes a similar claim for the stage in *An Apology for Actors* (London, 1612), sigs. G1v–G2v, F4v; G1v; B4.
31. Stephen Gosson, *Playes Confuted in Five Acts* (London, 1582), sig. E7v; Henry Ainsworth, for instance, writes 'these stony Saints have eyes and see not, have ears and hear not; like them be they that make them, and whosever trusteth in them,' *An arrow against idolatrie* (Amsterdam, 1624), p. 13. While Perdita's initial astonished response to the statue raises the fear that it has turned her into stone, Shakespeare rewrites the seemingly idolatrous scenario by turning her impulse to kneel to the statue into a daughter's obedient honoring of her mother (that is, from a violation of the second commandment to a fulfillment of the fifth commandment).
32. 'The Contents of a Book of Articles devised by the King' (1538), qtd. in John Foxe, *Actes and Monuments* (London, 1563), 5:163.
33. 'Shakespeare, Carnival and the Sacred: *The Winter's Tale* and *Measure for Measure*,' *Shakespeare and Carnival After Bakhtin*, ed. Ronald Knowles (London: Macmillan, 1998), pp. 190.
34. *The Idolatrous Eye*, pp. 138, 140.
35. Calvin, *The Catechisme, or Manner to teache children the Christian religion* (London, 1582), sig. G6v.

Works cited

Ainsworth, Henry. *An arrow against idolatrie*. Amsterdam, 1624.
Barkan, Leonard. ' "Living Sculptures": Ovid, Michelangelo, and *The Winter's Tale*,' *ELH* 48 (1981): 639–67.
Bate, Jonathan. *Shakespeare and Ovid*. Oxford University Press, 1993.
Bernard, Richard. *The faithfull shepheard, amended and enlarged: with the shepheards practise in preaching annexed thereunto*. London, 1609.
Bishop, T. G. *Shakespeare and the Theatre of Wonder*. Cambridge: Cambridge University Press, 1996.
Bucer, Martin. *A treatise declaryng [and] shewing dyvers causes ... that pyctures & other ymages which were wont to be worshypped, ar i[n] no wise to be suffred in the temples and churches of Christen men*. London, 1535.
Calvin, John. *The Catechisme, or Manner to teache children the Christian religion*. London, 1582.
——. *A commentarie on the Whole Epistle to the Herbrewes*. London, 1605.

Calvin, John. *A commentarie upon S. Paules epistle to the Corinthians.* Trans. Thomas Timme. London, 1577.
——. *A commentarie upon the Epistle of Saint Paul to the Romanes.* Trans. Christopher Rosdell. London, 1583.
——. *The commentaries of M. John Calvin upon the Actes of the Apostles.* Trans. Christopher Fetherstone. London, 1585.
——. *Institutes of Christian Religion.* Trans. Thomas Norton. London, 1562.
——. *The sermons of M. J. Calvin, upon the Epistle of S. Paule too the Ephesians.* Trans. Arthur Golding. London, 1577.
'The Contents of a Book of Articles devised by the King' (1538). Qtd. in John Foxe, *Actes and Monuments.* London, 1563.
Ebert-Schifferer, Sybille. *'Trompe l'Oeil*: The Underestimated Trick.' In *Deceptions and Illusions.* Ed. Sybille Ebert-Schifferer. Washington, DC: National Gallery of Art, 2002.
Gash, Anthony. 'Shakespeare, Carnival and the Sacred: *The Winter's Tale* and *Measure for Measure.*' In *Shakespeare and Carnival After Bakhtin.* Ed. Ronald Knowles. London: Macmillan, 1998.
Gosson, Stephen. *Playes Confuted in Five Acts.* London, 1582.
Greenblatt, Stephen. *Shakespearean Negotiations: The Circulation of Social Energy in Renaissance England.* Berkeley: University of California Press, 1988.
Heywood, Thomas. *An Apology for Actors.* London, 1612.
'An Homily Against perill of Idolatrie and superfluous decking of Churches in the time of Queen Elizabeth.' In *Certain Sermons or Homilies appointed to be read in Churches in the Time of Queen Elizabeth I.* London, 1623.
Lupton, Julia Reinhard. *Afterlives of the Saints: Hagiography, Typology, and Renaissance Literature.* Stanford: Stanford University Press, 1996.
Luther, Martin. *A commentarie of M. Doctor Martin Luther upon the Epistle of S. Paul to the Galathians.* London, 1602.
O'Connell, Michael. *The Idolatrous Eye: Iconoclasm and Theater in Early-Modern England.* Oxford: Oxford University Press, 2000.
Perkins, William. *A discourse of the damned art of witchcraft.* Cambridge, 1608.
——. *A reformed Catholike.* Cambridge, 1597.
——. *A warning against the idolatrie of the last times.* Cambridge, 1601.
Platt, Peter. *Reason Diminished: Shakespeare and the Marvelous.* Lincoln: University of Nebraska Press, 1997.
Rankins, William. *A Mirrour of Monsters.* London, 1587.
Roberts, Gareth. ' "An art lawful as eating"? Magic in *The Tempest* and *The Winter's Tale.*' In *Shakespeare's Late Plays: New Readings.* Ed. Jennifer Richards and James Knowles. Edinburgh: Edinburgh University Press, 1999.
Shakespeare, William. 'The Winter's Tale.' In *The Norton Shakespeare.* Ed. Stephen Greenblatt. New York: Norton, 1997.
A shorte Cathechisme: A briefe and godly bringing up of youth in knowledge and commandements of God. London, 1550.
Stoichita, Victor I. *Visionary Experience in the Golden Age of Spanish Art.* London: Reakton Books, 1995.
Torsellino, Orazio. *The History of our B. Lady of Loreto.* Saint-Omer, 1608.
Vanita, Ruth. 'Mariological Memory in *The Winter's Tale* and *Henry VIII.*' *Studies in English Literature* 40 (2000): 311–37.
Weimann, Robert. *Authority and Representation in Early Modern Discourse.* Ed. David Hillman. Baltimore: Johns Hopkins University Press, 1996.

2
Performance and Urban Space in Shakespeare's Rome, or 'S.P.Q.L.'

D. J. Hopkins

> Consider the case of a city – a space which is fashioned, shaped, and invested by social activities during a finite historical period.
>
> Henri Lefebvre[1]

In the decades bracketing 1600, English popular culture appropriated Rome as a valuable model for the reimagining of London and its spaces. Not only did Rome provide a precedent for those seeking to authorize and consolidate power, but it also served as a site of contest where existing social relations could be explored, reconsidered, and troubled. Caesarism was in the air, and Shakespeare's London 'saw its problems mirrored in the wide glass of Roman history,'[2] from the references to Rome that riddle John Stow's late Elizabethan *Survey of London*[3] to the elaborately Romanate royal entry of James I.

On the 15 March 1604, James Stuart made his way through the streets of London amidst a long train of nobles, courtiers, and retainers.[4] The occasion of James's arrival in the City was the king's decision to finally participate in a city-spanning theatrical celebration of his kingship. For the occasion, the City[5] erected seven temporary triumphal arches, most of which were accompanied by a theatrical performance. The first of these arches was conceived by Ben Jonson and designed by Stephen Harrison, 'artificer' for the entire entry.[6] This arch served as the gateway through which the king passed at the outset of his public progress through the city, and also as a stage for the actor Edward Alleyn who played the role of 'Genius Urbis,' the personification of the City of London. The arch itself was crowned by a fifty foot wide perspective portrait of the City of London. Beneath this elaborate rendering, a formal cartouche bore the title: 'Londinium.' The Londinium Arch offered James the spectacle of an idealized city: an abstract, Romanized space of classical references and new visual paradigms, a space that stood in stark contrast with the warren of medieval structures among which this arch had been built.

At the conclusion of his entry, James faced the second of Jonson's two arches, 'The Temple of Janus.' Situated at Temple Bar, the official boundary of the City, James saw the second appearance of Alleyn as *Genius Urbis*. That Jonson composed James's entry in relation to Roman historical and literary sources may not have been forcefully apparent in his first arch: only the Latin name for the city that the Romans founded on the Thames would have provided textual testimony to the Londinium Arch's classical associations. But unlike the Londinium Arch, the Temple of Janus was 'a towering mass of classical scholarship.'[7] Its surface densely inscribed with Latin text, the last structure of James's entry was less an architectural monument than a freestanding literary object. Much of this Latin was quoted from Roman sources, though some was of Jonson's invention, notably the neologism emblazoned on the Temple's facade: 'S.P.Q.L.'[8] This abbreviation appropriates a Roman source in the context of James's London. The original Roman form, 'S.P.Q.R.,' abbreviated *'Senatus Populusque Romanus'*: 'the Senate and People of Rome.' With the substitution of an 'L' for an 'R,' Jonson invented a new social category for a new space: 'the Senate and People of Londinium.' So doing, Jonson not only recalled his previous invention, the Londinium Arch, he also implied (on James's behalf) that the crown's authority and London's people – even London itself – were framed by discourses of Rome.

After James passed through the Temple of Janus, a door in the Temple closed behind him, concluding the entry by concealing James from the assembled 'People of Londinium,' while at the same time revealing additional text:

> IMP. JACOBUS MAX.
> CAESAR AUG. P. P.
> PACE POPULO BRITTANICO
> TERRA MARIQUE PARTA
> JANUM CLUSIT. S.C.

(Jonson 395)

It seems appropriate that James, in passing from the City of London, should be celebrated as a new Caesar Augustus, *'imperator'* of a newly united Britain. Not only were the language and imagery of James's entry Roman, the political designs of the king were equally imperial. Jonson's flamboyant new name for James, 'Jacobus Maximus,' would have been all the more appropriate in relation to Alleyn's last words, delivered from this arch at the limits of the City's domain. His valedictory included the lines: 'And may these Ides as fortunate appear / To thee, as they to Caesar fatal were' (Jonson 394). James's entry was performed on the 15 March, a detail that could not have been accidental. Jonson was careful not to associate James with Julius Caesar nor the Ides of March with assassination. Thus the 15 March served as a date from which was marked, not the death of a republic, but the beginning of an empire.

The 'S.P.Q.L.' blazon on the last arch gives a proper name to that empire, and locates the entire entry in a conceptual 'Londinium.' More than just a reference to London's Roman history, 'Londinium' was a representation of historical space in which a new city could be imagined in conjunction with the entry of its authorizing king. Jonathan Goldberg has suggested that a 'spectral kingdom of Augustus' was the masque-like 'setting' for all of Jacobean politics.[9] Jonson gave that kingdom a name, and as James exited the Temple of Janus, the king left behind the 'simultaneously real-and-imagined' city limits of Londinium.[10]

Rome influenced the representational site of James's entry; it provided James with a forceful paradigm of urban space, and it would do so for Shakespeare as well. Gail Kern Paster speculates that Shakespeare was 'drawn to those moments in the Roman past which brought the internal order of the city to a point of critical change, when one kind of city was giving way to another.'[11] On the occasion of the 1604 entry, Shakespeare's own city was at a point of critical change, but Paster's formulation must be reversed in the case of early modern London: it was not the present that was drawn to the past, but the past that was brought to the present: 'Rome' was introduced into the streets and even into the proper name of the city. Conceptually as well as topographically, a medieval town was on the verge of giving way to early modern urbanism,[12] and performance representations of a Romanized London participated in conceiving and convening that new cityspace.

The emphasis of this essay is on performance, and on the contributions of Shakespeare's theatre to the reinvention of the urban in early modern London. Articulating what has become a given of contemporary cultural and literary studies, Louis Montrose describes Shakespeare's theatre as not merely an 'inert product' of early modern British culture, but in fact 'a source of cultural production.'[13] My interest is in the ways in which performance events like James's entry and Shakespeare's theatre were productive of the space of London. The epigram from Lefebvre with which I began insists on the materiality and historicity of cities as spaces that are 'fashioned, shaped, and invested by social activities during a finite historical period' (73). But Lefebvre argued as well that social activity was in turn shaped by the city. Thus understood, performance in the physical space of early modern London can be seen to have conditioned as it was conditioned by the social practices of the city and its inhabitants.

This project traces a discrete genealogy of texts and performances that suggest the ways in which the city serves as the fragmentary repository of its own histories.[14] In contrast with James's entry, in which the king was compared to Augustus, I will consider *Julius Caesar*; the theatre practices inscribed in Shakespeare's 1599 text mark it as related to but significantly different from the representational strategies at work in James's entry. Richard Wilson locates in *Julius Caesar* 'the scars of a material struggle,' and I too see in this text the lasting marks of a cultural transformation.[15] Though performance may have a material effect on physical space, the trace of that effect remains elusive. In reading these texts together, this study seeks to theorize the effects of early modern performance on the emergence of new urban spaces in Shakespeare's London.

London calling

The imagery and language of James's entry introduced an idea of Rome into the space of London. The entry's triumphal arches were only the most visible examples of the event's Romanness, their architectural form drawn from Serlio, who himself drew from classical Roman forms.[16] The arches were adorned with quotations from a range of Latin texts. These quotations not only informed the entry pageants with constant reminders of Roman culture, they also worked to incorporate the *ideal* of Rome into the *idea* of London. In the representational strategies of the entry, a new conception of London emerged, a hybrid of early modern concepts of classical Rome and the material conditions of London's actual spaces. In Lefebvre's terms, a new *representation of space* was produced, one that offered a stark contrast with the *representational space* in which it appeared.[17] In the interaction of these spaces, not only was Rome quoted in the context of London, but London was quoted in the context of Rome: the Londinium Arch and the Temple of Janus themselves bracketed the physical city, framing the early modern English streets, houses, and churches between idealized classical Roman reference points. Like the image of the city on the first arch, all of London was temporarily defined in the space of 'Londinium': a city suspended between the real and the imaginary, the material and the representational.

Marjorie Garber provides a productive way of thinking about the quotational uses of Rome in the texts and performances of Shakespeare's London. Garber observes that 'the idea of Rome is itself [...] a quotation.'[18] The idea of Rome was not a daily presence in the city that James entered in 1604. Rather, a new idea – 'Rome' – was introduced into those streets by way of quotational sites and performances. Subsequent to this entry, the city was subject to the lingering quotation marks of the Romanate performance. In the streets of London, and in the Roman plays of Shakespeare,[19] 'Rome' was always already in quotation.

For Garber, the work of quotation is akin to the work of representation: something is introduced into a context where it had not been, and by use of quotation marks, a distinction between the two – the thing introduced and its new context – is maintained. As Garber observes, 'Notice that we put "in quotation" in quotation marks' (*Ghost Writers* 52). In the appositive phrase that starts the preceding sentence, notice how carefully 'Garber' is distinguished from its context, my sentence. This is the source of Garber's authority, that she and her words are distinguished from 'Hopkins' and my words; but this distinction is also the source of my authority: I, Hopkins, can deploy 'Garber' in the service of my argument. Quotation as a practice sets up boundaries that distinguish between inside and outside, past and present. Thus quotation is a function of difference; it is also a function of power.[20]

James had Roman ambitions. His claim of imperial status was justified by his unification of a Great Britain, and the seat of this latter-day Roman empire was London. James even had Roman ambitions for London, though in the course of his reign, James's grand vision for rebuilding the city was only marginally realized, and only at the city's margins.[21] But even in such incomplete achievement, James displays *romanitas*, for Julius Caesar, too, posthumously exerts his 'will' over the city, bequeathing in his final testament a civic space to Rome's masses. This civic space, however, does not come into being in the course of Shakespeare's play; though proposed, it remains a space deferred.

The Londinium Arch, though only a temporary monument, was a space of conflict for urban power and representational authority. Shakespeare's *Julius Caesar* is play composed of quotational performances through which his characters vie for authority over their representational city.

The setting of this play participates in the same kind of spatial suspension represented in the Londinium of James's entry. For Elin Diamond, representation is 'the making visible (again) of what is lacking or what has disappeared.'[22] The representational space of Londinium exists between the parentheses of Diamond's '(again)': a carefully constructed retrospective performance that locates discourses of the past in the present. *Julius Caesar* contains numerous internal quotations that provide points of juxtaposition between Roman past and early modern 'present.' The most productive points of juxtaposition are those in which representations of Rome would have worked to suggest a new urban space when performed in Shakespeare's London.

Michel De Certeau contends that the space of the modern city emerged in sixteenth-century Europe, and that this new space was marked by an obsession with representing the city as a static, unchanging image: 'The city, like a proper name, provides a way of conceiving and constructing space on the basis of a finite number of stable, isolatable positions.'[23] In Shakespeare's play, Caesar struggles to stabilize his identity; he is particularly concerned with fixing the meaning that he links to his 'proper name' (de Certeau 94).[24] But the play named for Caesar is not hospitable to the eponymous Roman's representational fixations. Londinium was not merely a name, but a space determined in performance.

Performance and the city

Shakespeare's *Caesar* has become 'one of the most quoted texts in debates about critical theory,' and the play continues to draw and focus critical attention as do few others.[25] Responding to this critical tradition, Wilson describes the play as 'a text that dreamed the past as a museum' (1). Resisting the pull of such a lovely metaphor, I prefer instead to read the play not as a 'museum' of static, inert objects, but as a *performance archive*. I regard *Caesar* as a flexible text, whose meanings are multiple, processual, and provisional. The importance of this play extends beyond the performance history of Shakespeare's plays to include the history of one of the major urban developments in London during this period: the emergence of the public theatre. Just as the city was a theatrical formation in early modern London, the professional theatre emerged as an urban formation. Shakespeare's *Caesar* corroborates this urban / theatrical dualism, and indeed collaborates with it. The representations of space in this play, and the performances in the space of representation that this play insists on, worked together to produce a theatrical event profoundly engaged with the early modern city.

The opening of *Caesar* presents an urban scene richly expressive of the cultural anxieties and representational possibilities that worked to shape dramatic literature and theatrical practice in early modern London. In the very first lines of the play, the tribunes Flavius and Murellus castigate a group of 'Commoners':

> FLAVIUS: Hence! Home, you idle creatures, get you home!
> Is this a holiday? What, know you not,
> Being mechanical, you ought not walk
> Upon a laboring day without the sign
> Of your profession? Speak, what trade art thou? (I.i.1–5)[26]

The Commoners respond with irreverent puns that play on the guilds and professions by which they are named: 'Carpenter' and 'Cobbler' in particular. The comic exchange reaches its culmination when the Commoners finally confess their reason for assembling.

> COBBLER: [...] But indeed, sir, we make holiday
> To see Caesar, and to rejoice in his triumph.
> MURELLUS: Wherefore rejoice? What conquest brings he home?
> What tributaries follow him to Rome,
> To grace in captive bonds his chariot-wheels?
> You blocks, you stones, you worse than senseless things! (I.i.30–5)

For an audience of 1599, this exchange would have begun in a space firmly anchored in the everyday placeworld familiar to the Elizabethan Londoners in attendance. Even before the first lines have been delivered, some number of actors playing the parts of the Commoners must already have been on stage before the tribunes entered, otherwise there would be no holiday mischief in progress to justify their outrage. Since the names and language given to these Commoners identify them with an Elizabethan population more than with Roman plebeians, one may well assume the 'holiday' disruptions were forms of Elizabethan performance juxtaposed with the representation of Caesar's Rome. Other more obvious juxtapositions like clocks, chimney-pots, hats, and billiards can be found throughout Shakespeare's Roman plays. Though in 1910 MacCallum could assert that Shakespeare included these anachronisms 'without any consciousness of the discrepancy' (85), I argue that Shakespeare's use of history (or indeed, abuse of it) was entirely intentional. As Coppélia Kahn concurs, anachronism isn't the issue: 'Through a kind of cross-pollination that isn't simply anachronism, Englishness appears in Roman settings, and Romanness is anglicized.'[27] Like the arches of James's entry, Shakespeare's juxtapositions of London and Rome are neither accidental nor incidental: they are strategic cultural hybridizations produced from the interaction of text and performance.

Speculative considerations of early modern performance are critically important to understanding the representational strategies employed in *Caesar*. The text of the play strongly suggests that the theatrical event would have begun before the point at which the text itself begins. In other words, performance by the actors would have preceded the authorized and 'authored' text attributed to the characters.[28] Wilson argues that this 'exposé' would have made it clear to the real-world commoners attending the theatre that 'they had no business to be there' (' "Is this a holiday?" ' 57). However, I find it difficult to conclude that the tribune's address was an expression of 'company policy' on the part of the Lord Chamberlain's Men (56) – after all, the tribunes would soon be 'put to silence' for their actions (I.ii.285–6). Robert Weimann suggests alternative terms by which to consider the play's opening:

> [O]ne of the ways by which the Elizabethan theatre appropriated power was to challenge the representation of authority by an alternative authority of theatrical representation.[29]

The actors playing the Commoners can be seen to have opened up a playful contestatory space, one in which the real-world conditions of theatrical performance remained visible along with (and even in opposition to) the representation of authority by Flavius and Murellus. While the tribunes may have chased the Commoners from the stage, the commoners in the audience would recognize that all the actors on stage were commoners like them.[30]

On the occasion of Platter's performance, by the time Murellus was delivering his monologue on the state of the empire,[31] a representational transition would have already begun. The 'holiday' dialogue that marked the opening of the play serves the dramaturgical function of tenuously anchoring the performance in the concrete world of London, 1599. Subsequent dialogue leads the audience toward the abstract space produced for the narrative: Rome. Before Murellus speaks, the scene is dominated by characters recognizable as similar to those in attendance at the Elizabethan playhouse, perhaps even indistinguishable from them. Murellus's accusations make anachronistic reference to the quotidian business of Elizabethan Londoners. His references locate the opening of the play not so much in Rome as in the very London where the performance itself would have taken place, and identify the speakers not so much as Romans but as part of crowd. Murellus interrupts the Commoners' playful banter, and the space of comic performance – with its references to the space of theatrical production – gives way to the production of an abstract space far removed from that of the playgoers.

'*Locus* and *Platea* revisited' revisited

Shakespeare's *Caesar* reveals a class of issues related to changing conceptions and practices of space in late Elizabethan culture.[32] In the case of London, a gradual shift in the conception of space introduced hybrid spaces, and new ways of practicing the space of the city.

Scenes such as the opening of *Caesar* rely on a 'double business' in the 'purposes of playing' that invokes a 'bifold authority' in representation. Such representational 'doubleness' in theatrical practice has received extensive, profound consideration in the work of Robert Weimann. In *Author's Pen and Actor's Voice* (2000), Weimann considers the early modern emergence of visually determined representational strategies to offer a reconsideration of the terms *locus* and *platea*, which he first discussed in his foundational *Shakespeare and the Popular Tradition*. I wish to extend Weimann's reconsideration of his own study so that the meanings governing the space of the city can be seen reflected in the city's complexly represented other: the space of the stage. There, the interaction between the ideal and the real, the abstract and the concrete, were made vivid and accessible to the city's inhabitants.

Weimann's expanded consideration of the *locus* and *platea* performance conventions on early modern stages takes into account 'the newly expanding space *in* (imaginary) representation and the recently institutionalized, material space *of* its performance' (*Author's Pen* 180, italics in original). Weimann frames the understanding of these terms in the context of considerations of representation in and of space. He re-defines *platea* as 'an opening in the *mise-en-scène* through which the place and time of the stage-as-stage and the cultural occasion itself are made either to assist or resist the socially and verbally elevated, spatially and temporally remote representation' (181). The *locus*, by contrast, 'can be seen as a strategic approximation to the uses of perspectival form: it implicated the establishment of a topographically fixed locality' (182). The players' occupation of the imaginatively fixed narrative space of the *locus* abstracted the theatrical performance from the world of the audience and the 'cultural occasion' of attendance at the public theatre, establishing a *counter-occasion*: a represented event separate from the theatre and the audience around the platform stage.

Importantly, *platea* and *locus* must not be seen as mutually exclusive. The interaction of these spaces demonstrates a consonance between Shakespeare's theatrical practice and that of hybrid spatial constructs such as the Londinium Arch – an object that integrated performance with self-contained representational location. In 1599, the space of *Caesar*, a dramatic fiction set in Rome, would never have ceased to be associated, however tenuously, with the space of the stage from which that fiction emerged. For example: the Cobbler says that he has come 'To see Caesar'; indeed, the audience members that he so closely resembles would have come to see *Caesar* too. In the Cobbler's punning phrase, 'Caesar' refers to both the character *in* the representation and the representation itself, the 'cultural occasion': a play at the Globe theatre.[33]

Beginning as it does in the space of the *platea*, the play suggests that the space of the stage would have produced an ambiguous intersection of London and Rome: Londinium. *Caesar* initiates its discourse on the power of the theatrical in urban life with a scene that conflates the city *in* performance with the city *of* performance, inviting continuous comparison between the characters' Rome and audience's London.

Performance is an essential tool for engaging theories of space. It is performance that activates the events that occupy space.[34] But the spatial activity of early modern performance cannot be fully understood without engaging with representation. As Weimann's work has consistently demonstrated, representation is the key to understanding *locus* and *platea* as much more than merely a relationship between 'upstage' and 'downstage' portions of the playing area, as these concepts are often reductively mistaken. Such terms of stage location are, at any rate, anachronistic in a discussion of early modern London's platform stages, where audiences would have been located on three (and in some cases on four) sides of the players. By collapsing the understanding of *locus* and *platea*, scholars of early modern literature and theatre run the risk of underestimating the complex meaning-making at work on the Elizabethan stage.[35]

In Shakespeare's plays, fictional agents operate and fictional events transpire in a location that is non-identical with the location in which the actual performance took place. (For example, Rome is real, but Caesar's Rome was far removed in time and geography from Shakespeare's London.) It is with such representation of space that *locus* is associated. But *platea* space is not merely a point 'downstage from' the *locus*; rather, the *platea* is a space produced by early modern actors when they acknowledged the actual event of performance while performing in relation to a representational event. There would have been no need to go 'downstage' to produce *platea* space: a performing agent need only acknowledge that *there is a stage* to invoke the space of the *platea*, and even to do so from within the *locus* of representation, thereby hybridizing the performance space. The strategy of negotiating the relationship between *locus* and *platea* provided Elizabethan performers (and writers) with opportunities to engage the audience, to comment ironically upon the action of the narrative, and (not unimportantly) to make a joke. In other words, the difference between *locus* and *platea* is found not in a particular stage location, but in a performance decision. And the agency of the player was to be found in the negotiation of representation and the representational in this performance.

In the uses of *locus* and *platea*, Shakespeare and his players found a multivalent source of individual authority and cultural productivity, and through Shakespeare and his players the city incurred a debt to the stage.

'It is performed'

Though the performance of Rome on the platform stage seems in stark contrast with the elaborate architectural pageantry of James's entry, this urban play participates in the cultural phenomenon of early modern hybrid space that I describe with the Latin word that Jonson appropriated for James: 'Londinium.' The space of Londinium serves as the unacknowledged *limen* connecting the abstract elsewhere of early modern representation with the very real place of the stage. While the idea of Rome may provide a paradigm of urban space in *Caesar*, it is through the gaps in this representation of Rome – the *platea* – that London's own spaces were produced. Though the innovations in visual culture that would eventually reshape the city were emergent in 1599, Shakespeare's London was still manifestly a city of performances and processions where, in Steven Mullaney's words, 'a community could chart, in its actual topography, the limits and coherence of its authority.'[36] However, the authority represented in the streets of *Caesar*'s Rome (as in Shakespeare's London) was one whose coherence was more vulnerable to challenge and disruption than Mullaney's statement admits.

The holiday against which Flavius and Murellus militate is the feast of Lupercal.[37] Their complaint is not with the holiday itself, but with Caesar's appropriation of it as an occasion for an urban triumph not unlike a royal entry. The character of Caesar is introduced in the course of his entry into Rome, orchestrating his own city-spanning theatrical event.

> CAESAR: Calphurnia!
> CALPH: Here, my lord.
> CAESAR: Stand you directly in Antonio's way
> When he doth run his course. Antonio!
> ANTONY: Caesar, my lord?
> CAESAR: Forget not in your speed, Antonio,
> To touch Calphurnia; for our elders say
> The barren, touched in this holy chase,
> Shake off their sterile curse.
> ANTONY: I shall remember:
> When Caesar says, "Do this," it is performed. (I.ii.1–10)

In his performance of urban ceremony, Caesar displays a thorough understanding of the theatricality of the (political) stage. Not content to be merely the object of his spectators' 'viewe,' Caesar actively performs in his Lupercal entry, instructing Calphurnia and Antony in their roles. Caesar displays a flexible understanding of his own public identity – so much so that he attributes transformational power to the civic triumph, and wishes to make sure that Calphurnia is touched by that power. Antony's response, 'When Caesar says "Do this," it is performed,' positions him as Caesar's performance-surrogate, not unlike Alleyn's role in James's entry. But Caesar, unlike James, does not hesitate to join the performance.

Throughout the play, the discourses of power in the city are directly compared to the discursive space of the theatre.[38] By continually referring to and metaphorizing theatricality, Shakespeare is also continually indexing the 'cultural occasion' of the theatrical event itself. The city represented in *Caesar* is a theatrical space where authority displays itself to the people, but where it is also judged by those same people.

When the conspirators take violent action, the discourses of the theatre are so strongly invoked that they suggest an infinite regress of the theatrical, a multiplication of violence in representation. Following the murder of Caesar, staged in Pompey's Theatre, it is Brutus's turn to orchestrate a public performance.

> BRUTUS: Stoop, Romans, stoop,
> And let us bathe our hands in Caesar's blood
> Up to the elbows, and besmear our swords;
> Then walk we forth, even to the market-place,
> And waving our red weapons o'er our heads,
> Let's all cry, "Peace, freedom, and liberty!"
> CASSIUS: Stoop then, and wash. How many ages hence
> Shall this our lofty scene be acted over
> In states unborn and accents yet unknown! (III.i.105–10)

Brutus's staging of the conspirators' public appearance is met with a reply that displaces the scene from civic performance to public theatre: Cassius's lines refer to Shakespeare's own production, in which, 'ages hence' the murderers' 'lofty scene' was indeed 'acted over.' These lines, delivered from the most narratively substantiated position of the *locus*, invoke the double vision of the *platea* in which both ancient Rome and contemporary London would have been equally in play on the stage. At this point, Shakespeare puts his entire play in quotation marks, reminding his audience that Caesar's death was not in fact actually happening in the past but was being 'acted over,' performed again in an accent that would have been 'unknown' to Caesar and in a state 'unborn' in his Caesar's age – though in a location that he himself had claimed, and which another writer would later name 'Londinium.'

The conspirators murder Caesar for their belief that he represented himself as greater than they, and their theatrical murder is itself 'deeply dependent on the mechanics of representation.'[39] They have little opportunity to secure their representation, however, before yielding the scene to Antony, whose own representation quickly displaces that of the murderers'. From the second line of his funeral oration, 'I come to bury Caesar, not to praise him' (III.ii.74), Antony seeks to appropriate the version of history recently established by Brutus and the other conspirators, and to produce for the Commoners a favorable retrospective image of Caesar. This is, in a sense, Caesar's last public performance: even in death, his identity remains available to theatrical interpretation, and Antony takes advantage of the performability of this late Roman actor.

At the outset of *Caesar*, the tribunes established and defined the *locus* in Rome, by disparaging the playful plebians: 'you blocks, you stones [...] you cruel men of Rome' (I.i.35–6). At the most critical point in Antony's oration to Rome's citizens, he flatters the plebians with the same words: 'You are not wood, you are not stones, but men' (III.ii.142). Antony's oration reverses the movement of the opening: Antony '*comes down from the pulpit*' and stands among the Commoners to read Caesar's will (III.ii.163 sd). Rather than asserting a *locus* distinct from the space of the audience, as Murellus and Flavius do, Antony moves from *locus* to *platea*. Antony is the only character in the play to perform in this way. Though this movement preserves the narrative fiction, Antony's gesture of inclusion nevertheless takes in London's groundlings along with Rome's plebeians. It is not above imagining that when he came '*down from the pulpit*,' the actor playing Antony may well have left the platform stage and joined the groundlings in the Pit. As Alessandro Serpieri observes, the theatre-loving Antony consistently demonstrates 'mastery of every stage space,' including Shakespeare's theatre as well as Pompey's.[40]

While the Commoners may have been chased from the stage at the outset of the play, Antony finds the authority to overturn the conspirators' victory by including the audience of commoners in his performance (III.ii.201). This victory was not the result of mere rhetoric, but of a performance decision: a careful agencing of (representational) space and (theatrical) event.

This interplay of concrete performance and abstract representation, located as it was in the permeable representational space of Londinium, created for the early modern audience an opportunity to compare 'the limits and coherence' of the Rome on display in *Caesar* to their own understandings and experiences of their own city and its authorizing urban performances (Mullaney 10). Thus considered, the Londinium Arch was both a material monument and a spatial concept, and it served as a nodal point in the urban history of early modern London.

A conclusion and an emergence

The hybrid spaces explored and developed in the 1599 performance of *Julius Caesar* contributed to the necessary preconditions for the elaborately hybridized event of James's royal entry. Though Shakespeare's play preceded James's entry by five years, both participated in the same 'real-and-imagined' space; Jonson just gave it a name. The Londinium Arch straddled not only a narrow, ancient street in the City, it served as a threshold across which traditional and emergent spaces briefly coexisted, suspended between representation and performance.

When Garber calls *Julius Caesar* 'in a way, the last play of its kind,' she is identifying this text as partial evidence of the cultural shift taking hold in late Elizabethan England.[41] I, too, view *Julius Caesar* as among the last of its kind, because of the way in which the text reveals the cultural traces, however atrophied, that linked the spatiality of medieval performance culture to the representational forms of late sixteenth-century London.

By contrast, a sense of 'the first of its kind' pervades James's 1604 entry. While the performed event of the entry displayed a doubled spatiality under the name of Londinium, the king (in the role of Caesar Augustus, not Julius) attempted to retire into fixity: de Certeau's 'proper' was James's ruling representational force. Though the character of Caesar is 'almost obsessively' concerned with fixing his political identity in his own name, nevertheless he sees his authority as something to be publicly performed.[42] James achieved the fixed identity that de Certeau describes, and to which Shakespeare's Caesar aspired, by eschewing performance. Instead, James made a spectacle of himself and his city. James refused to yield the *locus* of his own represented identity, choosing to remain on display in the stabilized site of his Latin-derived, Roman representation. If the hybridized Rome of *Julius Caesar* – in which the city's ruler willingly performed in the space of the city – was the 'last of its kind,' then what followed in James's entry was a hybrid, Romanized space in which the city's ruler absolutely refused to perform at all.

And this is the critical difference. The performance events considered here, demonstrate the brief trajectory of this period of hybrid spatiality. Shakespeare's *Julius Caesar* and James's royal entry stand on either side of a cultural threshold, offering a before-and-after view of this spatial transition: predecessor and successor; Julius and Augustus. While *Caesar* and other theatre texts of its ilk demonstrate 'a strategic approximation to the uses of perspectival form' (Weimann, *Author's Pen* 182), James's entry approximated nothing: the visual paradigms that would come to dominate perspective-based theatre were imported to England with this event. Such a cultural emergence is best understood as defined by Foucault: '*emergence*, the moment of arising,' an incident of historical 'apparition.'[43] Wilson locates one such emergence in *Caesar*, which shows 'the process of separation as the new theatre distanced itself from [...] an older participatory form' (*Julius Caesar* 43); this marks the beginning of the period of hybrid spatiality; that period began to end with James's entry. The force of visual representation at work in the entry superceded the role of performance that had been a traditional aspect of urban pageantry (and an essential feature of the public theatre). Within months, Inigo Jones would introduce both the self-contained theatrical narratives of the masque and the self-contained urban narratives of the piazza to Jacobean London, precipitating the end of this period of spatial hybridity.

For Shakespeare, James, and others in this transitional period, the city of Rome was as much an idea as a location, and this idea was suspended between a historical past and a material present. Shakespeare was not concerned that his Roman patricians spoke like English aristocrats, just as he was not concerned that the plebeians on his stage might be indistinguishable from the commoners in the audience. Shakespeare set his Roman plays in a kind of Londinium, a Romanized representation of his own city.

Londinium, a simultaneously real-and-imagined space, was the setting for James's first Arch. It inaugurated the king's Roman vision of himself and of his capital city. Similarly, Shakespeare produced his own version of Londinium, an urban paradigm of hybrid spatiality that responded to his own experience of increasingly multivalent cultural, social, and urban practices. Though Shakespeare's *Caesar* preceded James's entry by some five years, they participated in the same 'finite historical period' (Lefebvre 73): two hybrid spaces among the broader genealogy of spaces in Shakespeare's London. More than just a site in representation, early modern London was equally produced in performance. Interactions between bodies and spaces remained crucial to the production of the city – on the stage, on the printed page, and in the streets themselves. Shakespeare's idea of the world was a theatrical one – the name of his theatre, The Globe, was not chosen by accident. If Shakespeare indeed saw all the world as a stage, then in his Roman plays he conceived the city as theatrical too: a space that was meant to be, not passively viewed, but actively performed.

Notes

1. Lefebvre, *The Production of Space*, 73.
2. Wells, *The Wide Arch*, 4.
3. Stow, *A Survey of London*, 33–39.
4. Jonson, *King James's Royal and Magnificent Entertainment*, 377–99.
5. Following the usage of urban historian Francis Sheppard, references to 'the City' (capitalized) refer to the City of London, the territory traditionally bounded by London's medieval walls. 'London' or 'the city' (lower case) refer to 'the whole metropolitan urban area' (Sheppard xvi), including suburbs like Southwark and Shoreditch.
6. See Dekker 376; Bergeron, *Practicing Renaissance Scholarship*, 165–75.
7. Parry, *The Golden Age Restor'd*, 18.
8. See Jonson, 387–95.
9. Goldberg, *James I and the Politics of Literature*, 165.
10. Soja, *Thirdspace*, 33. This project owes an interdisciplinary debt to the fields of urban studies and human geography.
11. Paster, *The Idea of the City*, 58. See also Cantor, *Shakespeare's Rome*, 28.

12. John Schofield writes: 'In 1600, London was a medieval city on the edge of spectacular expansion in the century to come.' Schofield, 'The Topography and Buildings of London,' 319.
13. Montrose, *The Purpose of Playing*, 109; ' "Shaping Fantasies," ' 31.
14. The work of Joseph Roach, provides an important landmark to my methodology: 'genealogies of performance document – and suspect – the historical transmission and dissemination of cultural practices through collective representations.' Roach, *Cities of the Dead*, 25.
15. Wilson, *Julius Caesar* 40.
16. Serlio's *The Five Books of Architecture*; Italian, 1584; English translation, 1611. Serlio, i.
17. See Lefebvre 38–39 for the introduction of these terms.
18. Garber, *Shakespeare's Ghost Writers*, 52.
19. The field of study 'the Roman plays of Shakespeare' was established by Mungo MacCallum in *Shakespeare's Roman Plays and Their Background* (1910).
20. In the most remarkable use of quotation in recent critical history, Gayatri Chakravorty Spivak concludes her 'Translator's Preface' to Derrida's *Of Grammatology* with a short paragraph that begins in quotation marks. This short concluding paragraph is actually the beginning of Derrida's own preface to *Of Grammatology*, but Spivak quotes his preface at the end of her own. Moreover, Spivak interpenetrates this quotation with italicized text, addressing the reader: '*Now I insert my text within his and move you on, situating here*' (lxxxvii). Significantly, at the end of this eight-line paragraph, there is no second set of quotation marks, no closure to the open quotation. Instead, there is only an ellipsis, blurring the boundary between 'Spivak' and 'Derrida.' By opening but not closing the quotation at the end of her 'Preface,' Spivak situates all of Derrida's *Of Grammatology* as merely a supplement to her introduction to it.
21. See Baker, ' "Master of the Monuments," ' 266–87.
22. Diamond, *Unmaking Mimesis*, 85.
23. De Certeau, *The Practice of Everyday Life*, 94.
24. Platt argues that: 'By seldom or never speaking of himself as "I," ' Caesar 'is already a monument, a colossus.' *Rome and Romans*, 187.
25. Wilson, 'Introduction,' 1.
26. All quotes from Shakespeare are from *The Riverside Shakespeare*.
27. Kahn, 'Roman Virtue on English Stages,' 4.
28. For further consideration of the relationship between text and performance in Shakespeare, see Hopkins and Reynolds, 'The Making of Authorships,' 29–51.
29. Weimann, 'Towards a Literary Theory of Ideology,' 272.
30. For another reading of one of Shakespeare's Roman plays that incorporates a discussion of the role of the audience, see Reynolds, ' "What is the city but the people?" ' 107–32.
31. For discussions of this monologue, see Rose, 'Conjuring Caesar,' 256–57; and Wilson, *Julius Caesar*, 25–6.
32. This section title is an appropriation of the chapter title '*Locus* and *Platea* Revisited' in Weimann, *Author's Pen*, 187. For the introduction of the terms *locus* and *platea*, see Weimann, *Shakespeare and the Popular Tradition*, 73–85.
33. My thanks to Weimann for bringing this artful pun to my attention. See also Paster 61.
34. The architectural theorist Bernard Tschumi, proposes that architecture is engaged in 'the careful agencing of spaces and events.' Tschumi, *Event Cities*, 11.

35. Not to mention underestimating the contributions of Weimann to studies of the Elizabethan stage. See Howard's favorable review of *Author's Pen* for a well meaning example of this fallacy (311). In a rather more acerbic estimation of Weimann's work, Vickers limits the relevance of his remarks by oversimplifying *locus* and *platea* and other Weimanian concepts (214–71). Helms misconstrues *locus* and *platea* as specific 'venues' or stage locations (555), but her idea of a 'tragic platea' is suggestive.
36. Mullaney, *The Place of the Stage*, 10.
37. See Liebler, ' "Thou Bleeding Piece of Earth," ' 85–111; Sterling, ' "Or Else This Were a Savage Spectacle," ' 39–49.
38. Drakakis, ' "Fashion It Thus," ' 82.
39. See Ronan, '*Antike Roman*,' 24–7 and Wilson, *Julius Caesar*, 41–7.
40. Serpieri, 'Reading the signs,' 119–43.
41. Garber, 'Dream and Interpretation,' 46.
42. Barton, 'Rhetoric in Ancient Rome,' 86–7.
43. Foucault, 'Nietzsche, Genealogy, History,' 148, italics in original.

Works cited

Baker, David Weil. ' "Master of the Monuments": Memory and Erasure in Jonson's *Bartholomew Fair*.' *English Literary Renaissance* 31.2 (Spring 2001): 266–87.
Barton, Anne. 'Rhetoric in Ancient Rome.' Bloom 1988. 79–89.
Bergeron, David M. *English Civic Pageantry, 1558–1672*. London: Edward Arnold, 1971.
——. *Practicing Renaissance Scholarship: Plays and Pageants, Patrons and Politics*. Pittsburgh, Pennsylvania: Duquesne University Press, 2000.
Bloom, Harold, ed. *William Shakespeare's* Julius Caesar. New York: Chelsea, 1988.
Cantor, Paul A. *Shakespeare's Rome: Republic and Empire*. Ithaca, NY: Cornell University Press, 1976.
Certeau, Michel de. *The Practice of Everyday Life*. Trans. Steven Rendall. Los Angeles: University of California Press, 1984.
Diamond, Elin. *Unmaking Mimesis: Essays on Feminism and Theater*. New York: Routledge, 1997.
Drakakis, John. ' "Fashion It Thus": *Julius Caesar* and the Politics of Theatrical Representation.' Wilson 2002, 77–91.
Foucault, Michel. 'Nietzsche, Genealogy, History.' *Language, Counter-Memory, Practice*. Ed. Donald Bouchard. Ithaca, NY: Cornell University Press, 1977. 139–64.
Garber, Marjorie. *Shakespeare's Ghost Writers: Literature as Uncanny Causality*. New York: Methuen, 1987.
——. 'Dream and Interpretation: *Julius Caesar*.' *William Shakespeare's* Julius Caesar. Ed. Harold Bloom. New York: Chelsea, 1988. 43–52.
Goldberg, Jonathan. *James I and the Politics of Literature*. Baltimore: Johns Hopkins University Press, 1983.
Helms, Lorraine. ' "The High Roman Fashion": Sacrifice, Suicide, and the Shakespearean Stage.' *PMLA* 107.3 (May 1992): 554–65.
Hopkins, D.J. 'The Londinium Arch: Representing the Urban Subject in Performance and Print (London, 1604).' *Symbolism Yearbook*. Ed. Douglass Bruster and Robert Weimann. Forthcoming.
Hopkins D.J. and Bryan Reynolds. 'The Making of Authorships.' *Performing Transversally: Reimagining Shakespeare and the Critical Future*. New York: Palgrave, 2003. 29–51.

Howard, Jean. 'Rev. of Author's Pen and Actor's Voice: Playing and Writing in Shakespeare's Theatre by Robert Weimann.' *Shakespeare Quarterly* 53.3 (Fall 2002): 390–93.
Jonson, Ben. *The Royal and Magnificent Entertainment*. Nichols 1828, 377–99.
Kahn, Coppelia. *Roman Shakespeare: Warriors, Wounds, and Women*. London: Routledge, 1997.
Lefebvre, Henri. *The Production of Space*. Trans. Donald Nicholson-Smith. Oxford: Blackwell, 1991.
Liebler, Naomi Conn. ' "Thou Bleeding Piece of Earth": The Ritual Ground of *Julius Caesar*.' *Shakespeare's Festive Tragedy: The Ritual Foundations of Genre*. New York: Routledge, 1995. 85–111.
MacCallum, Mungo. *Shakespeare's Roman Plays and Their Background*. London: Macmillan, 1910.
Montrose, Louis. *The Purpose of Playing: Shakespeare and the Cultural Politics of the Elizabethan Theatre*. Chicago: University of Chicago Press, 1996.
——. ' "Shaping Fantasies": Figurations of Gender and Power in Elizabethan Culture.' *Representing the English Renaissance*. Ed. Stephen Greenblatt. Berkeley: University of California Press, 1988. 31–64.
Mullaney, Steven. *The Place of the Stage*. Chicago: University of Chicago Press, 1988.
Nichols, J. B., ed. *Progresses of King James the First*. Vol. 1. London: Society of Antiquaries, 1828.
Parry, Graham. *The Golden Age Restor'd: The Culture of the Stuart Court, 1603–42*. London: Manchester University Press, 1981.
Paster, Gail Kern. *The Idea of the City in the Age of Shakespeare*. Athens, GA: University of Georgia Press, 1985.
Platt, Michael. *Rome and Romans According to Shakespeare*. Rev. Ed. New York: University Press of America, 1983.
Reynolds, Bryan. ' "What is the city but the people?": Transversal Performance and Radical Politics in Shakespeare's *Coriolanus* and Brecht's *Coriolan*.' *Shakespeare Without Class: Misappropriations of Cultural Capital*. Ed. Donald Hedrick and Bryan Reynolds. New York: Palgrave, 2000. 107–32.
Riverside Shakespeare, The. Ed. G. Blakemore Evans and J.J.M. Tobin. New York: Houghton Mifflin, 1997.
Roach, Joseph R. *Cities of the Dead: Circum-Atlantic Performance*. New York: Columbia University Press, 1996.
Ronan, Clifford. *'Antike Roman': Power Symbology and The Roman Play in Early Modern England, 1585–1635*. Athens, GA: University of Georgia Press, 1995.
Rose, Mark. 'Conjuring Caesar: Ceremony, History and Authority in 1599,' *True Rites and Maimed Rites: Ritual and Anti-Ritual in Shakespeare and His Age*. Ed. Linda Woodbridge and Edward Berry (Chicago: University of Illinois Press, 1992), 256–69.
Schofield, John. 'The Topography and Buildings of London, ca. 1600.' *Material London, ca. 1600*. Ed. Lena Cowen Orlin. Philadelphia: University of Pennsylvania Press, 2000. 296–321.
——. *The Building of London: From the Conquest to the Great Fire*. London: Colonnade – British Museum, 1984.
Serlio, Sebastiano. *The Five Books of Architecture: An Unabridged Reprint of the English Edition of 1611*. New York: Dover, 1982.
Serpieri, Alessandro. 'Reading the signs: Towards a Semiotics of Shakespearean Drama,' *Alternative Shakespeares*. Ed. John Drakakis. London: Routledge, 1985. 119–43.
Sheppard, Francis. *London: A History*. New York: Oxford University Press, 1998.

Soja, Edward W. *Thirdspace: Journeys to Los Angeles and Other Real-and-Imagined Places*. Malden, MA: Blackwell, 1996.
Spivak, Gayatri Chakravorty. 'Translator's Preface.' *Of Grammatology*. By Jacques Derrida. Baltimore: Johns Hopkins, 1974.
Sterling, Brents. 'Or Else This Were a Savage Spectacle.' *Twentieth Century Interpretations of Julius Caesar*. Ed. Leonard F. Dean. Englewood Cliffs, NJ: Prentice-Hall, 1968. 39–49.
Stow, John. *A Survey of London Written in the Year 1598*. Phoenix Mill, UK: Sutton, 1994.
Tschumi, Bernard. *Event Cities*. Cambridge, Mass.: MIT Press, 1994.
Vickers, Brian. *Appropriating Shakespeare: Contemporary Critical Quarrels*. New Haven: Yale UP, 1993.
Weimann, Robert. *Shakespeare and the Popular Tradition in the Theater: Studies in the Social Dimension of Dramatic Form and Function*. Johns Hopkins University Press, 1978.
——. 'Towards a Literary Theory of Ideology: Mimesis, Representation, Authority.' *Shakespeare Reproduced: The Text in History and Ideology*. Ed. Jean E. Howard and Marion F. O'Connor. New York: Methuen, 1987.
——. *Author's Pen and Actor's Voice: Playing and Writing in Shakespeare's Theatre*. New York: Cambridge University Press, 2000.
Wells, Charles. *The Wide Arch: Roman Values in Shakespeare*. New York: St. Martin's Press, 1992.
Wilson, Richard. 'Introduction.' *Julius Caesar: Contemporary Critical Essays*. Ed. Richard Wilson. New York: Palgrave, 2002. 1–28.
——. ' "Is this a holiday?" Shakespeare's Roman Carnival.' *Julius Caesar: Contemporary Critical Essays*. Ed. Richard Wilson. New York: Palgrave, 2002. 55–74.
——. *Julius Caesar*. London: Penguin, 1992.

3
Shakespeare's Little Boys: Theatrical Apprenticeship and the Construction of Childhood

Catherine Belsey

I

Performances of *As You Like It* can have the effect of bringing home to the audience the centrality of Rosalind. Particularly as Ganymede, Rosalind dominates the stage. She buys the cottage, organizes the lovers, and successfully educates Orlando in the proprieties of courtship. More important, she makes the jokes, while the hero acts largely as her foil. In other words, she sets the tone, which means she has the primary responsibility for enlisting the audience's attention, maintaining the suspense and shifting the mood from comedy to romance and back. The actor who plays Rosalind has to be good: a weak Rosalind would entail a poor play all round. Like Cleopatra, like Juliet, Rosalind is at the heart of the play and, also like them, is required to display a range of moods, as she herself indicates. Adding Ganymede's role to Rosalind's own, the play asks its protagonist to 'grieve, be effeminate, changeable, longing and liking, proud, fantastical, apish, shallow, inconstant, full of tears, full of smiles' (3.2.410–12).[1]

All the evidence indicates that in 1599 Rosalind would have been played by a boy apprenticed to a member of the company. The records are exceptionally sketchy: boys were evidently fairly low on everyone's list of priorities, and where the sharers in the company are identified in the surviving documents with some respect, the boys often feature only by their first names, if that. Subsequent scholars, too, have paid more attention to the stars, Richard Burbage and Edward Alleyn, not least because a good deal more is known about them. But a certain amount of information can be gleaned from theatre history, in conjunction with the texts, to indicate that the period of apprenticeship played a part not only in training the boys for their future roles,[2] but also in the composition of the plays and, beyond that, perhaps in the construction of childhood itself as a distinctive phase entailing its own special state of consciousness.

II

How widespread was the practice of apprenticeship? According to evidence pieced together from scattered sources, many of the players took on boys as apprentice actors. Of the 98 players known to have belonged to the Shakespeare company at any one time between 1594 and 1642, at least 30 began as boy-players, and in some 18 of these cases there are clear indications that they were apprenticed to adult actors. During the course of his career, John Heminges, for instance, registered ten apprentices, including John Rice, 'a very proper Child, well spoken' in 1607; Augustine Phillips is known to have had three; Nicholas Tooley was Burbage's apprentice.[3] Meanwhile, Richard Jones, prominent in Philip Henslowe's company, the Admiral's Men, had an apprentice, James, who was listed some time between 1597 and 1602 as one of the boy actors in the plot of *Troilus and Cressida*.[4] Thomas Downton, of the same company, had two boys.[5] Even Henslowe himself, manager and entrepreneur but not a player, had an apprentice, James Bristow. Henslowe had bought him in 1597 from William Agusten, a player, and by April 1600, at least, the Admiral's Men were paying Henslowe 3 shillings a week for James Bristow's wages, so presumably he too had been co-opted for the stage.[6] Alleyn had a boy, John Pyk or Pig, who seems to have played Alice Pierce in a production of 1597, since in December that year Henslowe laid out £1 for taffeta and tinsel for a dress for her, as well as an additional 6s 7d to make the bodice and sleeves 'of pyges gown'.[7]

With such training on the job by such masters, there is no reason why the boys should not have been good. And it seems they were. According to Henry Jackson, who saw *Othello* in Oxford in 1610, the tragedies of the King's Men were generally 'decorously' and 'aptly' performed, but he singled out Desdemona, who, 'although she always put her case very well, after her death moved us still more when, lying in bed, she implored the pity of the spectators with her countenance itself'.[8]

The plays are often quite extravagant in the allocation of parts for boys. *As You Like It* includes three female roles, besides Rosalind's. Celia, Phebe and Audrey would surely have been played by boys. But in addition, the last act includes a scene where Touchstone and Audrey appear for the sole purpose, it seems, of listening to two boys sing a song. 'Here', Audrey announces, so that we know who they are, 'come two of the banish'd Duke's pages' (5.3.5–6), and with very little more ado the boys break into 'It was a lover and his lass'. When their performance comes to an end, Touchstone teases the 'young gentlemen' for having made a poor show of it, the pages insist that they have kept time (34–41), and everyone goes off.

The song is cheerful, lyrical, altogether appropriate to the last act of a comedy, and the treble voices of the pages would contrast well with the earlier songs of the grown-up Amiens in Act 2. But the introduction of two new speaking parts in the final act, and with no contribution whatever to the plot, looks remarkably like extravagance. Could the parts have been doubled with the female roles? Not easily. Audrey is on stage; Rosalind and Phebe appear in the scene immediately before this one; Rosalind, Phebe and Celia are in the one after it. Costume, according to Henslowe's inventories, was a major component of performance, and it seems reasonable to assume that in this respect the practices of the Admiral's Men were not radically different from those of the Shakespeare company. The boys could not possibly have changed from skirts to breeches and back in time. What could Shakespeare, as a working dramatist and professional man of the theatre, at the height of his powers in 1599, have been thinking of when he included two extra boys in a play that could perfectly well have done without them?

We do not, of course, have access to Shakespeare's thoughts, and recent biographies suggest that they might be disappointing if we had: they were apparently full of land acquisition, coats of arms and exploitation.[9] But if there is any truth in this current view, we have all the more reason to suppose that the presence of these boys is motivated. Moreover, the economy of Shakespeare's stage might have implications for other plays of the period, and perhaps beyond the theatre, for our understanding of the culture itself. 39 child characters appear in Shakespeare's plays.[10] At least 20 of the plays include minor parts for pages and young boys, and 21 if we include the boy player in *Hamlet*, who appears, though he does not speak, in his own person, but has one scene as the Player Queen. Little girls are very rare. Excluding the infant Elizabeth in *Henry VIII*, since she was probably a doll, there remains Clarence's daughter, who has a small part in *Richard III*. Among the little boys, the two pages who come and go so unexpectedly in *As You Like It* are not, as it turns out, an extreme case. A 'boy' sings a sad song to Mariana in the moated grange, and then disappears from *Measure for Measure*, though he might, of course, have doubled as a minor figure.[11] In *All's Well That Ends Well*, a page comes on in the first scene to say, 'Monsieur Parolles, my lord calls for you', then exits and is never seen again (1.1.187), though it is possible that he doubled as Mariana, or the silent and still less obviously motivated Violenta. Benedick has a boy, who is summoned only to be sent off to fetch a book (*Much Ado About Nothing*, 2.3.1–5). Gardiner's boy in *Henry VIII* is on stage for rather longer, but speaks only to confirm the time (5.1.1–2). These pages indicate the rank of their masters, of course. But is there an additional reason for their inclusion?

Though there is no unequivocal evidence, the comedy of Bottom's exchanges with Peasblossom, Cobweb, Moth and Mustardseed in *A Midsummer Night's Dream* would work well if the four fairies were played by boys (3.1.162–96). These elves are to hop and gambol, and steal honeybags from humble-bees. Ironically, Bottom calls them 'your worships', sends his compliments to Peaseblossom's parents, and contrasts Mustardseed with the 'giant-like' beef his kindred traditionally accompany. The tiniest of these small parts belongs to Moth, who says only 'And I' (163). The expansion of his part to include a 'Hail' (177), as well as a non-speaking appearance in 4.1, is editorial.[12] The problem here, however, is that, since all the principal female figures appear in 4.1, the play would require at least eight boys, with one doubling as the fairy of 2.1, and possibly another as Flute. Is it possible? David Bradley, who has calculated the requirements for the public theatre plays, assigns six boys to most Shakespeare plays of this period.[13] Were more available?

The hardest evidence we have of stage practice is provided by *The Battle of Alcazar*, which survives both as printed text of 1594 and as 'plot', or casting chart, for a revival by the Admiral's Men in or about 1598. This is a unique instance, of course, and may not be typical. Moreover, the text and what survives of the plot are not at first sight entirely compatible. Even so, taken together, they indicate that this play, at least, involved more than six boy-actors. There are three principal female parts, Calipolis, otherwise unidentified in the plot, Abdula Rais, played by Dick Jubie, Edward Dutton's apprentice, and Ruben Archis, played by 'Jeames', who doubles as a page. Was this Henslowe's apprentice, James Bristow, bought from William Agusten in 1597, or Richard Jones's boy, who was in *Troilus and Cressida*? In addition, Dab and Harry appear as little princes, smothered in their beds in dumbshow. They reappear as ghosts, crying 'Vindicta', and Dab later features as Ruben's son. The historical record throws no light on the status of Dab and Harry. Nemesis, who beats a drum in the second dumbshow is identified as female and is played by 'Tho. Drom', but he may be a musician, rather than an apprentice actor. Thomas Parsons, Thomas Downton's apprentice, plays a mute Fury. The plot also casts 'mr Allens boy' and 'mr Townes boy' as silent pages.[14] It thus names at least seven boy-actors, while leaving one unnamed, giving a total of eight. Have we been too ready to assume that the principle of thrift, which determined the allocation of adult roles, obtained for the boys as well? We shall probably never know for sure how many of the unidentified and mute 'attendants' in other plays were boys.

III

The incidental children who feature in so many plays have been barely visible to the critical tradition, at least until recently. Whereas there has been a good deal of attention to the role of the boy actors impersonating women, and even more to the boys playing women dressed as boys, the younger boys played by boys have generated relatively little excitement. What are the likely motives for including so many minor parts for little boys? Most obviously, plays written for children to perform had already demonstrated the charm of witty pages who offered a sceptical alternative to high sentiment and lyrical romance. The tradition, familiar from John Lyly's courtly comedies, goes back at least to *Damon and Pythias* (1564–65), written by Richard Edwardes, then Master of the Chapel Children.[15] Nicholas Udall's school play, *Ralph Roister Doister*, written some time before 1553, includes a whole crew of children, servants of the protagonist and the widow he seeks to marry. Dame Custance has two little girls and a boy in her service; Roister Doister employs the 'little wagpastie' (line 793), Dobinet Doughtie, to press his suit, as well as the very nearly silent Harpax.[16] These children sing a variety of songs. In addition, the comedy owes a good deal to the byplay between them, and the attempts to impose discipline practised by their 'elders', played, presumably, by slightly older boys.

From the 1570s on, the choirboys of St Paul's, as well as the Children of the Chapel Royal, put on public performances of plays. In the early 1590s, however, these children's companies were temporarily silent, at least in London. The Paul's Boys did not resume their public performances until towards the end of the decade, and it was 1600 before the Chapel Children took back the Blackfriars.[17] If Shakespeare's plays of the 1590s included boys, it seems unlikely that there was any plan to *rival* the children,[18] but the adult companies might well have learnt from their former successes what boy-actors were capable of. Further, in a theatre where what is heard is as important as spectacle, the diversity of voices might well be a consideration, rather like the range of instruments in a musical performance.[19] When Hamlet hopes that the boy-player's voice 'be not crack'd', perhaps he has an ear to acoustic variety as well as mimetic plausibility (*Hamlet*, 4.2.428).[20]

Above all, however, the duration of the apprenticeship, whether seven years or rather more, was the time available for learning the skills required to play Rosalind, Juliet or Desdemona. Surely, no company in its right mind would let a boy loose with any of these parts until he had shown his capabilities in roles where considerably less was at stake?[21] There must have been a good deal to learn, not least how to move, as well as stand still, speak audibly and intelligibly, use the range of the voice, and cope with an audience, especially one that was probably less deferential and less silent than our own. Then as now, we may assume, boys did not do any of these things by nature.[22] While adult casting was driven by the effort to extract the maximum number of characters from the fifteen or so people Thomas Platter saw in *Julius Caesar* in 1599,[23] it seems likely that the inclusion of so many fictional children was motivated by the imperative to train apprentices in the arts of acting, in preparation for their leading roles.

Additional skills would be necessary, however, before they were ready to play Rosalind or Juliet. Shakespeare's little boys are not always quite as incidental as the pages in *As You Like It*, and sometimes they contribute significantly to the action. Prince Arthur, for example, plays a crucial part in *King John*. Arthur's thematic role might be read, indeed, as larger than his part. In this play, curious to modern eyes, part mirror for princes, part analysis of the condition of England, John himself represents the nominal hero, but almost as in the old moral plays, two contrasting figures mark out his ethical state: on the one hand, Philip the Bastard, strong and courageous but illegitimate; on the other, Prince Arthur, legitimate but weak. Each is the son of one of John's dead elder brothers, Philip of Richard Coeur de Lion and Arthur of the second brother, Geoffrey. John therefore addresses both as 'cousin' (3.2.12, 16).[24] The Bastard, blunt, pragmatic and invincible, personifies English heroism, and to the degree that the King recognizes and fosters these qualities, he deserves to rule. But Philip's bastardy has an emblematic dimension: John's reign is illicit. By contrast, as the rightful heir to the throne, Prince Arthur is, he insists in his first speech, helpless. In France to seek the support of England's hereditary enemies, and reduced to enlisting in his own cause the Duke of Austria, Arthur greets the man who killed Richard I with, he says, 'a powerless hand/ But with a heart full of unstained love' (2.1.15–16). His heart is unstained in two senses: purged of hatred for a former foe, but also innocent; and Arthur is powerless in two parallel senses: deprived of rule, and a little boy. The play emphasises his vulnerability throughout. Its thematic turning-point comes in Act 3, at the moment when John, having promised Arthur land, titles and love, gives instructions for his murder (3.2.76). Arthur's role thus throws into relief the tyranny of the usurping king, and the child's fate becomes evidence of John's – and England's – moral and political decline.

The prince himself has, however, only one big scene. At other times he is present and highly visible, but mostly silent. He is apparently onstage for some 500 lines of 2.1, but with only two short speeches, while the grown-ups quarrel and threaten each other around him and on his behalf. In the second of these speeches, he once again presents to the audience his own innocence and the pathos of his situation, begging his mother to desist: 'I would that I were low laid in my grave:/ I am not worth this coil that's made for me' (164–5). The little prince represents the occasion, as well as the incongruity, of the adult quest for power, while the adults themselves ironically make his childish virtue the justification of their rapacity.[25] He has one line in 2.2, again an ineffectual effort to pacify his mother (42) and another single line in 3.2, where he registers for the audience the predictable horror of Constance at his capture by King John (15). In 4.3 he jumps to his death, leaving the English nobles to speak, resolve and exchange vows over his inert body. At the emblematic high point of this scene, which is paradoxically the low point morally and politically for the kingdom, the Bastard orders Hubert to carry the dead prince, exclaiming:

> How easy dost thou take all England up!
> From forth this morsel of dead royalty
> The life, the right and truth of all this realm
> Is fled to heaven. (4.3.142–5)[26]

The editor of Arden 2 sees 4.1, where Arthur pleads with Hubert not to put out his eyes, as the 'central' scene of the play, arguing that Shakespeare rewrites his sources to focus John's problems on Arthur.[27] While the blinding scene is unequivocally theatrical, its dramatic mode is emphatically not mimetic: Arthur does not talk quite as we should expect of a frightened child. Robert Weimann makes a distinction between two modes of representation, the one in the process of supplanting the other on the early modern stage. On the one hand, 'presentation' specifies an emotion or a state of mind, points to it, defines it, as if from outside; on the other, 'impersonation' enacts it mimetically. Weimann attributes presentation to an earlier form of drama, before the author took control of the stage with a view to creating the illusion of a self-contained fictional world.[28] In this sense, Prince Arthur 'presents' his own pathos to Hubert and to the audience in a succession of conceits that we should not expect a modern child to utter. When, for instance, in response to Arthur's plea to spare his eyes, Hubert insists, 'with hot irons must I burn them out', 'Ah, none but in this iron age would do it!', Arthur punningly replies (59–60). The iron has cooled, Arthur points out; it 'would not harm me'. He can heat it up again, Hubert counters. 'No, in good sooth; the fire is dead with grief', the prince returns. But Hubert can rekindle it. 'And if you do, you will but make it blush/ And glow with shame of your proceedings, Hubert' (103–13). This repeated wordplay draws attention to Arthur's innocence and helplessness, but does not mimic it.

We might find nothing childish about these exchanges, but as Weimann's distinction indicates, there is more than one way to hold the mirror up to nature. When Hamlet urges the players 'to show virtue her feature, scorn her own image' (3.2.22–3), he names allegorical personifications, not characters. Bertolt Brecht, for one, wanted to create a drama that would discourage emotional identification in order to foreground a point, without sacrificing our interest in the story. Arguably, at least, John's tyranny is made more apparent in this non-illusionist presentation of the brutality of the crime, and Arthur's innocence is made more pitiable, not less, as his un-child-like eloquence persuades Hubert to relent.

In medieval drama, where the moral purpose is never far away, characters are as likely to 'present' their own condition as to impersonate it. As an extreme instance, the Northampton play of *Abraham and Isaac* sustains intense pathos in a long dialogue between a father obedient to the will of God and the child he loves. Isaac does not resist his own sacrificial death but, like Arthur anticipating Constance's grief (3.2.15), he visualizes on Sara's behalf her sorrow at his loss: 'of my modre, I wot wel, I shall be myst./ Many a tyme hath she me clipt and kyst,/ But farewel nowe, for that is do' (lines 213–25). Isaac asks his father to take off his gown. He cannot do it himself, he explains, 'For I may not. I falle in swownne'.[29] It is as if the dialogue stands in for stage directions or a third-person narrative. At the beginning of *The Castle of Perseverance* the human protagonist announces his own helpless infancy in the accents of an adult:

>   This nyth I was of my modyr born.
>   Fro my modyr I walke, I wende,

Ful feynt and febyl I fare you beforn.
I am naked of lym and lende
As Mankynde is schapyn and schorn. (lines 276–80)[30]

While he speaks, three powerful kings tower above him on their scaffolds. The World, the Flesh and the Devil have already announced their intention to destroy their human victim (lines 266–70). Mankind was almost certainly not played by a child since, as the action goes on, the same character will become first a young man and then an old one. But the physical disposition of the figures makes a visual contrast between the three kings elevated on their platforms and the human figure, who probably rises, as he is 'born', from the bed the stage plan places on the ground at the centre of the circular playing area.[31] Mankind looks small. A similar contrast would emphasize Arthur's vulnerability as Hubert stands over the boy with the blinding iron, and this is presumably intensified when the keeper calls in the executioners.

In addition, Arthur's littleness is repeatedly indicated all through the play. At the beginning of this scene, Hubert calls him 'little prince', and Arthur puns on his 'great title' to be 'more prince' (4.1.9–11). At the end of it, Hubert addresses him as 'pretty child' (129). His mother thinks of him as 'pretty Arthur' (3.3.89) and in the text he is consistently a 'child'.[32] The legitimate heir is a condensed version of his father, and the King of France goes on to re-emphasize his small stature in the comparison that follows:

This little abstract doth contain that large
Which died in Geoffrey: and the hand of time
Shall draw this brief into as huge a volume. (2.1.101–3)

Size matters in the visual economy of the play. The Bastard's claim to be Richard's son depends explicitly on his 'large composition' (1.1.88) and his evident muscularity (237–40). By contrast, the Earl of Pembroke will allow the true heir a three-foot grave (4.2.100), which, if we took it literally, would make Prince Arthur very little indeed. Holinshed, one of several sources, offers a choice of emphasis. In 1199, when Richard died, Eleanor supported her son John's claim to the throne, according to Holinshed, on the grounds that Arthur 'was but a babe to speake of'. Three years later, however, Arthur was to be found leading an army against the English, and possibly taking his grandmother prisoner.[33] In a play that rewrites history in several respects, Shakespeare seems to have opted for the first account: his Arthur is not much more than a baby.

How little, then, was the boy who played Prince Arthur? This was not, I have urged, a mimetic play. All audiences know that if the text repeatedly reaffirms a character's smallness, or beauty or muscularity, the actor tends to acquire these qualities in the eyes of the audience for the duration of the play. In addition, any illusion of littleness there was might well be reinforced by costume. Aristocratic boys wore petticoats while they remained in the care of women, until the age of six or seven, when they were put into breeches and taught manly pastimes like hunting and falconry. Mamillius, who plays with his mother and her ladies-in-waiting in *The Winter's Tale*, is explicitly 'unbreech'd' (1.2.155). Probably Macduff's son is too, since he is also to be found with his mother. Ross addresses him as 'My pretty cousin' and the First Murderer calls him an 'egg' (*Macbeth*, 4.2.25, 83). Arthur is twice identified as an 'infant' (2.1.97; 3.3.132). In the first half of the play he appears always with his mother, and when Constance remembers her son, it is as a little boy in her care that she portrays him:

> Grief fills the room up of my absent child,
> Lies in his bed, walks up and down with me,
> Puts on his pretty looks, repeats his words ... (3.3.93–5)

There is, as far as I know, no direct evidence, but the performance would have made a point if the boy who occasioned the quarrels of Act 2 was in petticoats, and Arthur appeared in breeches for the first time when he was captured and handed over to Hubert.

It seems likely that the actor was older than Arthur. No evidence exists of any apprentices in the adult companies under 11 or 12 years old,[34] though it is possible that little boys acted on stage before they were bound.[35] Allowing for a later age of puberty, however, many would still be children when they were first apprenticed.[36] They were also actors, of course, and part of their skill must have included playing roles younger than their actual age. There is some evidence that the companies saw their junior apprentices as 'little'. An inventory of the Admiral's Men's stock on 10 March 1598 includes, among assorted doublets, jerkins and gowns, 'j lyttell dublet for boye'. A list of costumes made three days later lists 'j littell gacket for Pygge'. Pig was Edward Alleyn's apprentice, and the same inventory includes a damask gown for him, as well as various suits.[37] The surviving 'plot' of *1 Tamar Cam* (?1602) includes among its boy players, 'Little Will Barne'. The document also names Thomas Parsons, who was Thomas Downton's apprentice, and – separately – Mr Downton's 'little boy'.[38] Henslowe records that in 1597 he 'Layd owte for copper lace for the littell boye & for a valle for the boye' 29 shillings 'A geanste the playe of dido & enevs'.[39] Here, too, a distinction is made in terms of size. Presumably, the veil was for Dido, played by the boy, while the copper imitation of gold or silver lace indicated the high birth of Ascanius, young son of Aeneas, the little boy.

If Arthur was played by a younger boy in training for a leading role in due course, what would he learn from the experience? In addition to the primary skills of speech and movement and reacting to an audience, he would also have the opportunity to display precisely the kind of pathos Henry Jackson praised in the boy who played Desdemona. Arthur's long silences in Act 2 would work best if he were able to 'implore the pity of the spectators with [his] countenance itself', like the heroine of *Othello*. The influence of the children's companies might be evident here, since they specialized in pathetic protagonists, including Griselda, Susanna and Dido. In *Two Gentlemen of Verona* Julia, disguised as Sebastian, claims to have played the part of Ariadne and to have made her mistress weep bitterly in the process (4.4.158–71). This is Julia's invention, of course, and the tears of her 'mistress' are for her own betrayal, not Ariadne's, but it implies that pathos is among the skills boy-heroines were known for. Shakespeare's little boys might have learnt to move their audiences to tears as Macduff's son, or Mamillius. And if they played these parts in petticoats, they would also have become accustomed to managing skirts in preparation for their reappearance as heroines in due course.

IV

Rosalind's accomplishments include comedy too. As the youthful Ganymede, in particular, she is required to be worldly, knowing, and altogether wittier than the lover, Orlando. Shakespeare had appropriated the unruly page from the children's companies as early as *Love's Labours Lost* in 1594–95, where a sceptical Moth consistently outwits the fantastical lover Armado, playing 'tender juvenal' to the Spaniard's 'tough signior' (1.2.8, 17). Like Moth, Lyly's servant-boys, too, are cleverer than their adult masters. The pages in *Mother Bombie*, for instance, descend directly from Terence's ingenious slaves, who outwit their betters to bring about a happy ending.

But Lyly's servants are explicitly little. The boys' plays repeatedly exploit the discrepancy between inventiveness and size. Lyly's Halfpenny, for example, is a hop o' my thumb, scarcely as high as a pint pot (*Mother Bombie*, 2.5.45–6), but an accredited trickster for all that. Like Arthur, he may not be a large volume yet, but appearances do not do him justice: 'bound up in *decimo sexto* for carriage, yet a wit in *folio* for coosnage' (2.1.45–6).[40] Moreover, small stature is no bar to self-confidence: already in *Roister Doister* Dobinet Doughtie's name points to a similar paradoxical combination of small size and grand pretensions.

In the same way as Ganymede (*As You Like It*, 3.2.334), or Arthur, Macduff's son and, indeed, Halfpenny (*Mother Bombie*, 3.4.140), the cheeky Moth is 'pretty'. In response to his wit, Armado comments, 'Pretty and apt'. Moth immediately dissects this: 'How mean you, sir? I pretty, and my saying apt? or I apt, and my saying pretty?' 'Thou pretty', Armado replies, 'because little' (1.2.18–21). The term has a wider range of reference in the early modern period than it has now. It can indicate general approval of ingenuity or good manners, as well as appearance, but it very often acts as a kind of diminutive, more appropriate then as now to women and children (*OED*).

As Armado makes clear, 'pretty' and 'little' belong together. Prince Hal provides Falstaff with a page, and the jokes depend almost entirely on their relative sizes. Falstaff tells him: 'I do here walk before thee like a sow that hath overwhelm'd all her litter but one.... thou whoreson mandrake, thou art fitter to be worn in my cap than to wait at my heels' (*2 Henry IV*, 1.2.11–16). When the boy reappears as Robin in *The Merry Wives of Windsor*, Ford calls him a 'pretty weathercock' (3.2.17, cf. 3.3.22, 27). Evidently just as small, he is also equally precocious. In one instance, Mistress Page asks the 'little gallant' whether he would rather attend her or Falstaff. 'I had rather, forsooth', he replies, 'go before you like a man than follow him like a dwarf'. 'O, you are a flattering boy', she comments fondly. 'Now I see you'll be a courtier' (3.2.1–7).

But here again Robert Weimann's distinction between presentation and impersonation makes possible a tentative distinction. This is sometimes no more than a nuance, open to debate, certainly not a binary opposition. Once again, however, in my view, these children are not inevitably *childish* in the modern sense of the term. Here is an exchange between Lyly's Dromio and his master, Memphio, who is complaining that his own son is a fool:

> Mem. I maruell he is such an asse, he takes it not of his father.
> Dro. He may for anie thing you know.
> Mem. Why, villain, dost thou think me a foole?
> Dro. O no, sir, neither are you sure that you are his father.
> (*Mother Bombie*, 1.1.19–23)

Like Moth, Dromio is ready with a witty insult, and equally quick, when the offence is spotted, to find an alternative which is not much more flattering. These pages are prematurely knowing: there is nothing here of the guileless innocence we tend to associate with childhood. By contrast, Mamillius, who tells his mother a nursery tale of sprites and goblins (*The Winter's Tale*, 1.2.64–5), apparently makes nothing of his father's jealous ravings. His affirmation to Leontes, 'I am like you, [they] say' (*The Winter's Tale*, 1.2.208), surely owes its appeal to dramatic irony, not a design to reassure. The little Macduff seems more knowing, but his precocity is framed as unconscious by his mother's fond diminutives, 'poor monkey' and 'Poor prattler' (*Macbeth*, 4.2.59, 64).

In other words, both Macduff's little boy and Mamillius are presented as naively playful. There is a difference of genre, certainly; and they are younger than the pages. But do they not also mark a shift of style from presentation to impersonation? The date of *King John* is uncertain, but most of the evidence points to the first half of the 1590s, the period of *Love's Labours Lost*. *Macbeth* is conventionally assigned to 1606, *The Winter's Tale* to three or four years later. In the interval the image of childhood seems to develop a certain autonomy, derived from the previous drama but not bound

Illustration 7 Marcus Gheeraerts, Barbara, Lady Sidney and her Children, 1596.

by it, as a period of play, of artless teasing, when the precocity that invites our indulgence is un-self-conscious, and the more charming in consequence. Polixenes nostalgically remembers how he and Leontes were 'as twinn'd lambs that did frisk i' th' sun' (1.2.67), 'wags', certainly (66), but innocent: 'we knew not/ The doctrine of ill-doing, nor dream'd/ That any did' (69–71).

Visual styles were also changing in this period towards a new fidelity to what the eye actually sees. My own tentative researches indicate a gradual, though irregular, movement from the formal representation of the child as a miniature person, with adult proportions and features, to a much more mimetic depiction of childish contours.[41] The little boy, still wearing petticoats and slumped in misery, who appears on the tomb of Jane, Lady Waller, in the 1630s, meets our own expectations of infant proportions (Illustration 6). The size of the head, the length of the arms and the rounded cheeks all go to distinguish this child from an adult in a similar pose. Indeed, the incongruity of his conventional posture of adult melancholy has the effect of deepening the pathos of his grief, in mourning for his mother. But a generation earlier, when Marcus Gheeraerts portrays Barbara, Lady Sidney with her children, there is not a great deal to differentiate their silhouettes from their mother's (Illustration 7). Moreover, the white dresses of both mother and children seem to emphasize the similarities. The costume of the four daughters is more or less adult, though the youngest wear no ruffs.[42] The faces of the standing children are all much the same size, and while the smallest girl seems to have a childishly large head in consequence, her waist is drawn in to particularly un-childlike effect. Lady Sidney extends one protective hand to each of the boys, as if to affirm their genealogy. Sir Robert's heir occupies the central foreground, his hat deferentially in his hand and his miniature sword in place, despite the petticoats. He reaches only to his mother's waist, but looks taller than he is, in consequence of his relatively grown-up proportions. William Sidney would have been five or six in 1596. (He died of smallpox in 1612, while his father was still living, so that in practice it was his brother Robert, only months old at the time of the portrait, who went on to become Viscount Lisle, and then Earl of Leicester.)

This image shows exactly how we might see Arthur in Act 2, shielded by his mother and still in petticoats, but with indications of incipient authority. Arthur nursed Hubert when the keeper was ill, he reminds him, just as an adult might (*King John*, 4.1.29–30; 41–52). Arthur names his suffering; he does not demonstrate it by a doleful inertia. It is hard to imagine Arthur or William Sidney at play, and yet it is exactly the *absence* of playfulness that defines the pathos of the child on the monument. Surely, *this* little boy *ought* to be carefree?

V

John Pyk or Pig, Edward Alleyn's apprentice, who played Alice Pierce and wore one of the little jackets, wrote a playful letter to Alleyn's wife. Or that, at least, is the pretence, in a document in Alleyn's own writing and addressed to Mistress Alleyn. What gives the game away is that in a postscript 'Pig' pretends that Thomas Downton wrote the letter on his behalf behind his master's back. The handwriting suggests otherwise. Alleyn had married Henslowe's stepdaughter, Joan, in 1592, and to judge from the surviving letters between them, written when Alleyn was on tour, the relationship was affectionate: he calls her his 'mouse' and 'Jug'; she addresses him as 'My Intyre & welbeloved sweete harte'.[43] The letter pretending to be from the apprentice evidently represents one of Alleyn's own light-hearted contributions to this marital correspondence, but for precisely that reason, it gives some indication of the way these grown-ups thought of the boy.

Apprentices lived with their masters and were members of the family as it was conceived in the period. John Pyk was evidently at home there. In his supposed letter he sends his commendations to Henslowe and his wife, as well as to Mistress Alleyn. He also includes Joan's sister, Bess, 'for all her harde delyng with me', but looks forward to being beholden to her again for opening the cupboard. Was Bess, perhaps, the disciplinarian of the household, who kept him in order, but also had sweet things among her stores that boys might like, to reward good behaviour? He sends good wishes to 'my neyghbore doll for calynge me vp in a mornyng' and 'my wyf sara for making clean my showes'. Were Doll and Sara servant-girls in this large household, sleeping in an attic room next to John's, and were the family perhaps in the habit of teasing John for getting on well with Sara? He also mentions 'that ould Jentillman mounsir pearle that ever fought with me for the blok in the chemeney corner'. In the absence of any other evidence, I would conjecture that Pearl was a cat, and that the animal and the apprentice are seen as competing for a warm place in the hearth.

'Pig' himself is evidently a kind of pet too. Moreover, his charm depends on the comic self-regard of a favourite whose bravado solicits adult indulgence.[44] 'Though you all Look', he assures them, 'for the redy retorne of my proper person yett I swear to you by the fayth of a fustyan kinge never to retorne till fortune us bryng with a Joyfull metyng to lovly london'. John Pyk proves engaging in much the same way as Mamillius, 'this kernel,/ This squash, this gentleman'. When Leontes pretends to treat him as an adult, 'Mine honest friend,/ Will you take eggs for money?', the child replies, 'No, my lord, I'll fight' (*The Winter's Tale*, 1.2.159–62), and the comedy depends on the child's pastiche of grown-up behaviour. It has the effect of distracting the king from his jealousy for a moment, so that he turns to Polixenes to compare experiences of fatherhood, and finds that his unsuspecting guest feels much the same about young Florizel (1.2.166–71).

Pastiche depends on difference, as well as similarity. In these instances the discrepancy between the children they are and the grown-ups they aspire to be is hard to resist. While Arthur speaks like an adult to present his childish vulnerability, these playful little boys disarm by asserting themselves as the adults they so evidently are not. Concluding his letter with the flourish, 'I sesse', Alleyn's apprentice signs himself, 'yor petty prety pratlyng parlyng pyg/ by me John Pyk'.[45] The letter is undated, but Pig's little jacket was listed in 1598; the gown for Alice Pierce was being made in December 1597; he was in *The Battle of Alcazar* in about 1598, and *Troilus and Cressida* in (probably) 1599. The letter may belong to about this period.

My own view is that these depictions of playfulness, Alleyn's as well as Shakespeare's, contribute to the cultural shift they also reproduce, towards a new definition of childhood. These children are not yet endowed with an inner life and self-consciousness: in British culture that would have to wait for Wordsworth. A hundred years later still, Freud would invest them with unconscious desires. Child-like early modern children, by contrast, suppose there is no more behind than 'such a day to-morrow as to-day,/ And to be boy eternal' (*The Winter's Tale*, 1.2.64–5). But they are distinguished from adults to the degree that they are without responsibility, unburdened and, in spite of the best efforts of Protestant theology, innocent (1.2.69).

A boy who had played Prince Arthur *and* Moth (or, later, Mamillius) would be well trained in the rudiments of Rosalind's part, able to move with relative ease between the oppressed heroine, banished by Duke Frederick, and the saucy lackey who teases Orlando. The additional ingredient, not practised by the children, would be romantic love. Once that is added, we begin to have the recipe for Juliet and Cleopatra as well. When Robert Weimann makes the distinction he draws between presentation and impersonation, he does so in order to define the difference between an earlier mode of acting that allows the player a certain autonomy to clown, sing, or dance, and the gradual subjection of the actor's skills to a new kind of theatre. This emerging mimetic drama insists on bringing the players into line with a fictional world invented by the author, but at its most successful, it also incorporates those traditional skills into the fictional world itself, with the effect that the actor's voice exerts an influence on the activities of the author's pen.[46] If the presence of so many little boys in Shakespeare's plays owes something to the material imperative to train apprentices in the new kinds of skills that such a drama required, the plays are not best understood as feats of pure imagination born out of airy nothing more than the desire to mimic the world. Instead, we should have to acknowledge that the exigencies of the developing profession of actor exert their influence on the nature of the world the author creates, that the material conditions of the early modern theatre leave their mark on the shape of the plays.

And perhaps that they also exert an influence on the culture at large. There was probably no more powerful cultural apparatus than the theatre in this period. The new 'family values', I have argued elsewhere, were given a major boost at this time, for better or worse, by the theatre's insistence on romantic love as the proper basis of marriage.[47] It seems to me altogether likely that the drama helped at the same moment to construct an image we still recognize of 'petty pretty pratlyng parling' little boys, capable of mischief, disarming precocity or deep sadness, and also of inviting adult indulgence towards the distinctive phase they represent.[48] As in so much else, Shakespeare's theatre, and the subsequent influence of his plays, helped to produce an account of childhood that is now widely taken for granted in Western culture.

Notes

1. All references to Shakespeare's plays, with the exception of *King John*, are to *The Riverside Shakespeare*, ed. G. Blakemore Evans *et al.* (Boston, MA: Houghton Mifflin, 1997).
2. See Scott McMillin, 'The Sharer and His Boy: Rehearsing Shakespeare's Women', *From Script to Stage in Early Modern England*, ed. Peter Holland and Stephen Orgel (Basingstoke: Palgrave, 2004), pp. 231–45.
3. Andrew Gurr, *The Shakespeare Company, 1594–1642* (Cambridge: Cambridge University Press, 2004), pp. 217–46; 21. See also Roslyn Lander Knutson, *Playing Companies and Commerce in Shakespeare's Time* (Cambridge: Cambridge University Press, 2001).

4. R. A. Foakes, ed., *Henslowe's Diary* (Cambridge: Cambridge University Press, 2002), p. 32. This was a version by Dekker and Chettle, not Shakespeare's *Troilus and Cressida*. For the plot see David Bradley, *From Text to Performance in the Elizabethan Theatre: Preparing the Play for the Stage* (Cambridge: Cambridge University Press, 1992), p. 111.
5. *Henslowe's Diary*, pp. 75, 77; Bradley, *From Text to Performance*, pp. 116–17.
6. *Henslowe's Diary*, pp. 241, 167.
7. *Henslowe's Diary*, pp. 73, 85.
8. Reproduced in *The Riverside Shakespeare*, p. 1978 (my translation).
9. Katherine Duncan-Jones, *Ungentle Shakespeare: Scenes from His Life* (London: Thomson, 2001). See also Richard Wilson, *Will Power* (London: Harvester, 1993).
10. Mark A. Heberle, ' "Innocent Prate": *King John* and Shakespeare's Children', *Infant Tongues: The Voice of the Child in Literature*, ed. Elizabeth Goodenough, Mark A. Heberle and Naomi Solokoff (Detroit, MI: Wayne State University Press, 1994), pp. 28–43.
11. It has been argued that this episode is a later theatrical interpolation (Gary Taylor and John Jowett, *Shakespeare Reshaped, 1606–1623* (Oxford: Clarendon Press, 1993), pp. 123–40). If so, the question of the motive for its inclusion is simply deferred to a later date.
12. I owe this observation to Alan Dessen, who has entered into the spirit of my quest for invisible boys, and contributed a mine of information in the process.
13. Bradley, *From Text to Performance*, pp. 230–43. In an essay arguing for the reassignment of *2 Seven Deadly Sins* to Shakespeare's company in 1597-8, David Kathman points out that this 'plot' names six boy-actors ('Reconsidering *The Seven Deadly Sins*', *Early Theatre*, 7.1 (2004), pp. 13–44).
14. Reproduced by T. J. King, *Casting Shakespeare's Plays: London Actors and Their Roles* (Cambridge: Cambridge University Press, 1992), pp. 260–1. One of them is probably the boy who finds his master a horse and speaks a total of six lines in the printed text, but the plot does not mention this brief episode (W. W. Greg, ed., *The Battle of Alcazar* (Oxford: Malone Society Reprints, 1907), lines 1387–1426). It would be satisfying to think that this was Mr Alleyn's boy, since Edward Alleyn played his master, the Moor.
15. G. K. Hunter, *John Lyly: The Humanist as Courtier* (London: Routledge and Kegan Paul, 1962), pp. 229–43.
16. Nicholas Udall, *Roister Doister*, ed. W. W. Greg (Oxford: Malone Society Reprints, 1935).
17. Michael Shapiro, *Children of the Revels: The Boy Companies of Shakespeare's Time and Their Plays* (New York: Columbia University Press, 1977), pp. 14–26.
18. On the contrary, possibly. Andrew Gurr suggests that when Rosencrantz and Guildenstern tell Hamlet of the threat to the tragedians from the children, this is 'a discreet advertisement' designed to increase their takings and the income of their landlord at the Blackfriars, Richard Burbage (*Shakespeare Company*, p. 33, n. 48; 142, n. 30). He does concede, however, that they had probably become 'an irritant' (p. 135).
19. See Bruce R. Smith, *The Acoustic World of Early Modern England* (Chicago, IL: University of Chicago Press, 1999), pp. 206–84.
20. It seems that apprentices went on playing women into their late teens and beyond, after their voices must have broken (Michael Shapiro, *Gender in Play on the Shakespearean Stage: Boy Heroines and Female Pages* (Ann Arbor, IL: University of Michigan Press, 1996), p. 34; Richard Madelaine, 'Material Boys: Apprenticeship

and the Boy Actors' Shakespearean Roles', *Shakespeare Matters: History, Teaching, Performance*, ed. Lloyd Davis (Newark: University of Delaware Press, 2003), 225–38, p. 232).
21. Some, of course, had learned their skills from the children's companies, like Nathan Field, William Ostler and John Underwood, who moved on from the Blackfriars to the King's Men (Gurr, *Shakespeare Company*, 227, 235, 245).
22. A fictional account of the training of a boy-actor appears in Nicholas Wright, *Cressida*, 2.2 (London: Nick Hern, 2000).
23. See *The Riverside Shakespeare*, p. 1964.
24. William Shakespeare, *King John*, ed. E. A. J. Honigmann (London: Methuen, 1954). All references are to this edition.
25. Lines 18; 99–106; 115; 122–33; 156–63; 166–82.
26. Punctuation modified.
27. Shakespeare, *King John*, pp. lx–lxi.
28. *Author's Pen and Actor's Voice: Playing and Writing in Shakespeare's Theatre* (Cambridge: Cambridge University Press, 2000).
29. Norman Davis, ed., *Non-Cycle Plays and Fragments*, EETS (London: Oxford University Press, 1970), pp. 32–42.
30. Mark Eccles, ed., *The Macro Plays*, EETS (London: Oxford University Press, 1969), pp. 1–111.
31. See Catherine Belsey, *The Subject of Tragedy: Identity and Difference in Renaissance Drama* (London: Methuen, 1985), pp. 13–23.
32. 2.1.159–60; 179; 189; 245; 3.1.113; 3.3.75; 92; 4.2.97; 259; 4.3.124; 156.
33. Shakespeare, *King John*, pp. 150, 152–3.
34. I owe this observation to John H. Astington, who has been generous with his time and kept a restraining eye on my wilder speculations on this topic. See especially 'John Rhodes: Draper, Bookseller and Man of the Theatre', *Theatre Notebook*, 57 (2003), 83–9, p. 83; 'The Career of Andrew Cane, Citizen, Goldsmith, and Player', *Medieval and Renaissance Drama in England*, 16 (2003), pp. 130–44. The traditional minimum age of apprenticeship was 14. In 1631 William Trigge petitioned to be discharged from his apprenticeship on the grounds that he had been only 13 at the time of the contract (David Kathman, 'Grocers, Goldsmiths and Drapers: Freemen and Apprentices in the Elizabethan Theater', *Shakespeare Quarterly*, 55 (2004), 1–49, p. 11).
35. Kathman also points out that William Patricke, who must have been the son of an actor of the same name, was acting with the King's Men four years before he was apprenticed ('Grocers', p. 11).
36. Richard Rastall estimates the likely age of male puberty as 17–18 in the late middle ages ('Female Roles in All-Male Casts', *Medieval Drama in English*, 7 (1985), pp. 25–50). Although Bruce Smith opts for 14 for early modern boys and 12 for girls, on the basis that this interpolation in the English version of *The Problemes of Aristotle* was based on observation (*The Acoustic World*, p. 227), the translator probably simply reproduces convention: 14 was the legal age of marriage for boys and 12 for girls in ecclesiastical law (Ralph Houlbrooke, *The English Family 1450–1700* (London: Longman, 1984), p. 166).
37. *Henslowe's Diary*, pp. 317–23.
38. Reproduced in Bradley, *From Text to Performance*, pp. 116–17.
39. *Henslowe's Diary*, p. 86.
40. John Lyly, *Mother Bombie*, *The Complete Works*, ed. R. Warwick Bond (Oxford: Clarendon Press, 1902), 3 vols, vol. 3, pp. 163–228.

41. As evidence of the irregularity, Holbein's portrait of a childlike Edward Prince of Wales, c. 1538, is well ahead of its time. A more typical work at Longleat shows William Brooke, 10th Lord Cobham, with his stiffly formal family in 1567.
42. The oldest girl, nine or ten at this time, would go on to become Lady Mary Wroth, and would refer in *Urania* (1621) to the acting style of boys in female roles (see Michael Shapiro, 'Lady Mary Wroth Describes a Boy Actress', *Medieval and Renaissance Drama in England*, 4 (1989), pp. 187–94).
43. *Henslowe's Diary*, pp. 274–5; 276–7; 297.
44. Compare David Lee Miller, 'The Father's Witness: Patriarchal Images of Boys', *Representations*, 70 (Spring 2000), 115–41 (p. 119).
45. *Henslowe's Diary*, pp. 282–3. (I have modernized the contractions.)
46. Weimann, *Author's Pen and Actor's Voice*.
47. Catherine Belsey, *Shakespeare and the Loss of Eden: The Construction of Family Values in Early Modern Culture* (London: Macmillan, 1999).
48. This is not, of course, to argue that boys were not boys until the drama made them so (see Keith Thomas, 'Children in Early Modern England', *Children and Their Books*, ed. Gillian Avery and Julia Briggs (Oxford: Clarendon Press, 1989), pp. 45–77). On the contrary, cultural history should not be mistaken for social history, or the image of children for the experience of childhood (see Belsey, *Shakespeare and the Loss of Eden*, pp. 1–25).

Works cited

Astington, John, 'The Career of Andrew Cane, Citizen, Goldsmith, and Player', *Medieval and Renaissance Drama in England*, 16 (2003), pp. 130–44.

Astington, John, 'John Rhodes: Draper, Bookseller and Man of the Theatre', *Theatre Notebook*, 57 (2003), pp. 83–9.

Belsey, Catherine, *Shakespeare and the Loss of Eden: The Construction of Family Values in Early Modern Culture* (London: Macmillan, 1999).

Belsey, Catherine, *The Subject of Tragedy: Identity and Difference in Renaissance Drama* (London: Methuen, 1985).

Bradley, David, *From Text to Performance in the Elizabethan Theatre: Preparing the Play for the Stage* (Cambridge: Cambridge University Press, 1992).

Davis, Norman, ed., *Non-Cycle Plays and Fragments*, EETS (London: Oxford University Press, 1970).

Duncan-Jones, Katherine, *Ungentle Shakespeare: Scenes from His Life* (London: Thomson, 2001).

Eccles, Mark, ed., *The Macro Plays*, EETS (London: Oxford University Press, 1969).

Evans, G. Blakemore *et al.*, eds, *The Riverside Shakespeare*, (Boston, MA: Houghton Mifflin, 1997).

Foakes, R. A., ed., *Henslowe's Diary* (Cambridge: Cambridge University Press, 2002).

Greg, W. W., ed., *The Battle of Alcazar* (Oxford: Malone Society Reprints, 1907).

Gurr, Andrew, *The Shakespeare Company, 1594–1642* (Cambridge: Cambridge University Press, 2004).

Heberle, Mark A., ' "Innocent Prate": *King John* and Shakespeare's Children', *Infant Tongues: The Voice of the Child in Literature*, ed. Elizabeth Goodenough, Mark A. Heberle and Naomi Solokoff (Detroit, MI: Wayne State University Press, 1994), pp. 28–43.

Houlbrooke, Ralph, *The English Family 1450–1700* (London: Longman, 1984).

Hunter, G. K., *John Lyly: The Humanist as Courtier* (London: Routledge and Kegan Paul, 1962).

Kathman, David, 'Grocers, Goldsmiths and Drapers: Freemen and Apprentices in the Elizabethan Theater', *Shakespeare Quarterly*, 55 (2004), pp. 1–49.
Kathman, David, 'Reconsidering *The Seven Deadly Sins*', *Early Theatre*, 7.1 (2004), pp. 13–44.
King, T. J., *Casting Shakespeare's Plays: London Actors and Their Roles* (Cambridge: Cambridge University Press, 1992).
Knutson, Roslyn Lander, *Playing Companies and Commerce in Shakespeare's Time* (Cambridge: Cambridge University Press, 2001).
Lyly, John, *Mother Bombie, The Complete Works*, ed. R. Warwick Bond (Oxford: Clarendon Press, 1902), 3 vols, vol. 3, pp. 163–228.
McMillin, Scott, 'The Sharer and His Boy: Rehearsing Shakespeare's Women', *From Script to Stage in Early Modern England*, ed. Peter Holland and Stephen Orgel (Basingstoke: Palgrave, 2004), pp. 231–45.
Madelaine, Richard, 'Material Boys: Apprenticeship and the Boy Actors' Shakespearean Roles', *Shakespeare Matters: History, Teaching, Performance*, ed. Lloyd Davis (Newark: University of Delaware Press, 2003), 225–38.
Miller, David Lee, 'The Father's Witness: Patriarchal Images of Boys', *Representations*, 70 (Spring 2000), pp. 115–41.
Rastall, Richard, 'Female Roles in All-Male Casts', *Medieval Drama in English*, 7 (1985), pp. 25–50.
Shakespeare, William, *King John*, ed. E. A. J. Honigmann (London: Methuen, 1954).
Shapiro, Michael, *Children of the Revels: The Boy Companies of Shakespeare's Time and Their Plays* (New York: Columbia University Press, 1977).
Shapiro, Michael, *Gender in Play on the Shakespearean Stage: Boy Heroines and Female Pages* (Ann Arbor, MI: University of Michigan Press, 1996).
Shapiro, Michael, 'Lady Mary Wroth Describes a Boy Actress', *Medieval and Renaissance Drama in England*, 4 (1989), pp. 187–94.
Smith, Bruce R., *The Acoustic World of Early Modern England* (Chicago, IL: University of Chicago Press, 1999).
Taylor, Gary and John Jowett, *Shakespeare Reshaped, 1606–1623* (Oxford: Clarendon Press, 1993).
Thomas, Keith, 'Children in Early Modern England', *Children and Their Books*, ed. Gillian Avery and Julia Briggs (Oxford: Clarendon Press, 1989), pp. 457–57.
Udall, Nicholas, *Roister Doister*, ed. W. W. Greg (Oxford: Malone Society Reprints, 1935).
Weimann, Robert, *Author's Pen and Actor's Voice: Playing and Writing in Shakespeare's Theatre* (Cambridge: Cambridge University Press, 2000).
Wilson, Richard, *Will Power* (London: Harvester, 1993).
Wright, Nicholas, *Cressida* (London: Nick Hern, 2000).

Part II
What's the Matter? Revisions and Reversions in Pen and Voice

4
Rematerializing Shakespeare's Intertheatricality: The Occidental/Oriental Halimpsest

Jonathan Gil Harris

> I, from the orient to the drooping west,
> Making the wind my post-horse, still unfold
> The acts commenced on this ball of earth.
>
> *2 Henry 4*, Induction 3–5

At the beginning of *2 Henry 4*, Rumour represents himself as a global communications system that spans 'orient' and 'drooping west.' These compass points demarcate a space conceived both temporally (from sunrise to sunset) and geographically (from Asia to Europe). They also circumscribe the space of the theatrical, providing the imaginative limits within which Rumour can 'unfold/ The acts commenced on this ball of earth' – if not the Globe (built in 1599), then at least the stage on which the Lord Chamberlain's Men first performed *2 Henry 4*. 'Orient' and 'drooping west' are not simply outer limits for the play's spatio-temporal fields of representation. Indeed, throughout the Henriad, the theatrical 'unfold[ing]' of 'acts' also entails a persistent *palimpsesting* of 'orient' and 'west,' in both their temporal and geographical senses. *Henry 5*'s palimpsests of different eras, particularly the Chorus's 'loving likelihood' that typographically cross-hatches the medieval Henry with both the classical Caesar and the Elizabethan Earl of Essex (*H5*, 5.0.28, 30), have attracted much commentary.[1] By contrast, the Henriad's palimpsests of geography have escaped critical attention. They are most legible in the plays' ambivalent (dis)identifications of their English characters with a string of oriental despots from antiquity to more recent times: Cambyses of Persia, Tamburlaine of Scythia, Herod of Jewry, and Amurath of Turkey. With these occidental/oriental palimpsests, the Henriad complicates Rumour's promise to 'unfold' the 'acts' of 'the orient to the drooping west': instead the orient becomes *folded into*, or inscribed within, the west. This 'orient' is not the orient of historical fact, however, or even of Elizabethan 'orientalism.' It is rather the orient of the English theater: an orient of over-the-top, histrionic bodily gestures and deafening verbal delivery.

The repeated allusions to oriental despots, all of whom were familiar to English theatergoers as larger-than-life stage villains, contribute to the metatheatrical quality of the Henriad in general. Of course, readers have long been attuned to the theatricality of the three plays. The tendency of critical readings since the 1980s, however, has been to subsume this theatricality within a statist politics: in Stephen Greenblatt's well-known essay on the Henriad, for example, Hal theatrically performs his power in much the same way the Elizabethan state apparatus performed its own, staging subversion so that it may be contained.[2] By contrast, I will argue that the plays' theatricality – in particular, their staging of oriental kings – is less about the *theatrum politicum* of the monarchical state than about theater itself. Or if the plays adumbrate a politics of playing, the power they seek to explain is primarily their own. They do so with a keen self-reflexivity about styles of acting, past, present and future: the ranting tyrants of the late medieval mysteries and moralities, the Marlovian-era bombast popularized by Edward Alleyn and the Admiral's Men, and an emergent style – what I call the 'new histrionicism' – practiced by Shakespeare's company.[3] The plays' palimpsests of history and geography, then, are just as much palimpsests of performance styles. In the process, Shakespeare's Henriad offers what might be described as a politics of intertheatricality, where what is at stake is less the *realpolitik* of the king than the skillful versatility, relative to both earlier and contemporary English actors, of the Lord Chamberlain's Men.

To decode this intertheatricality, what is required is not a synchronic mode of analysis that would trace the circulation of discourse between the theater and larger social formations cotemporal with it, but a diachronic or even anachronic hermeneutic that attends to the haunting of Shakespeare's present by its theatrical pasts (or 'orients') and futures (or 'occidents'). Such a hermeneutic might have something in common with the method of criticism known as intertextuality, though it is also significantly different. This is partly because, in contrast to intertextuality's narrower focus on language (whether specific phrases or 'discourse' in general), intertheatricality attends to the bodies of actors and their techniques of movement, gesture and verbal delivery. A purely intertextual reading of, say, *2 Henry 4*'s allusions to Amurath might investigate the play's verbal and thematic echoes of sixteenth-century treatises about Ottoman emperors or literary representations of Turks, but will neglect the conventions of performance that shaped the Elizabethan actor's presentation of the oriental despot.[4]

An even bigger difference between intertextuality and intertheatricality concerns the temporality of their hermeneutics. Though intertextuality is less invested in definitive origins than source study, it has often lent expression to a similar antiquarian impulse, showing how texts dialogue with what has come before – the 'already-written,' in Barthes's words (21).[5]

This relation to the past can take many forms, be it wistful nostalgia (Zumthor's 'désir d'intégration'), Oedipal anxiety (Bloom's filial revisionism), or playful assimilation (Kristeva's mosaic *idéologème*).[6] By contrast, even as the intertheatrical reading turns to the acting techniques of the past, its primary concern is the new ground opened up by histrionic versatility. The intertheatrical Shakespearean actor has at his command a variety of performance styles that he reproduces masterfully; the success of the performance, however, depends on audience recognition – of the styles, of their masterful rendering, but also of future opportunities that their performance engenders. Intertheatricality serves as a reminder that the matter of the stage is not simply physicality existing in the here and now of the performance; it is also dynamic materiality, in both Aristotle's and Marx's senses of the term – material that is worked upon and transformed by theatrical praxis, thereby presuming and inducing a future.[7] Thus if intertextuality voices a desire for the past, Shakespearean intertheatricality generates a desire for what is to come. Despite its express nostalgia for a medieval Golden Age of English kingship, the Henriad's occidental/oriental palimpsests work the past to produce new theatrical possibilities. In doing so, they demand materialist analyses sharply different from those of mainstream historicism.

Robert Weimann, transversal theory, and the palimpsested stage

Amongst the many virtues of Robert Weimann's work is the complexity with which it theorizes authority, and in ways that greatly illuminate the problematic of Shakespearean intertheatricality that I have sketched here. Weimann's formulations of early modern authority provide an important counterbalance to those of historicist criticism, at least in its 1980s incarnation. Whereas early historicism tended to reify authority on the model of the centralized, monarchical state, Weimann has repeatedly emphasized the multiple forms of authority produced on and by the space of the stage. In the process, he has proposed an alternative understanding not only of authority, but also of performance – one in which theater is not subsumed within an all pervasive, synchronic 'discourse,' as it has tended to be in historicist criticism, but regarded as its own semi-autonomous semiotic field, requiring special methods of critical analysis that, in their diachronic sweep, illuminate the evolving spatio-temporalities of the medieval and Elizabethan stages.

While Weimann's famous distinction between 'locus' and 'platea' in his germinal *Shakespeare and the Popular Tradition in the Theater* (1967) might suggest a synchronic understanding of Elizabethan theatrical space, this is no mere mapping of a static physical grid. Rather, his subdivision of the stage is also a distinction between competing theatrical chronotopes.[8] The more representational 'locus,' specified in place and time, serves what might be termed a historicist chronotope: its historical and geographical setting is determinate, and remote from that of the playhouse or its audience. The 'platea,' by contrast, is 'an entirely nonrepresentational and unlocalized setting,' from where the actor both comments on the action of the locus and speaks directly to the audience (79). This space is typified by the 'contrariety' of the theatrically ambidextrous Vice, who plays, in the words of *Cambyses*, 'with both hands' (l. 744), participating in the dramatic illusion and stepping outside it. Just as this palimpsested space breaks down the barrier between audience and actor, so does it potentially intermingle past (as depicted in the playworld) and present (as instanced in the space of the playhouse and audience).

Weimann's theorization of the platea and its anachronic 'contrariety' anticipates what I see as the more intertheatrical focus of his recent work. Of course, Weimann has always been attentive to how the Elizabethan theatre mined the forms of older popular conventions, including those of the mysteries and moralities. But in *Author's Pen and Actor's Voice* (2000), he supplements his earlier theorizations of theatrical authority with explicit attention to the bodies of actors. Building on Peter Quince's direction in *A Midsummer Night's Dream* 'to disfigure, or to present, the person of Moonshine' (3.1.61), Weimann theorizes a regime of theatrical representation that exploits the unclear gap between 'what is to be represented and what or who is doing the (re)presenting' (82). For Weimann, this 'disfigurement' invokes an earlier style of playing that highlights the permeable partition between the object and agency of representation. In cycle drama and early Tudor entertainments, this partition was generated through unusually histrionic techniques of performance: 'the *excessive*, the eccentric thrust in corporeal movement ... most contrariously and, of course, visibly plays with what is different from the Renaissance regime of holding the mirror up to nature' (85). Hence when the actor playing Bottom channels the ranting 'Ercles' vein' (1.2.40), he enacts a 'bi – fold authority' that refracts not just theatrical space, but also time.[9] Displaying both the representational quality appropriate to the locus and the burlesque typical of the platea, he overlays his contemporary performance of a Graeco-English weaver with archaic styles of acting (the histrionic techniques demanded by both Seneca's *Hercules Furens* and medieval cycle drama's 'tyrants'). In doing so, he generates a theatrical palimpsest that compresses the historically specific forms of the classical, medieval and Elizabethan stages.

The palimpsest is a particularly useful tool with which to understand the Henriad's intertheatricality. Admittedly, to read Shakespeare through the lens of the palimpsest is a long established practice. But it is one that has been applied exclusively to the archaeology of Shakespeare's playscripts, with their tell-tale traces of rewriting, rather than to the plays in performance.[10] Weimann's study of Shakespearean disfigurement and 'excessive' corporeality suggests a different framework within which to decode the palimpsests of the Henriad. I would add, however, that Weimann's understanding of intertheatricality is sometimes wistfully oriented towards a golden past of folk-drama. For example, Weimann claims that Shakespeare's aesthetic of disfigurement 'does not go as far as the mainstream of folklore had gone,' implying that the Elizabethan theater stands at the twilight of a vital demotic tradition (*Author's Pen*, 88). As I have suggested, however, the intertheatrical palimpsests of the Henriad are not simply reprises of the past. Like Bottom's channeling of Seneca and medieval tyrants, the Henriad compulsively recycles old histrionic conventions. Unlike Bottom's performance, however, the Henriad transforms these into something new. My name for this innovative style, 'the new histrionicism,' itself performs some of the palimpsestic qualities it designates: even as it visibly re-inscribes familiar terms from the recent past of our critical landscape – not just the hegemonic 'new historicism' of Stephen Greenblatt et al., but also the 'new histrionicism' that Harry Berger Jr. in *Imaginary Audition* (1989) cheekily applies to Shakespearean performance criticism – it tweaks those terms into something else, something recognizable yet strange, something *transverse*.

'Transverse' is a key term in Michel de Certeau's account of the distinction between place and space. Place, in his analysis, is a coordinate within a synchronic grid such as a map, optically available to an omniscient viewer. By contrast, space is not a static location, but metamorphic terrain marked and changed by everyday practice. For de Certeau, walking is the practice *par excellence* that transforms place into space: 'it is like a peddler, carrying something surprising, transverse or attractive compared with the usual choices' (101). The 'transverse' is thus the instrument of metamorphic praxis. Transversal theory, as outlined by its leading practitioner Bryan Reynolds, has adapted de Certeau's analysis to theorize the ways in which dramatic and cultural performance similarly transforms place into space. Like intertheatricality, transversal theory is itself a palimpsest: yoking the theoretical sophistication of French poststructuralism to the political commitments of British cultural materialism, it examines how subjects can break free of their social interpellations in order to occupy, transform, and be transformed by new, transversal spaces.[11] Weimann's theorization of the medieval and Elizabethan stage, particularly the platea as a dynamic, critical space that displaces the univocal mimetic authority of the locus, resonates with de Certeau's and Reynolds's theorization of transversal space. What transversal theory adds to Weimann's work, however, is a keen attention to the future possibilities generated by Shakespeare's theatrical codes of 'contrariety' and 'bifold authority.'

These possibilities are particularly evident in Don Hedrick and Reynolds's shrewd account of 'projective transversality' in *Henry 5*. For Hedrick and Reynolds, the play engenders new transversal experiences in its audience through Henry's charismatic performances of his versatility. This versatility is grounded in what Hedrick and Reynolds call 'translucency,' a kind of performance in which one semiotic code is 'incompletely concealed within another' (171). Thus defined, translucency is remarkably similar to the palimpsests of intertheatricality. Although Hedrick and Reynolds view *Henry 5*'s transversality as an ultimately failed project, they nonetheless insist on its heterodox potential. Following Hedrick and Reynolds, I wish to show how such translucency is the signature of Harry/Hal/Henry's palimpsested performances *throughout* the Henriad. He is a Halimpsest in which are visible both old styles of staging the orient (temporal and geographical) and a new histrionicism. I am more interested than Hedrick and Reynolds, however, in folding such translucency back into an analysis of the claims the Henriad makes about the skill of the Lord Chamberlain's Men. In doing so, I want to show how a more institutionally specific transversal approach to Shakespeare's theatricality can bolster a reading of the palimpsested stage in sympathy with Weimann's work. But I shall argue also that transversal theory must take stock of the problematic emplotments of historical progress that seemingly transversal movements can presume. This is especially the case with Shakespeare's intertheatricality. For all their transversal potential, the Henriad's occidental/oriental palimpsests entail a conception of cultural progress that uncannily resembles a much later, Eurocentric philosophy of 'world' history.

'In Cambyses's vein'

As many readers have noted, the Henriad's tavern scenes are suffused with self-conscious theatricality. Hal and Falstaff are constantly play-acting, turning the Eastcheap tavern into their pre-modern karaoke-cum-drag bar. Adding to these scenes' performativity is their specification of venue. Although the playscript never explicitly names its tavern the 'Boar's Head,' it would have been readily recognizable as the watering-hole of that name in the Eastcheap parish of St. Michael's, not least because of the pun in *2 Henry 4*: 'Doth the old boar feed in the old frank?' (*2H4*, 2.2.133). The Boar's Head was famous as not only a tavern, but also a venue for contemporary theatrical performances. The playing companies patronized by the Earl of Oxford and Earl of Worcester performed there often in the 1590s, and when the two joined into one company, they requested that the Lord Mayor grant them the Boar's Head as their playhouse in residence.[12] Hence the tavern scenes neatly undo Weimann's distinction between locus and platea, inasmuch as they present *both* a spatio-temporally circumscribed past *and* a performance space shared by Shakespeare's audience in the present.

The many dramatic and literary forms held up for playful scrutiny in the tavern scenes include morality drama and John Lyly's euphuism. But the only work explicitly name-checked is *Cambyses*, Thomas Preston's 'Lamentable Tragedy, Mixed full of Pleasant Mirth' of the 1560s. Why does Falstaff play-act in the Persian 'Cambyses's vein' (*1H4*, 2.4.385)? Some readers have suggested characterological and thematic parallels between Preston's and

Shakespeare's dramas. *Cambyses* sternly chronicles the consequences of its title character's drunkenness, and is hence a suitable intertext for the soused Falstaff, whose 'give me a cup of sack' (*1H4*, 2.4.384) seems to recall Cambyses's 'give it me to drink it off, and see no wine be waste' (l. 530). Preston's Vice character, Ambidexter, also anticipates Falstaff, whom Hal identifies with 'that reverend Vice, that grey iniquity' (*1H4*, 2.4.453–4).[13]

Yet these readings strike me as too literal – or rather, literary – minded. What they cannot account for is that, simply as a *literary* parody, Falstaff's rendition of Cambyses is bafflingly wide of the mark. The metronomic fourteeners of Preston's play are not reproduced by Sir John, who instead speaks lines written in more up-to-date pentameter. If Falstaff parodies anything in *Cambyses*, it is not its literary or thematic qualities (such as they are), but its pervasive histrionicism. Preston's play calls for not only an inordinate amount of weeping, but also self-commentary on its occurrence. Before his execution by Cambyses, the wicked Judge Sisamnes says to his son Otian: 'O childe thou makes mine eyes to run, as rivers doo by streme' (l. 455); Praxaspes and his wife not only weep, but discuss their weeping over the death of their son: 'It is even so, my Lord I see, how by him he dooth weep' (l. 575), and 'With blubred eyes into mine armes, from earth I wil thee take' (l. 582); and, most crucially, the Queen weeps pitifully when, having heard the story of the three lion-club brothers who refused to kill each other, she recalls Cambyses's cruel murder of his own brother: 'These words to hear makes stilling teares, issue from Christal eyes' (l. 1030). Even the Vice weeps at the Queen's death: 'A, A, A, A, I cannot chuse but weep for the Queene' (l. 1127). It is the play's weeping that Falstaff comically replays: 'Give me a cup of sack to make my eyes look red, that it may be thought I have wept'; 'Weep not sweet Queen, for trickling tears are vain'; 'For God's sake my Lords, convey my trustful Queen, /For tears do stop the floodgates of her eyes' (*1H4*, 2.4.384–6, 391, 393–4).[14]

Why Falstaff's comic obsession with the tears of *Cambyses*? Did Shakespeare's macho company find such theatrical displays of weeping effeminate, and enjoy poking fun at them? Macduff, like many characters, has to apologize for his 'woman'-like tears. Revealingly, however, he also associates weeping with playing the 'braggart' with his 'tongue,' as if he were remembering the lachrymose braggadocio of *Cambyses* (*Macbeth*, 4.3.232–3). Thus Macduff's outburst serves to draw attention not just to weeping but also to the histrionic conventions that accompanied its staging. In this, it is typical of Shakespeare's other references to the mechanics of crying: the Page in the Induction of *The Taming of the Shrew* is advised to use an onion to perform wifely tears (Induction 1.120–4), and Katherina herself says of Bianca that her tears are created by putting a 'finger in the eye' (1.1.78–9). These scenes provide compelling instances of translucency: the audience sees or hears about weeping, but is also clued into the theatrical skill needed to stage it.[15] At such moments, in other words, Shakespeare's company allows its dramatic characters to become visible as actors who can move in and out of the codes of histrionic performance. We find ourselves in the presence not of heightened emotion, but of self-regarding skill in archaic performance techniques – like a contemporary rock singer at a sound-check who cannot resist channeling the histrionic vocal stylings of Elvis, and in a manner that is equal parts parody, homage, and flagrant self-display.

Hence Falstaff's acting 'in Cambyses vein' is far more than just a robust send-up of excessive weeping. It also advertises the self-conscious art of the Shakespearean actor, who simultaneously rehearses *and* distances himself from excessive styles of performance. Throughout the Henriad, the histrionicism on which such art draws is repeatedly given a local habitation and a name: the orient. Falstaff's turn as the Persian Cambyses is just one of several occasions where the Henriad codes histrionic excess as oriental. Inasmuch as this tactic works to valorize its actors' 'occidental' prowess, it recalls Edward Said's famous schematization of the orient as Europe's constitutive other. But as Rumour suggests, the Henriad's 'orient' does not just participate within a synchronic logic of *othering*; it is equally cast as the occident's point of temporal and geographical *origin*. This logic is apparent in Falstaff's occidental/oriental palimpsest. Three discrete but linked 'oriental' and 'occidental' layers are implied by his performance of the Persian Cambyses:

1. An orient of *time*, seen as a *past* style of performance metonymically identified with the over-the-top techniques of English actors who have played eastern despots; and
2. An orient of *space*, viewed as a synchronic geographical type of histrionic excess in an eternal *present*;
3. An occidental *space* and *time* of the *future* that not so much opposes the spatio-temporal orients I have sketched above, as dialectically *transcends* them under the sign of theatrical 'self-consciousness,' or what I am terming the new histrionicism.

As this schema suggests, Falstaff's palimpsest hints at a Eurocentric teleology, in which a (theatrical) orient must give rise to a more perfect (theatrical) west. In the Henriad, Cambyses is but the first in a series of oriental stage-despots who enable this maneuver.

'Not Amurath an Amurath succeeds'

In a canny reading, Richard Hillman has underlined 'the principle of English–Turkish "shadowing" as a key factor in the Henriad's intertextuality' (38). His test-case is Hal's speech upon his ascension to the throne. Hal seeks to reassure his brothers that, rather than the fratricidal king they fear he might become, he will prove a benign monarch:

> This is the English, not the Turkish court;
> Not Amurath an Amurath succeeds,
> But Harry, Harry.
>
> (*2H4*, 5.2.48)

Noting that historically no Amurath ever succeeded another, and that indeed Amurath here has no clear historical referent – the name may refer to Murad I, the Ottoman emperor who died in 1389 and who inflicted enormous cruelty on his son and brother, or anachronistically to Murad III, the Ottoman emperor who died in 1596 and notoriously killed his brother upon his own ascension in 1574 – Hillman concludes that 'the cultural projection that goes with the name Amurath is effectively detached from historical specificity and released into "discursive space," to resonate ... amongst and beyond particular bearers of it' (27). Having liberated 'Amurath' from any specific historical figure, Hillman nonetheless rehistoricizes the signifier in relation to sixteenth-century continental literature, citing a variety of 'intertexts' that include Paul Giovo's and Jacques La Vardin's histories of the Christian warrior George Scanderbeg's battles with the Ottomans. In the process, he shows how Hal, and indeed, the entire Henriad, is haunted by a series of 'Turkish' foils and specular doubles.

Despite Hillman's express interest in the Henriad's 'complex set of intertexts, written and unwritten' (38), he notably omits one set of 'unwritten' intertexts, or rather, intertheatrical codes. Overlooked in his reading of Amurath is any consideration of the character as he was performed on the Elizabethan stage. Shakespeare's original audience may very well have called to mind whatever 'historical' knowledge they possessed of the medieval Murad I and the early modern Murad III. Yet the Amurath with whom Shakespeare's audiences were most familiar was neither of these historical figures, but a generic character from the theater – or rather, a specific theater, the Rose.[16] The earliest instance is the Amurath referred to in George Peele's *Battle of Alcazar*, performed at the Rose in 1589. Peele's character is not based on any historical figure, but is instead an entirely conventional oriental despot. Though he is never seen, he is described as 'angrie Amurath' (sig. D4). And it is as an almost comically over-the-top angry ranter that Amurath takes the stage in other Elizabethan drama. In the popular *Soliman and Perseda* (possibly by Thomas Kyd, and performed in the early 1590s), Amurath is again a generic rather than a historically specific character. Channeling Preston's Cambyses, he is an irascible hothead and fratricide who whips out his sword at the slightest provocation, and meets a suitably violent end at the hands of his other brother, Soliman (1.5.77–80).

The Amurack, or Amurath, of Robert Greene's *The Comicall Historie of Alphonsus, King of Aragon* (c. 1591) is a King of the Turks again based not on any identifiable historical figure, but on the recognizably histrionic techniques of the oriental stage despot. He responds to his 'prattling' wife, Fausta (who has rejected his plan to marry their daughter Iphigina to Alphonsus), in a ranting fashion that recalls Cambyses's outbursts against his Queen. His outburst is prefaced by a telltale stage direction, '*Amurack rise in a rage from thy chair*':

> What threat'ning words thus thunder in mine ears?
> Or who are they amongst the mortal troops
> That dares presume to use such threats to me?
> The proudest Kings and Kaisers of the land
> Are glad to feed me in my fantasy;
> And shall I suffer, then, each prattling dame
> For to upbraid me in this spiteful sort?
> (3.2.179–85)

In this speech, and throughout the play, we can hear echoes of another oriental stage despot familiar to playgoers at the Rose: Tamburlaine. Like Marlowe's megalomaniacal atheist, Amurack rails against Mahound (i.e. the Prophet Muhammed), so that 'Mahound, provoked by Amurack's discourse ... Denies to play the Prophet any more' (IV.prologue, 13, 15). Indeed, Greene's imitation of *Tamburlaine* is slavish: it is visible in the play's glorification of conquest, invocations of fortune's wheel, and wooing of its war-bride heroine. Yet *Alphonsus* parallels Marlowe's play less in any thematic or linguistic respect than in the histrionicism it calls for. To this extent, we might see Greene's Amurack/Amurath as a reprise of – and a synonym for – the theatrical Tamburlaine-effect, an effect generated primarily by excessive bodily techniques.

With its opening lines, *Tamburlaine* underscores the inadequacy of anything less than 'great and thund'ring speech in a king' (I.1.1.3); and it constantly refers to Tamburlaine's fierce 'looks' and body language (I.1.2.56, 3.2.66, II.1.4.76–8, 4.1.173–5, etc.). It is in the testimony of Elizabethan audience members, however, that we can recognize the impact of Tamburlaine's body language. In his *Virigidemiarium* (1597), Joseph Hall satirizes an actor's performance of 'the Turkish Tamberlaine'; in the process, Hall furnishes considerable information about the standard theatrical presentation of the character. Tamburlaine speaks loudly, resorting to 'huf-cap termes and thundering threats/ That his poore hearers hayre quite vpright sets,' and he employs melodramatic gesture or 'stalking and high-set steps' (Hall 14–15). A pamphlet from 1597 tells of a man who 'bent his browes and fetcht his stations vp and downe the rome, with such furious Iesture as if he had been playing Tamberlaine on a stage' (E. S. sig. C2v). Such 'furious Iesture' may also have included stamping: in Thomas Dekker's *Satiromastix*,

Tucca asks a player: 'doest stampe mad Tamberlaine, does stampe?' (IV.iii.369; Dekker, I. 364).

The actor Edward Alleyn became famous as a result of his performances as Tamburlaine, and many of his other star turns – such as the leads in *Tamar Cham* and Greene's *Orlando Furioso*, and Muly Mahomet in Peele's *Battle of Alcazar* – seem to have been custom-made for his Tamburlainian style of '*scenicall* strutting, and furious vociferation' (Jonson VII. 587). I would argue that the Amuraths we find in plays performed in the 1590s name a loose set of acting conventions associated with Alleyn's Tamburlaine. Even if these Amuraths were not played by Alleyn, they and other characters in these plays typify the histrionic 'oriental' style that had become his hallmark. An exemplary instance is the Turkish mercenary Brusor in *Soliman and Perseda*. Bragging about his past exploits, Brusor claims that

> Against the Sophy in three pitched fields,
> Under the conduct of great Soliman,
> Have I been chief commander of an host,
> And put the flint-heart Persians to the sword;
> (And) marched (a) conqueror through Asia.
> The desert plains of Affricke have I stained
> With blood of Moors, and there in three set battles fought;
> Along the coasts held by the Portinguze,
> Even to the verge of gold-abounding Spain,
> Hath Brusor led a valiant troop of Turks.
>
> (1.3.51–60)

Waving his sword in the air and ranting vaingloriously, Brusor emerges as another incarnation of Alleyn's histrionic Tamburlaine-effect. For playwrights in the 1590s, the temptation to imitate or burlesque this effect proved irresistible. Shakespeare arguably succumbed to the temptation in Bottom's ranting disfiguration of a 'lofty ... tyrant'; but he seems also to have remembered the specific details of Brusor's speech when writing the part of Morocco in *The Merchant of Venice*. This Barbary cousin of Brusor likewise swears noisily by his 'scimitar/ That slew the Sophy and a Persian prince/ That won three fields of Sultan' (2.1.25–7). When Morocco is beaten for Portia's hand by the less bombastic and more calculating Bassanio, the Venetian's success is arguably a triumph not only for European wooing skills, but also for a different, less 'oriental' style of acting than Alleyn's.

A similar geo-theatrical differentiation seems to be at play in *2 Henry 4*. As his dismissive remark about Amurath suggests, Hal pointedly valorizes supposed English moderation over oriental histrionicism. But the Henriad delights in staging Amurath/Tamburlaine's theatricality nonetheless – albeit in displaced or dis-oriented fashion. This histrionicism might be glimpsed in

Hotspur's many dazzling tantrums, but it surfaces even more unmistakably with the arrival of Pistol in *2 Henry 4*.[17] The ghost of Tamburlaine is conjured by Pistol's declamation about 'hollow pampered jades of Asia' (*2H4*, 2.4.141; cf. *Tamburlaine* II.2.3.1). He also channels Muly Mahomet – another role played by Alleyn – from Peele's *Battle of Alcazar* (*2 H4*, 2.4.155).[18] As with Falstaff's Cambyses, however, Pistol's occidental/oriental palimpsest is comprised primarily of intertheatrical rather than strictly intertextual references. His first entrance is prefaced by numerous remarks about his 'swaggering,' a term that describes not only his quarrelsome disposition, but also his bodily techniques – specifically, the 'furious vociferation and scenicall strutting' associated with Alleyn's Tamburlaine. These techniques serve a complicated theatrical purpose. Pistol's versions of Tamburlaine and Muly Mahomet, again like Falstaff's turn as Cambyses, are not simply occasions for theatrical parody; they also pay homage to the skill of the Shakespearean actor, who can move in and out of the codes of 'oriental' histrionicism with self-conscious 'occidental' versatility. So even as Hal seems to assert an absolute difference between his own techniques and those of Amurath, Pistol's performances ensure that oriental histrionicism is less a dispensed with *other* than a vital, if transfigured, set of techniques in the Lord Chamberlain's Men's repertory.

Something similar happens in *Hamlet*. The Danish prince's advice to the players to avoid 'o'erdoing Termagant' and 'out-Herod[ing] Herod' (3.2.13–14) may seem to assert a sharp distinction between occident and orient so that the latter can be exorcised: not only does Hamlet ridicule two stock oriental characters from the mystery plays, but his antipathy to actors who 'split the ears of the groundlings' and who 'have so strutted and bellowed' (3.2.11, 35) arguably glances also at Alleyn's Tamburlaine, Muly Mahomet or Amurath. Yet Hamlet himself fails to uphold the absolute difference he asserts between genteel acting styles and the barbarous primitivism of past and present oriental stage despots. As Weimann has noted, Hamlet's 'plea for a poetics of neoclassical discretion' is upended by his 'rehearsal' of 'stale' jokes and acting styles, including the histrionic ranting of Herod (Weimann, *Author's Pen*, 24).

Despite his explicit self-differentiation from Amurath in *2 Henry 4*, I would argue that Hal likewise 'rehearses' the very oriental histrionicism he inveighs against. For Weimann, Hamlet's channeling of Herod marks a return to the older excessive style of acting that distinguishes the platea and the 'contrariety' of the Vice. Hal's – or rather Harry's – rehearsals of the orient do not so much echo older demotic styles, however, as willfully transform and transcend them. If Herod is simply one intertheatrical layer within *Hamlet*'s palimpsested Tamburlaine-effect, the character re-emerges in the Henriad as a crucial layer of another occidental/oriental palimpsest. In his version of Herod, Harry does not distance himself from Amurath and his ilk. Like Falstaff with Cambyses, Harry instead harnesses the oriental despot's histrionic energies in order to underline his versatile mastery of acting styles.

'Herod's bloody-hunting slaughtermen'

As a child in Stratford, Shakespeare may well have attended a performance of the nearby Coventry Corpus Christi cycle play, which was discontinued in 1579. If so, he would have seen in the Shearmen and Taylors' pageant of the Slaughter of the Innocents an extraordinary scene of oriental histrionic strutting and bellowing. Having discovered that the three kings have eluded his trap for them, Herod the Great responds with an angry outburst: 'I stampe! I stare! I loke all abowte!' (Craig 779). Herod's tantrum is punctuated by an equally noteworthy stage direction, moreover, one that translates his previous remark into a bravura performance of sustained stamping, staring, and looking all about: *'Here Erode ragis in the pagond and in the street also'* (Craig 783).

Shakespeare stands alone among the major playwrights of the early modern London stage in making repeated reference to Herod. Inasmuch as Herod does make an appearance in the drama of Shakespeare's contemporaries, such as Elizabeth Cary's *Tragedy of Maryam*, the anonymous *Second Maiden's Tragedy*, and *Herod and Antipater*, it is as a historical character lifted from the pages of Josephus's *Of the Antiquities of the Jews*, and unrelated to the pageant Herod. When Shakespeare alludes to Herod, by contrast, it is in almost every instance less the Herod of classical history or of scripture than his histrionic cycle-drama incarnation that informs the reference, whether it is Hamlet's 'it out-Herods Herod,' or Mistress Page's denunciation of Falstaff as 'a Herod of Jewry' who puts on a false 'show' (*The Merry Wives of Windsor*, 2.1.18, 20). There are also recognizable echoes of the Coventry Herod in other Shakespeare plays; when Petruchio advises Katherine and the wedding guests to 'look not big, nor stamp, nor stare' (*Taming of the Shrew*, 3.2.230), it is less his word-choice than the implied techniques of over-the-top histrionic performance that recall the Coventry Herod's 'I stampe! I stare! I looke all abowte!'[19]

Shakespeare's most complex reference to the cycle-drama Herod appears in the Henriad. In *Henry 5*, Harry warns the besieged citizens of Harfleur that they can soon expect to see

> Your naked infants spitted upon pikes,
> Whiles the mad mothers with their howls confused
> Do break the clouds, as did the wives of Jewry
> At Herod's bloody-hunting slaughtermen.
>
> (*H5*, 3.3.115–18)

Editors tend to gloss Harry's speech with a reference to the pertinent passage concerning the Slaughter of the Innocents in St. Matthew (2:13–18). But the dominant detail in Shakespeare's rendition of the episode – the description of the 'howls' of upset mothers that 'break' the clouds – arguably derives less from an acquaintance with Scripture, which refers in any case only to the single voice of Rachel mourning for her children (2:18), than from a memory of an entertainment such as the Coventry Shearmen and Taylor's pageant. The latter directs the actors playing the mothers of the slaughtered children to create a hullabaloo of distress: after the children have been murdered, the first soldier asks 'Who hard eyuer soche a cry/ Of wemen that there chyldur haue lost?' (870–71).

In the Harfleur scene, then, the Hal of *1 Henry 4* has become a Halimpsest, one of whose layers is the Coventry Herod. The relation between the two characters unfolds in what transversal theory terms the 'subjunctive space' of *as if*.[20] Harry does not have Harfleur's infants put to death; but he can raise the specter of such a massacre by performing codes of histrionic excessiveness *as if* he were a stage Herod. His, however, is a Herod that can be channeled and discarded at will, as is suggested by his melodramatic yet calculated response to the Dauphin's jest: 'for many a thousand widows/ Shall this mock mock out of their dear husbands, / Mock mothers from their sons, mock castles down' (*H5*, 1.2.284–6). This is a display of versatility that both draws on and departs from the infanticidal Herod of cycle drama. To some readers, such a display might seem of a piece with the Henriad's constant identification of Hal/Harry/Henry with other powerful figures from antiquity. Fluellen likens Harry to Alexander the Great by correlating the geography of their birthplaces (*H5*, 4.3.22), a comparison that Hillman sees as exemplary of the Henriad's pervasive typological mode of figuration (Hillman 57). The subjunctive space in which Harry aligns himself with Herod, however, entails something quite different from a typological relation. This is not an instance of the past-oriented 'loving likelihood[s]' suggested by Fluellen and the Chorus; it is instead altogether more future-oriented, calculating, and, ultimately, triumphal. Harry's theatrical versatility, his self-conscious ability to move in and out of the archaic codes of histrionic performance from the cycle drama and the Marlovian stage, seals his success not only on stage or in war, but also within the Henriad's narration of England's privileged place in history.

The new histrionicism, Hegel, and *Aufhebung*

A recent television ad starts with an actor saying, in a soft voice that gradually crescendos into a roar, 'Don't you love commercials where everybody ... SHOUTS A LOT?' The camera cuts to a stage audience, who scream their assent. The character proceeds to holler his pitch for 'Shout' stain remover in the antic manner of 1950s ads (accompanied by a version of the Isley Brothers' hit tune of the '50s, 'Shout!'). This ad captures something of the intertheatricality of Shakespeare's company and their relationship to older histrionic playing styles. The difference is that the ad seems to offer little more than the pleasure of recognizing a now archaic code of performance, even if that pleasure is produced in the service of retailing a commodity. Shakespeare, by contrast, presents the Halimpsest as much more than just an opportunity to laugh at old styles. Like Falstaff's performance of Cambyses, Harry's version of Herod demands the rehearsal of a primitive orient to produce a superior occident characterized not just by its versatility but also by its sublime self-consciousness. He is no Amurath, but he can play him on (French) television. But while Falstaff's routine only hints at the Eurocentric teleology that narrates the advance from histrionic orient to versatile west, Harry's works *both* within the space of the platea to assert his theater company's superiority on the Elizabethan stage *and* within the representational locus to cement his nation's privileged place in world history. In doing so, the Halimpsest not only draws on its 'oriental' theatrical past, but also gestures towards an 'occidental' philosophical future. And that future's name is Hegel.

In his *Philosophy of History* (1822), Hegel offers an insistently theatrical account of the dialectic of Spirit, arguing that it perfects itself through time and space by taking 'the history of the World for its theatre' (54). Hegel's idealist *theatrum mundi*, like Marx's materialist counterpart in the *Communist Manifesto*, enlists Shakespeare to play a key role on its stage. Speaking about the will required to impose Spirit on the world, Hegel invokes Hamlet's 'hue of resolution' (24) – though for the German idealist philosopher this hue is, tellingly, no longer sicklied o'er with the pale cast of thought, for a Hamlet-like self-consciousness is Spirit's very objective. But it is less *Hamlet* than the Induction of *2 Henry 4* that arguably provides the theatrical template for Hegel's world history. Just as Rumour plots the 'acts commenced on this ball of earth ... from the orient to the drooping west,' so does Hegel narrate the orient as the first 'scene' in a global drama that finds its culmination in the occident: 'The Sun – the Light – rises in the East ... The History of the World travels from East to West, for Europe is absolutely the end of History' (103).

With its *theatrum mundi*, *The Philosophy of History* reprises the three layers of the occidental/oriental palimpsest that I identified in Falstaff's performance of Cambyses, and which we can now recognize as more aggressively at play in Harry's version of Herod. First, the Orient is for Hegel, as it is in the Henriad, a (past) *time* prior to our own, an early scene within a diachronic global drama: 'it is the childhood of History' and, like a child, suffers from a surfeit of 'unreflected consciousness' (99). Second, the Orient is also a theatrical *place* in the present, characterized by its eternal embrace of '*Despotism*': 'The East ... knows only that *One* is Free.' Hegel thus situates the Orient in synchronic opposition to the German world, which knows 'that *All* are free' (104). Hegel's conflation of Orient-as-past-time and Orient-as-present-place is enabled by his conviction that, even though the Orient is the first scene of world history, it is also a region incapable of change. He pronounces India, for example, as 'a phenomenon antique as well as modern; one which has remained stationary and fixed' (139). Indeed, Hegel sees all of Asia standing outside of history in an eternally primitive present: the history of the Orient 'is, for the most part, really *unhistorical*, for it is only the repetition of the same majestic ruin' (106).

The sterility of oriental repetition underwrites Hegel's commentary on the myth of the self-resurrecting phoenix. This myth, Hegel claims, 'is only Asiatic; oriental, not occidental.' By contrast, 'Spirit – consuming the envelope of its existence – does not merely pass into another envelope, nor rise rejuvenescent from the ashes of its previous form; it comes forth exalted, glorified, a purer spirit' (73). He thus sees the development of Spirit as a process of dialectical transformation rather than one of mere phoenix-like repetition. And here we might recognize the third layer of Falstaff's occidental/oriental palimpsest: the potential for 'occidental' growth in the future. Hegel's embrace of Spiritual transformation may in some ways amount to an idealist transversal praxis, but the geographical-temporal qualifiers in his critique of the phoenix myth betray his Eurocentrist agenda. For true rebirth to take place, and for Spirit to become self-conscious, it must move from the Orient, 'the region of origination' (99), to the West: 'for what is most remarkable in it, this land has not kept for itself, but sent over to Europe. It presents the origination of all religious and political principles, but Europe has been the scene of their development' (101). Hegel imagines the Orient less as Europe's *other* than as its immature theatrical *origin*; hence Occidental spirit is, fundamentally, Oriental Spirit captured, transcended and cancelled – the tripartite dialectical process that Hegel calls *Aufhebung*. For Hegel, this process 'necessarily implies that the present form of Spirit comprehends within it all earlier steps' (79); it is in the West, therefore, that the 'majestic ruin' of the Orient is redeemed. As a result, Hegel's Europe becomes an occidental/oriental palimpsest.

The relations between the layers of this palimpsest disclose the same teleologism as the Henriad. In Shakespeare's as well as Hegel's theater of history, a bivalently spatial and temporal orient associated with a despotic unselfconsciousness must pass on its 'majestic ruin' (how else to define the histrionicism of the stage-tyrant?) to an occident that dialectically refines it and, under the superior mark of self-consciousness, moves to a position of power on the world stage. The Halimpsest, in other words, is Hegelian *Aufhebung* incarnated in the bodily techniques of the Shakespearean actor. For all their transversal potential, both the Henriad's intertheatricality and Hegel's dialectic of Spirit instantiate a recognizable poetics of imperialism. Each licenses – one metaphorically, the other 'historically' – an unreciprocal exchange between orient and occident: the former is reified and appropriated for use by the latter, which extracts surplus value from it in the form of 'self-consciousness.' Hence the Western looting of both temporal and geographical orients can narrate itself as 'progress.'

To be sure, the Henriad does not advocate the looting of the orient in the economic guises it had taken by the time Hegel wrote *The Philosophy of*

History. The claims the Henriad makes for an occidental prowess based on appropriation and transformation of oriental materials are much more institutionally local: Shakespeare's occidental/oriental palimpsests are occasioned not by the future prospect of East India Company activity in the orient, of course, but by contemporary local competition between London theater companies for playgoers' money. Shakespeare and the Lord Chamberlain's men had a vested interest in positioning themselves as superior actors to rival companies such as the Admiral's Men, who with Edward Alleyn had performed many of the most financially successful 'oriental' plays at the Rose. Seen through this end of the critical telescope, the Henriad's intertheatricality is less about English colonial ambitions; it is instead, tautologically but crucially, about the power of Shakespeare's own theater. To acquire this power, and the financial profit that came with it, the Lord Chamberlain's Men re-oriented the 'orients,' temporal and geographical, of their own theatrical traditions. The transversal spaces opened up by their occidental/oriental palimpsests were less those of Cambyses, Amurath, Tamburlaine and Herod *per se*, than of the interstitialities traversed by their movements in and out of those roles. In this way, Shakespeare's and his company's versatile re-orientations did more than just model state power or legitimize English militarism. They also suggested affinities between the company's new histrionicism and new acquisitive modes of cultural and economic production that sought to capture, transform and cancel 'oriental' commodities, making them the basis for 'occidental' wealth and power.

It is precisely in these affinities, however, that we might recognize the rhetorical as well as material preconditions for the more blatantly colonial-imperialist logic of Hegel's philosophy of world history. Hence when Rumour promises to 'unfold/ The acts commenced on this ball of earth ... from the orient to the drooping west,' he speaks – at least for us in the twenty-first century – with a 'bi-fold authority' that tweaks Weimann's theorization of early modern performance and points it in a new, anachronic direction. We may see in Rumour's remark another palimpsest, albeit one that compresses Shakespeare's present less with its histrionic pasts than with its world historical future: the Elizabethan English vociferation of Shakespearean intertheatricality now underwrites the Enlightenment German accent of Hegelian *Aufhebung*.

Acknowledgements

Many thanks to Will West, Bryan Reynolds, Robert Cohen and Madhavi Menon for their invaluable suggestions about earlier drafts of this essay.

Notes

1. On the widespread typographical association of Essex with Henry, see Harrison, 214–15.
2. Greenblatt, 21–65.

3. The phrase was used originally by Harry Berger Jr. to refer to the (then) new theater history that privileged performance over text; see Berger, *passim*. I am using it differently, to refer to an Elizabethan style of acting that is equally a mode of criticism.
4. See, for example, Hillman, 26–57, which I discuss in more detail below.
5. Indeed, some critics have suggested that for all its promise of playful dialogue between texts, intertextuality is little more than traditional source study: see Culler, 118.
6. See Zumthor, 336; Bloom; and Kristeva, 262.
7. See Aristotle, II. 555; and Marx, 400.
8. Weimann, *Shakespeare and the Popular Tradition*, 73–85. I appropriate Mikhail Bakhtin's term 'chronotope' here; although he applies it specifically to the form of the novel, it remains a useful tool with which to illuminate different epistemological and theatrical formations of space and time. See Bakhtin, *passim*.
9. The phrase is, of course, from *Troilus and Cressida*, but Weimann has adapted and popularized it in his theorization of the space of the stage. See, for example, Weimann, 'Bifold Authority in Shakespeare's Theatre.'
10. For a study of Shakespeare that reads the playtext through the prism of the palimpsest, see Lecercle. On the palimpsest of Falstaff and Oldcastle, see Goldberg.
11. See, in particular, Reynolds and Fitzpatrick. See also Reynolds, *Becoming Criminal*, and Reynolds, *Performing Transversally*.
12. The new company's letter to the Lord Mayor, written in March 1602, is reprinted in Pollard, 326.
13. And like Ambidexter, Falstaff does a comic turn as a *miles gloriosus*. See Weimann, *Shakespeare and the Popular Tradition*, 124.
14. Indeed, at the level of textual style, Falstaff's remarks recall not the clumsy fourteeners of Cambyses, but the language of drama contemporary with the play. Falstaff's reference to 'tears' that 'stop the floodgates of her eyes' potentially alludes to *Soliman and Perseda*, 4.1.94–5: 'How can mine eyes dart forth a pleasant look,/ When they are stopped with floods of flowing tears?'
15. For a discussion of performing tears in Shakespeare, see Cohen, 7–18.
16. Of the plays I consider here, Peele's *Battle of Alcazar* and Marlowe's *Tamburlaine* were both performed by the Admiral's Men at the Rose; the production details of *Soliman and Perseda* and Greene's *Alphonsus* are not clear, though Henslowe's 1598 inventory of the Admiral's Men's stage properties includes an 'owld Mahametes head' that corresponds to the most spectacular stage effect, in 4.1, of Greene's play; see Foakes and Rickert, 319.
17. When the two parts of *Henry 4* are performed in repertory, Pistol can easily be played by the same actor who played Hotspur, thereby linking the two characters. This was the case in the recent 2004 Washington DC Shakespeare Theatre repertory productions, directed by Bill Alexander, of *Parts 1 and 2*.
18. When Pistol tells Mistress Quickly 'feed and be fat, my fair Calipolis,' the actor palimpsests the character with the scene in which Muly Mahomet offers his starving wife the raw flesh of a lion.
19. I have written elsewhere about the links between Petruchio's remark and the Coventry Herod; see Harris, esp. 367–9.
20. See Reynolds, *Performing Transversally*, 4–5, 120.

Works cited

Adams, Joseph Quincy, ed. *Chief Pre-Shakespearean Dramas*. Boston: Houghton Mifflin, 1924

Aristotle. *The Basic Works of Aristotle.* Trans. Richard McKeon. New York: Random House, 1941
Bakhtin, Mikhail. *The Dialogic Imagination: Four Essays.* Trans. Caryl Emerson and Michael Holquist. Austin: University of Texas Press, 1981
Barthes, Roland. *S/Z.* London: Jonathan Cape, 1974
Berger Jr., Harry. *Imaginary Audition: Shakespeare on Stage and Page.* Berkeley, CA: University of California Press, 1989
Bloom, Harold. *The Anxiety of Influence: A Theory of Poetry.* New York: Oxford University Press, 1973
de Certeau, Michel. *The Practice of Everyday Life.* Trans. Steven Randall. Berkeley: University of California Press, 1984
Cohen, Robert. *More Power to You.* New York: Applause Theatre & Cinema Books, 2002
Craig, Hardin, ed. *Two Coventry Corpus Christi Plays.* London: Oxford University Press, 1957
Culler, Jonathan. *The Pursuit of Signs: Semiotics, Literature, Deconstruction.* Ithaca, NY: Cornell University Press, 1981
Dekker, Thomas. *The Dramatic Works of Thomas Dekker.* Ed. Fredson Bowers. 5 vols. Cambridge: Cambridge University Press, 1953
Foakes, R. A. and R. T. Rickert, eds. *Henslowe's Diary.* Cambridge: Cambridge University Press, 1961
Greenblatt, Stephen. *Shakespearean Negotiations: The Circulation of Social Energy in Renaissance England.* Berkeley, CA: University of California Press, 1988
Greene, Robert. *The Comicall Historie of Alphonsus, King of Aragon.* London, 1599
Goldberg, Jonathan. 'The Commodity of Names: "Falstaff" and "Oldcastle" in *1 Henry IV*.' *Reconfiguring the Renaissance: Essays in Critical Materialism.* Ed. Jonathan Crewe. London: Associated University Press, 1992. 76–88
Hall, Joseph. *The Collected Poems of Joseph Hall, Bishop of Exeter and Norwich.* Ed. Arnold Davenport. Liverpool: Liverpool University Press, 1947
Harris, Jonathan Gil. ' "Look not big, nor stamp, nor stare": Acting Up in *The Taming of the Shrew* and the Coventry Herod Plays.' *Comparative Drama* 34 (2000–2001): 365–98
Harrison, G. B. *The Life and Death of Robert Devereux Earl of Essex.* London: Cassell, 1937
Hedrick, Donald and Bryan Reynolds. ' "A little touch of Harry in the night": Translucency and Projective Transversality in the Sexual and National Politics of *Henry V*.' Bryan Reynolds. *Performing Transversally: Reimagining Shakespeare and the Critical Future.* New York: Palgrave, 2003. 171–88
Hegel, Georg W. F. *The Philosophy of History.* Transl. J. Sibree. Prometheus Books: Amherst, NY, 1991
Hillman, Richard. *Intertextuality and Romance in Renaissance Drama: The Staging of Nostalgia.* New York: St. Martin's Press, 1992
Jonson, Ben. *Collected Works of Ben Jonson.* Ed. C. H. Herford and Percy and Evelyn Simpson. 12 vols. Oxford: Clarendon Press, 1947
Kristeva, Julia. *Semeiotikè: Recherches pour une sémanalyse, Tel Quel.* Ed. Phillipe Sollers. Paris: Seuil, 1969
Lecercle, Ann. 'Hamlet's Play within the Play as Palimpsest.' *The Show Within: Dramatic and Other Insets: English Renaissance Drama (1550–1642).* Ed. François Laroque. Montpellier: Paul-Valéry University Press, 1990. 207–15
Marlowe, Christopher. *Tamburlaine Parts One and Two.* Ed. Anthony B. Dawson. London: A & C Black, 1997
Marx, Karl. *Writings of the Young Karl Marx on Philosophy and Science.* Trans. Lloyd D. Easton and Kurt H. Guddat. New York: Doubleday, 1967

Peele, George. *The Battell of Alcazar, Fought in Barbarie, Betweene Sebastian King of Portugall, and Abdelmec King of Marocco*. London, 1594

Pollard, Tanya, ed. *Shakespeare's Theater: A Sourcebook*. London: Blackwell, 2003

Preston, Thomas. *A Critical Edition of Thomas Preston's* Cambises. Ed. Robert Carl Johnson. Salzburg: Institut fur Englische Sprache und Literatur, 1975

Reynolds, Bryan. *Becoming Criminal: Transversal Performance and Cultural Dissidence in Early Modern England*. Baltimore: Johns Hopkins University Press, 2002

——. *Performing Transversally: Reimagining Shakespeare and the Critical Future*. New York: Palgrave, 2003

Reynolds, Bryan and Joseph Fitzpatrick. 'The Transversality of Michel de Certeau: Foucault's Panoptic Discourse and the Cartographic Impulse.' *Diacritics* 29:3 (1999): 63–80

S., E. *The Discovery of the Knights of the Post*. London, 1597

Shakespeare, William. *The Norton Shakespeare*, ed. Stephen Greenblatt et al. New York: Norton, 1997

Soliman and Perseda. London, 1599

Weimann, Robert. *Shakespeare and the Popular Tradition: Studies in the Social Dimension of Dramatic Form and Function*. Ed. Robert Schwartz. Baltimore: Johns Hopkins University Press, 1978

——. 'Bifold Authority in Shakespeare's Theatre.' *Shakespeare Quarterly* 39 (1988): 401–17

——. *Author's Pen and Actor's Voice: Playing and Writing in Shakespeare's Theatre*. Cambridge: Cambridge University Press, 2000

Zumthor, Paul. 'Le Carrefour des rhétoriqueurs: intertextualité et rhétorique.' *Poétique* 27 (1976): 317–37

5
The Politics of Shakespeare's Prose

Douglas Bruster

During the late 1580s English playwrights developed a conventional system for picturing the world in the commercial playhouses.[1] Employing an unprecedented density of representational material, such dramatists as Christopher Marlowe, George Peele, and Robert Greene offered the world as a sequence of secular actions undertaken by eloquent characters. For their plays' eloquence these university-educated writers drew upon a rich variety of media, including diverse forms and subgenres of verse and prose alike. As important as their astounding fluency of expression in dramatic dialogue was the use of this representational variety in the service of a system that charted social distinctions among, and psychological distinctions within, linguistically self-aware characters. Ironically, the very success of these dramatists' system would lend it a kind of cultural invisibility. Indeed, so natural does this system strike us still that, despite a renewed interest in the material basis of culture and of cultural representations, we too seldom attend to its profoundly heterogeneous outlines and effects. To shed light on a crucial element of Shakespeare's career, I examine his adoption of this world-picturing system and how he changed it – in particular, his increasingly sophisticated, functional alternation of verse and prose in dramatic dialogue. Notwithstanding the findings of foundational studies of Shakespeare's prose by Jonas Barish and Brian Vickers, we tend to overlook the centrality of this distinction to Shakespeare's development as a playwright, and to the larger significance of his dramatic works.[2] For if, as Robert Weimann has noted, Shakespeare's theatre 'bestows upon us an unsurpassed paradigm in artful communication,'[3] this paradigm – at once linguistic and social – was profoundly affected by Shakespeare's early decision to mimic the verse/prose representational system developed by his dramatic contemporaries.

More than the simple fact of his writing scripts for an acting company at the outset of his career, Shakespeare's adoption of the world-picturing system that alternated verse and prose in conventional ways may have prompted Greene's well-known but still elusive indictment of this 'upstart Crow, beautified with our feathers.'[4] Whatever the prompt of this famous phrase, looking closely at the functional alternation of prose and verse in Shakespeare's work helps to contextualize his plays in meaningful relation to those of his contemporaries. It also reveals a paradox of form and sequence: What remain arguably the greatest works of our best dramatic writer owe their poetic achievement to Shakespeare's reliance on and mastery of prose, a medium he took up and then abandoned before returning to it as the vitalizing basis of his most productive years in the theater.

To describe the representational system that Shakespeare inherited and worked within, my analysis begins with an examination of prose's role in theatrical world-picturing as it came into being prior to his career as a playwright. An important if little-known text in the development of this system was the anonymously authored drama *The Rare Triumphs of Love and Fortune* (1582), which helped solidify in a systematic way the decorous correspondence of speaking style and social station. The next section of the essay explores the range of contemporary opinion on the relative merits of prose and verse, as well as the reasons behind some of these evaluations. Shakespeare's own tendencies with verse and prose (especially the grounds of their distinction) preface a concluding section that takes up several passages of verse and prose from *The Taming of the Shrew* (1590–91) and *Hamlet* (1600–01).[5] Here I seek to foreground a significant development in Shakespeare's deployment of the two media. This development, which involved the redefinition of prose as a significant element of aristocratic speech, constitutes one of his most meaningful contributions to the system of representation he adopted for the basis of his dramatic fictions.

Prose in English drama before Shakespeare

Philip Sidney's often-cited regret over the 'mingl[ing]' of 'Kings and Clowns' in English drama of his time anticipated a number of patterns of productive difference that would characterize plays of the commercial repertory during Shakespeare's lifetime. Among the more familiar of such differences are the dynamic relation of plots and subplots, the functional interplay of various domains of action and existence, and, notably, the contextual alternation of verse and prose in spoken dialogue. So familiar do the workings of this world-picturing system seem that it is sometimes hard for us to imagine English theaters featuring another mode of representation, much less a linguistic arrangement based on anything other than the use of blank verse and prose.

Prior to the 1580s, however, such was not only possible but the norm. For all our uncertainty connected with the rise of the theatrical industry in England during the second half of the sixteenth century (the number of plays extent is frustratingly small), enough evidence survives to show that the world-picturing system of representation we associate with Shakespeare came into existence through four stages. During the sixteenth century, playgoers and readers of published dramatic texts would encounter, in successive order (1) plays written entirely in verse; (2) plays written in verse and plays written in prose; (3) the sporadic intermingling of prose and verse within single plays; and, finally (4) a theatrical industry that alternated prose and verse – particularly blank verse – in a dynamic and regular way.

Medieval drama had been written entirely in verse, a convention that much Tudor drama accepted and continued.[6] Indeed, following the early and sole exception of a brief, conspiratorial stage-whisper in Henry Medwall's *Nature* (1496), plays written in an England influenced by humanism most often kept verse and prose apart, typically sorting them by the classical genres.[7] Playwrights tended to use prose for comedy – thought, of course, to be a 'low' form involving the middle and lower orders of society – and verse for the more aristocratic plots and characters of tragedy.[8] We can see this precise separation of the media in two plays that George Gascoigne wrote for presentation in Gray's Inn in 1566: *Supposes*, which he translated from Ariosto's *I Suppositi* (itself a play written first in prose then later revised in verse); and, with Francis Kinwelmershe, *Jocasta*, which they translated from Lodovico Dolce's *Giocasta*.[9] Significantly, Gascoigne executed his comedy (*Supposes*) in prose, and the tragedy (*Jocasta*) in blank verse. Thus if medieval drama represented a first stage in the history of representational media in the English theater, the mid-century years – which witnessed not only the inauguration of dramatic blank verse in Sackville and Norton's *Gorboduc* (1562) but also the beginnings of the theatrical industry in the commencement of playing at the Red Lion in 1567 – constituted a second stage, during which both prose and verse were used, though, as both the example of Gascoigne and of John Lyly's courtly comedies from the 1580s shows us, in separate places.

The third stage in the history of prose's relation to verse in drama comes with the late 1570s and 1580s. In such plays as George Whetstone's *Promos and Cassandra* (1578), Robert Wilson's *The Three Ladies of London* (1581) and Anthony Munday's *Fedele and Fortuno* (1584), prose began to appear sporadically as an external voice (sometimes the voice of authority) in plays otherwise wholly in verse. In the second part of Whetstone's play, a royal proclamation in bureaucratic prose is read, whereas in the play's first part a similar proclamation is in verse. Wilson's drama features the administration of a legal oath in prose; Munday's play, a love letter. Yet such developments remain piecemeal when compared with the most significant play relating to the multiple-form system for theatrical representation in early modern England. Here I am referring to the anonymously-authored, and little-known drama, *The Rare Triumphs of Love and Fortune*, almost certainly performed by the Earl of Derby's Men at Court in 1582. This combination of mythological morality and romance points the way for later drama in coordinating an overplot (a 'contest' of the pagan gods), a romantic plot, and an underplot with clownish actions. Even more important, however, is the play's decorous coordination of a compendious variety of forms of discourse. The play has 14 speaking characters and 1,778 lines of dialogue. Remarkably, it features 11 distinct modes of expression: blank verse, heroic couplets, rhyme royal, ababcc-stanzas, unrhymed and rhymed hexameter, poulter's measure, fourteeners, abab-stanzas, and doggerel, in addition to prose.

More than a virtuoso display of mastery regarding poetic form, *The Rare Triumphs* deploys its forms along a clear social hierarchy: blank verse, for instance, is spoken only by the most powerful mythological figures (Jupiter, Mercury, and Venus), with the earthy cuckold Vulcan speaking the same doggerel that the clowns employ (and which one of the aristocrats from the mortal plot speaks when comically disguised as a foreign doctor). The Fury, Tysiphone, who precipitates the Olympic contest, speaks in blank verse when confronted by Jupiter but 'descends' to hexameter and heptameter as the play unfolds. The play lends its mortal characters a similar hierarchy, with the younger, romantic characters occasionally speaking in heroic couplets (though never in blank verse) when in duets but employing hexameter, poulter's measure, and heptameter when engaged in conversations with two or more other characters. In addition to its decorum of social rank, the play offers moral and experiential distinctions by ensuring that its romantic plot's figure of civil authority, King (sometimes Duke) Phizantius, speaks almost entirely in hexameter couplets, poulter's measure, and fourteeners rather than in the heroic couplets that its younger, romantic figures sometimes employ.

Though contributing to a virtuoso production, the 11 discursive forms of *The Rare Triumphs of Love and Fortune* would be too unwieldy for adoption in London's commercial theaters. During the later 1580s hexameter and heptameter lines seemed more and more obsolete, as would what Marlowe referred to, in the famous preface to *Tamburlaine* (1587), as 'the jigging veins of rhyming mother wits.' Marlowe's play is perhaps best known for its introduction of blank verse as a staple of theatrical representation. But it is also remarkable for inaugurating the functional alternation of verse and prose in drama. This system has its beginnings when Tamburlaine turns to a caged Bajazeth, a captured king who has (along with the play's other characters) previously spoken only in blank verse, and taunts his captive in an extrametrical line: 'And now, Bajazeth, hast thou any stomach?' To which the captive replies in prose: 'Ay, such a stomach, cruel Tamburlaine, as I could willingly feed upon thy blood-raw heart.' Tamburlaine then responds in kind: 'Nay, thine own is easier to come by; pluck out that, and 'twill serve thee and thy wife. Well, Zenocrate, Techelles, and the rest, fall to your victuals'[10] Perhaps sensing that this tennis-like volley ('Ay ... thy' / 'Nay, thine') no less than its vocabulary ('stomach,' 'blood-raw,' 'victuals') could diminish the elevated stylistic comportment of his central character, Marlowe has

Bajzaeth's next response come in blank verse:

> Fall to, and never may your meat digest!
> Ye Furies, that can mask invisible,
> Dive to the bottom of Avernus' pool ...
> (4.4.10–18)

Along with *The Rare Triumphs of Love and Fortune*, the First Part of *Tamburlaine* – and this sequence in particular – constitutes a key moment in the history of early modern drama in England. When Marlowe has this caged, humiliated king speak differently owing to his visible humiliation, and in a medium itself characterized as humble over and against the golden-throating blank verse that dominates the larger drama, he hits upon a simpler version of the complex hierarchy of forms offered in *Rare Triumphs*.

It is unclear whether such prose exchanges (of which there are several in the play) form what the play's printer would refer to as 'fond and frivolous jestures' ideally left out of printed drama.[11] Whatever their original effect and status, Marlowe extended them into *The Jew of Malta* (1589) and *Doctor Faustus* (1592), where the lead characters as well as figures from the underplots and lower registers of society speak prose. Marlowe would be joined in this, of course, by Kyd and by the small but influential group of playwrights we know as the University Wits. In Kyd's *The Spanish Tragedy* (1587), in Greene's *Friar Bacon and Friar Bungay* (1589), *James IV* (1590) and *George a Greene, the Pinner of Wakefield* (1590), and in Greene's and Thomas Lodge's *A Looking Glass for London and England* (1590), prose and verse were united in a representational economy that not only saw prose employed for 'low,' comic scenes and verse for 'higher,' more aristocratic elements of the plot, but that offered some flexibility for various characters to use either medium depending upon context and situation. As J. F. Macdonald observed, the fifth scene of Greene's *Friar Bacon* features a group of disguised young noblemen who speak in prose until confronted in verse by Bacon (who is aware of their deception), whereupon they revert to blank verse, leaving the 'real' clowns, Rafe and Miles, to continue in prose by themselves.[12] If early modern literature is notable for what Thomas Greene has called 'the flexibility of the self,' in the dramatic practice of those who followed Marlowe and Greene that flexibility is largely expressed within discursive media.[13]

By 1590 the world-picturing system that the 'upstart Crow,' William Shakespeare, would mimic had been solidly established in London's commercial playhouses. We can perhaps sense the influence of this system by looking at how it affected two playwrights who wrote both before and after its instantiation. Where Robert Wilson, for example, had employed heptameter in *The Three Ladies of London* in 1584, four years later and only a year after *Tamburlaine* he would write *The Three Lords and Three Ladies of*

London in iambic pentameter lines, with some blank verse alternating with prose. Similarly John Lyly, who had written courtly prose comedies during the 1580s, by 1593 would pen *The Woman in the Moon* largely in blank verse, with the clownish servant Gunophilus frequently delivering comic prose. So quickly did the system originate which keyed blank verse and prose to social and experiential hierarchy that we may suspect the appropriation of it by a newcomer to the theatrical scene – rather than the mere fact of this newcomer's composing plays – lied behind Greene's notorious characterization of Shakespeare as an 'upstart Crow, beautified with our feathers.' Greene, after all, had witnessed the amazing success that Marlowe, Peele, and Lodge had enjoyed, writing in this system. And Greene had experienced such success himself in half a dozen plays prior to writing *A Quip for an Upstart Courtier* in 1592. However unjustified a sentiment, Greene may have felt a proprietary relationship less to playwrighting itself than to the *system* of verse and prose which, as we will see, Shakespeare adopted for his first plays. '[O]ur feathers,' then, could be understood not only generally, as referring to the composition of scripts for the theater, but also more specifically, as the variegated plumes of prose and verse in the new world-picturing system.

Prose in context

Before turning to Shakespeare's deployment of this system, it may be helpful here briefly to examine the relative value of dramatic prose as it was defined over and against verse during Shakespeare's time as a playwright. Sir John Davies's *Microcosmos* (1603), for example, offers a representative characterization in a set-piece *antithesis*:

> Yet let me give this *Cæsar* but his due
> (*Cæsar of speech* that monarchizeth *Ears*)
> Sweet Poësie, that can all *Souls* subdue,
> To *Passions*, causing joy or forcing *Tears*,
> And to itself each glorious *sp'rite* endears:
> It is a speech of most majestic state,
> As by a well-penn'd *Poëm* well appears;
> Than prose, more cleanly couched and delicate,
> And if well done, shall live a longer *Date*.
>
> For it doth flow more fluent from the *Tongue*,
> In which respect it well may termèd be
> (Having a *Cadence* musical among),
> A *speech* melodious, full of harmony,
> Or *Ear*-enchanting matchless melody:
> Succinct it is, and easier to retain
> (Sith with our *sp'rits* it better doth agree)

> Than that which tedious *ambage* doth contain,
> Albeit the *Wit* therein did more then reign.
>
> It's decked with *Colours* fresh, and figures fine,
> Which doth the *Judgment* aye inveigle so
> (Making the *Ear* to it of force incline)
> That *Judgment* often doth herself forgo
> And like *Wax*, bends *Opinion* to and fro;
> In *Prose* the speech is not so voluble,
> Because the *Tongue* in *numbers* doth not flow,
> Ne yet the *accent* half so tunable,
> Then, to our *spirits* much less suitable.[14]

Davies's comparison itself offers a microcosm of early modern opinion on prose and verse (what he calls 'Poësie;' other synonyms then current include, of course, 'numbers' and, as we have seen, 'meter').[15] When contrasted with verse (as it so often was), prose was typically held to feature opposite traits and aspects, or, at the very least, less positive attributes than those which Davies and others saw in poesie. Prose, when it was praised at all, was often said to be less formal, less authoritative, less beautiful – in short, lesser in every positive aspect ascribed to verse. For instance, where many commentators lauded what we would call the compression of verse ('Succinct it is'), prose was sometimes held to feature a 'multitude of words' and to be 'full of tedious ambage and long periods.' The phrases here are Puttenham's, but as we have seen, they are echoed precisely in Davies's description of prose as 'that which tedious ambage doth contain.' Something of prose's paradoxical status under such a 'thin' description – that is, under a definition that would lump together the prose of Lyly's *Euphues* (1579/80) or Bacon's *Essays* (1597–) with that of a play-bill or tavern reckoning – appears in the fact that while prose was held by some to be too wordy (an 'ambage' is a circumlocution, periphrasis, or delaying speech), it could likewise be characterized as useful for its bluntness.

Such bluntness appears in a humorous way in Chapman's *The Widow's Tears* (1604), where Lycus's blank verse magniloquence – 'Humanity broke loose from my heart, and / Streamed through mine eyes' – is glossed brusquely by Tharsalio: 'In prose, thou weptst.'[16] Marston's Freevill in *The Dutch Courtesan* (1605) prefaces a breathless narration with the phrase 'In most sincere prose, thus ...' (1.1.16), and Jonson similarly reminds us that prose is more efficacious than verse in certain situations when he has the 2nd Prisoner in *Eastward Ho!* (1605) praise Quicksilver for his facility in each medium: 'O he has penned the best thing, that he calls his "Repentance" or his "Last Farewell", that ever you heard. He is a pretty poet, and for prose – you would wonder how many prisoners he has helped out, with penning petitions for 'em, and not take a penny' (5.3.54–8).[17] The quest for such a plain, more direct mode of writing is perhaps implied in Longaville's declaration to 'tear' his 'numbers' and instead 'write in prose.'

Because of the everyday, utilitarian nature of some of its varieties ('In most sincere prose, thus'), prose invariably found a place lower on the ladder of renaissance forms.[18] With hierarchy constituting a central habit of thought for the period, the implied correspondence between prose and the lower orders of society was never far to seek. As Chapman put it in the Epistle Dedicatory to Prince Henry prefacing his translation of *The Iliads* (1609):

> So Truth, with Poesie graced, is fairer far,
> More proper, moving, chaste, and regular,
> Than when she runs away with untruss't Prose;
> Proportion, that doth orderly dispose
> Her virtuous treasure, and is Queen of Graces;
> In Poesie, decking her with choicest Phrases,
> Figures and numbers: when loose Prose puts on
> Plain letter-habits; makes her trot, upon
> Dull earthly business (she being mere divine):
> Holds her to homely Cates, and harsh hedge wine ...
>
> (ll. 102–11)[19]

Chapman articulates a widespread prejudice concerning the merits of verse and the lower nature of prose. Poesie valuably graces truth with 'choicest Phrases, / Figures and numbers.' Prose, an 'untruss't,' 'loose' person, adopts 'Plain letter-habits' (presumably, unattractively simple appearance or garb) and is made by proportion to 'trot, upon / Dull earthly business' and is given only 'homely Cates, and harsh hedge wine' for nourishment. Chapman's personified 'Proportion' 'dispose[s]' her 'virtuous treasure' in a manner he calls 'orderly,' calling up with its decorum of distribution the felt equivalence between an ostensibly lower medium, prose, and the lower orders of early modern society in England. As we will see, this equivalence would come under considerable pressure in the playhouses of early modern London during the late 1590s and early 1600s, when playwrights began to question the easy distinctions among the media.

Shakespeare's prose: tendencies

If it is difficult to appreciate how quickly the functional alternation of verse and prose solidified into a conventional mode of representation in London's theatrical industry from 1587 to 1590, the characterizations of verse and prose we have examined plainly suggest the extensive social and political implications that such a system carried with it. A hierarchy of forms that signalled contextually – albeit with verse generally the higher form and prose the lower – meant that English stages could represent with facility a dizzying range of social ranks, relationships, and experiences, and could chart these over and against various aspects of social life by means of formal variety.

Shakespeare and his fellow dramatists would of course retain something of the complex range of forms offered in *The Rare Triumphs of Love and Fortune*, with a kind of 'wheel' of forms offering itself for selection – from blank verse and rhymed pentameter through prose, hexameter and heptameter, song meters (folk and courtly alike) and even doggerel. If a simple choice of verse or prose does not account for the range of options available during the period, it is nonetheless true that the majority of dramatic works during the late-Elizabethan and Jacobean eras would see the most important distinction coming in the functional alternation of verse and prose.

Playwrights of the late 1580s fashioned a system offering ready-made distinctions along the lines of George Puttenham's famous linguistic differentiation of court and countryside.[20] Shakespeare would follow the lead of Marlowe, Greene, Peele, and Lodge in constructing playworld environments that feature artful switching between verse and prose, often with the clear implication that the characters themselves are not only conscious but fully responsible for choosing the media they employ. It is worth emphasizing this last point because the creation of profoundly self-aware speakers would prove central to Shakespeare's achievement and that of the early modern English theater generally. So sophisticated did Shakespeare's experimentation with this system become, in fact, that we often take for granted the fusion of metatheatrical discourse, self-aware characters, and linguistic sophistication that marks his dramatic practice and that of many who wrote after his example.

While long a part of the early modern repertory, this linguistic self-awareness reached a kind of peak at around 1599 to 1604. No doubt influenced by the exaggerated attention given to discursive style during the Wars of the Theaters, a number of plays at this time offered winking acknowledgments not just of their artificiality but of how that artificiality worked in and through language. We remember, of course, Jacques leaving the stage in *As You Like It* (1599) with a complaint that indicates his hyper-sophisticated awareness of representational media in the theater. Following Orlando's iambic pentameter 'Good day and happiness, dear Rosalind,' Jacques mutters, before exiting, 'Nay, then God buy you, and you talk in blank verse' (4.1.30–2). But Jacques may well have been anticipated by Chettle's and Munday's *The Downfall of Robert, Earl of Huntingdon* (1598), where Much begins a narrative in iambic tetrameter before breaking off with an aside, '(I'll speak in prose, I miss this verse vilely)' and continuing as promised with his exposition in prose.[21] Likewise the Second Part of *The Return from Parnassus* (1601–02) has Defensor interrupt a prose induction to say 'No more of this, I heard the spectators ask for a blank verse.'[22] Two years later, in Marston's *Parasitaster, or The Fawn* (1604), the Princess Dulcimell would respond to her waiting-woman's query ('By what means, sweet Madam?') with a metatheatrical acknowledgment of her discursive choices: 'Oh, Philocalia, in heavy sadness and unwanton phrase there lies all the brain work! "By what means"? I could fall into a miserable blank verse presently.'[23]

All these characters imply that, within the boundaries of their playworlds, they not only recognize the distinction between verse and prose but are themselves free to choose between them. I have suggested that such linguistic flexibility remained a crucial element in the representational economy of the early modern theater in England – particularly in scripts produced during Shakespeare's lifetime. Left to be answered, however, is the question of what prompted early modern dramatists and their characters when choosing between verse and prose. As with so much else concerning the drama, we know more about the practice of Shakespeare than that of his fellow dramatists. Since the later nineteenth century, in fact, scholars have reconstructed and gradually augmented a loose set of 'rules' to explain the use of prose in Shakespeare's plays. Jonas Barish summarizes these in offering, as 'rough guidelines,' what we could call the 'three Rs' of prose: 'rank, realism, and … risibility.' That is, in determining whether verse or prose would be more appropriate or efficient for a dramatic situation, Shakespeare appears to have had the criteria of social rank, of 'realism' (with all that term's ambiguous valences), and seriousness or jocularity as determinants of a scene's discursive medium.

The usefulness of this trio of determinants could be enhanced by a more analytical description, with certain caveats in mind. First, any 'list' of criteria offers tendencies rather than rules, and even these tendencies have clear exceptions across Shakespeare's career. Second, every choice that Shakespeare and his dramatic contemporaries made in terms of discursive media was overdetermined, being influenced in most cases not only by the complexities of a dramatic situation (in which various characters may well seem to have competing interests and interpretations of the contexts of their interactions with other characters), but also by the changeful market of discourse in which the highly competitive early modern repertories had a special investment. Third, there are various *kinds* of prose in Shakespeare, just as there are various kinds of verse, and many speakers seem to possess, if not idiolects, then idiosyncratic styles and competencies relating to the discursive media they use.

To these cautions I would add only that elements in the following dichotomy represent possible criteria for discursive situations rather than comprehensive or binding descriptions of what verse and prose 'were,' in Shakespeare and early modern drama. For instance, taking only the first set of alternatives – 'characters of high rank' (verse) and 'characters of middle and low rank' (prose) – one immediately notes that many characters of high rank speak sometimes in prose, and that some characters of middle- and lower rank speak in verse. Likewise, the suggestion (later in the table) that prose is more often employed for obscenity, and verse for decorous topics is meant to imply neither that verse is constitutionally decorous nor that most prose is obscene, but instead that, given a bawdy topic, and with other determinants (social rank, formality of circumstance, reigning linguistic medium already in operation) firmly in play, dramatists more often turned to prose than verse, and contrarily for decorous topics. The utility of this and any such schema, then, comes as a kind of handlist for those wishing to understand the range of things that may have contributed to a playwright's decision to employ one medium over another in a given situation.

verse	prose
characters of high rank	characters of middle and low rank
educated characters	uneducated characters
formal	informal
serious	playful
tragedy	comedy
functional	decorative
temporal	atemporal
ceremonial	commercial
sentiment	satire, criticism
proper English	non-standard English
tension	relaxation
decorum	obscenity
sobriety	drunkenness
sanity	insanity

Of course, each element in the schema above deserves (and in some cases, has received) extensive discussion in and of itself. Most of them have been recognized by scholars concerned with the function of prose in Shakespeare's plays. The one contribution I have made (something that is, to my knowledge, original with this essay) is the observation concerning prose's atemporal nature in Shakespeare and much early modern drama. That is, in many instances verse conveys the forward movement of time in a play and prose functions as a space and a discourse somewhat outside of time. Thus criticism, extended quibbling upon words and phrases, hypothetical imaginings, and *descriptio* of various types are often executed in prose, as though an imaginary clock were stopping while the speaker analyzes some action, object, or idea outside the normal pace of the dramatic event.

Prose and time

We could trace how Shakespeare began to deploy this atemporal mode in prose as early as *The Taming of the Shrew*, where the bridegroom Petruchio's bold appearance prior to the wedding is framed by two crucial passages of 'telling' rather than 'showing' (3.2.42–86; 158–79). In the second of the two passages, the pantaloon, Gremio narrates in blank verse Petruchio's comically obnoxious behavior at the marriage ceremony. Germio's speech 'tells' the story of the ceremony in the order of its happening, with careful attention not only to the event's physical actions and utterances but also to the precise order of its unfolding. The sequence is highlighted in the use of adverbs of time not only in Gremio's narration and Tranio's interruption, but in quoted speech within the narration itself: 'when ... and as ... "Now" ... when ... after ...' (3.2.158; 162; 165; 166; 169). Regularly embedded within the story, these markers of time give the audience and reader a sense of having witnessed, through Gremio's eyes, the slapstick scene unfold. The scene's rough, physical humor involving a priest and a religious book may have made it practically unperformable on public stages in early modern London. In any case, Gremio's status (like Baptista, he is regularly addressed as 'Signior') means that he often speaks in iambic pentameter; and even though the actions he describes are farcical and 'low,' Shakespeare has him narrate their unfolding in blank verse.

This stands in stark contrast to Biondello's narration of Petruchio's 'coming' earlier in this same scene. Equally a set-piece of dramatic writing, this description functions as an early masterpiece of comic prose. We could notice that, unlike Gremio's insistence on temporal sequence in his blank-verse account, Shakespeare carefully establishes an atemporal atmosphere for Biondello's telling. He does so by means of some significant quibbling prior to the description. When Baptista hears Biondello ask 'is it not news to hear of Petruchio's coming?', he responds with a question that allows the clown to defer the action outside time:

> *Baptista*: Is he come?
> *Biondello*: Why, no, sir.
> *Baptista*: What then?
> *Biondello*: He is coming.
> *Baptista*: When will he be here?
> *Biondello*: When he stands where I am, and sees you there.
>
> (3.2.33–41)

Biondello calls this 'old news,' a phrase that Baptista repeats as prologue to the clown's longer recitation (30, 42). With this paradox of 'old news' Shakespeare prepares us for the timeless dilation of the prose speech that follows:

> Why, Petruchio is coming in a new hat and an old jerkin; a pair of old breeches thrice turn'd; a pair of boots that have been candle-cases, one buckled, another lac'd; an old rusty sword ta'en out of the town armory, with a broken hilt, and chapeless; with two broken points; his horse hipp'd, with an old mothy saddle and stirrups of no kindred; besides, possess'd with the glanders and like to mose in the chine, troubled with the lampas, infected with the fashions, full of windgalls, sped with spavins,

ray'd with the yellows, past cure of the fives, stark spoil'd with the staggers, begnawn with the bots, sway'd in the back, and shoulder-shotten, near-legg'd before, and with a half-cheek'd bit and a head-stall of sheep's leather, which being restrain'd to keep him from stumbling, hath been often burst, and now repair'd with knots; one girth six times piec'd, and a woman's crupper of velure, which hath two letters for her name fairly set down in studs, and here and there piec'd with packthread.

(3.2.43–63)

While Gremio's speech follows Katherina and Petruchio through time, Biondello's description, having been prefaced with the figure of 'old news,' gives us a kind of perpetual present between the 'old' and the 'new.' This conjunction is taken up at the outset of the speech in the phrase 'a new hat and an old jerkin' (43–4). It is worth noting that the important history in this speech is not Petruchio's movement itself (he 'is coming'), but rather the mouldy history of the objects with which the Quixotic bridegroom has chosen to adorn himself. Even the first few objects the clown describes illustrate this history: the 'old breeches' have been 'thrice turn'd,' the boots 'have been candle-cases, one buckled, another lac'd,' and so on throughout the speech until its concluding description of a studded velure crupper 'here and there piec'd with a packthread.' For the prose speech, time can be deferred to the before and the after, the 'old' and 'new' with which Shakespeare prefaces the set-piece. But in the closing of this frame, in 3.2, upon the bridegroom Petruchio, Gremio's oration devotes itself to the experience of time, and to conveying that experience through the regular rhythms of blank verse.

We could pause for a moment to notice how 'natural' it seems for the clown to speak in prose and the 'Signior' to use verse, even though they are each describing, in approximately the same conversational setting, the indecorum of the same individual. This appearance of naturalness – a sense that such could well go without remark – is of course a goal as well as an effect of the world-picturing system that, as we have seen, functionally alternated verse and prose in its representation of socially- and psychologically 'thick' characters and discourse. The reasons for Shakespeare choosing prose in one instance and verse in another are multiple. Biondello, a clownish servant, is a 'low' character; Gremio, a wealthy pantaloon, is higher on the social ladder. We could also note, following Frank Kermode, that 'prose is the language of criticism,' and Biondello's comic set-piece can be seen as making claim upon Petruchio as an object of critical dilation through its wonderful suspension of time.[24] Gremio's speech, in contrast, commits itself to sequence, with Petruchio more of a subject than an object of discourse. In a carnivalesque fashion, the almost frozen 'present' by which Biondello has Petruchio not 'come' but 'coming' affords the clown a large measure of comedic agency over his social superiors, Baptista and Petruchio.

Viewed in the context of works from later in the playwright's career, Biondello's speech helps us notice something about the politics of prose in Shakespeare. In his early plays Shakespeare tends to observe a series of inherited conventions regarding the allocation of verse and prose in his fictional worlds, largely relegating prose to those from the lower orders of society. By the end of the 1590s, however, a new emphasis on prose as capacious expression would see him make that medium important to various of his aristocratic characters. By 1600–01, in fact, prose had become crucial to the agency of such 'playwright' figures as Hal and Hamlet. Hal famously boasts, in *1 Henry IV* (1596–7), of having learned to 'drink with any tinker in his own language' (2.4.18–19). And later in this scene he similarly brags 'I am now of all humours that have show'd themselves humors since the old days of Goodman Adam to the pupil age of this present twelve a' clock at midnight' (92–5). Although in this speech Hal refers to the *longue durée* of recorded history ('Goodman Adam to the pupil age of this present twelve a' clock'), a powerful subtext of the speech is its very motivation by 'wit' and 'humors' comedy, those fashionable elements of London society and its print culture during the 1590s. This development, still largely unchronicled by literary historians, appears to have been a strong prompt to Shakespeare's rising deployment of prose from 1595 to 1600.[25]

Hal's almost athletic proficiency at speaking verse and prose would soon be joined, of course, by Hamlet's exhibition of competence in the two media. Like that of Portia before them, and of Iago, Lear, and Vincentio after them, Hal and Hamlet's ability to speak eloquently in both verse and prose, and to switch between the media at will, demonstrates what Brian Vickers calls the gradual movement of Shakespeare's prose 'from clown to character.' During the 1590s, many of prose's elements, as Vickers points out, 'become less the province of type-characters such as the clown or of set-scenes, [and] are slowly integrated to more realistic personalities and to the dramatic texture.'[26] It seems no accident that at the same time Shakespeare is regularly giving various characters the ability to 'plot' – to conceive, arrange, and direct action – from within his dramatic fictions themselves, he sees fit to lend these playwright figures a clear mastery of verse and prose alike. What fitter accompaniment to a playwright's organizational powers than the writerly control of various discursive media? When Shakespeare makes Portia, Hal, Hamlet, and Iago de facto dramatists within their respective dramatic worlds, he allocates to them a particular facility with the verse/prose function of the world-picturing system. This is a facility, we will remember, that Shakespeare had himself labored to acquire during his apprenticeship in the theater.

Prose and politics

A passage from *Hamlet* suggests some of what is at stake, in Shakespeare's works, for a character's relation to verse and prose and for readers interested in the contours of these media as they unfold in the play. The passage is the less-familiar conclusion of Hamlet's meditation on mortality, a meditation prompted by Yorrick's skull (5.1). Spurred to philosophical comment by the omnipresence of death in their surroundings, the thoughtful prince begins what seems like a lecture:

> *Hamlet*: To what bases uses we may return, Horatio! Why may not imagination trace the noble dust of Alexander, till 'a find it stopping a bunghole?
> *Horatio*: 'Twere to consider too curiously, to consider so.
> *Hamlet*: No, faith, not a jot, but to follow him thither with modesty enough and likelihood to lead it: Alexander died, Alexander was buried, Alexander returneth to dust, the dust is earth, of earth we make loam, and why of that loam whereto he was converted might they not stop a beer-barrel?
>
> (202–12)

Hamlet winds 'curiously,' to use Horatio's word, through a mock-logical proof based on the process of decay, ending with a rhetorical question: 'and why ... might they not stop a beer-barrel?' Such mock-logic had formerly been the province of Shakespeare's clowns. Biondello's 'He is coming' exchange with Baptista is only one instance of the Tudor clown's easy mastery of the genre. Shakespeare seems to offer us a memory of these clowning routines when he precedes Hamlet's logical proof with the first Gravedigger's 'argal' summation: 'But if the water come to him and drown him, he drowns not himself; argal, he that is not guilty of his own death shortens not his own life' (5.1.18–20). Hamlet's subsequent exchange of wits with the gravedigger shows that, like Hal, he can speak that laborer's 'language.'

The most important thing about this shared language is that it is prose. As we have seen, prose and verse had multiple, and differing, resonances for writers, readers, and audience members. These resonances shifted over time. Early in the 1590s, prose registered largely as a medium for characters lower on the social ladder. By 1600, Shakespeare and other playwrights had accommodated prose to aristocratic character within the world-picturing system. Thus we see him demonstrating something like the range of discursive possibility for such characters when he has Hamlet turn suddenly and surprisingly to rhymed pentameter immediately upon the prose of what Harold Jenkins calls this meditation on 'Death the leveler.'[27] That is, just after the words 'might they not stop a beer-barrel?' Hamlet continues:

> Imperious Caesar, dead and turn'd to clay,
> Might stop a hole to keep the wind away.
> O that the earth which kept the world in awe
> Should patch a wall t' expel the winter's flaw!
>
> (213–16)

Hamlet offers Horatio a second notable instance for his own 'argal' demonstration, but switches from prose to verse as he does so. Jenkins seems troubled enough by the shift to account for it with an explanation that only leads to other questions: 'The citation of *Caesar* along with Alexander was traditional, but the burst of rhyme must be taken to be one of Hamlet's impromptus.'[28] Among the questions that Jenkins's explanation asks us to ask: Why does Hamlet change suddenly from prose to verse here? And What does it mean that Shakespeare gives him the appearance of choice over the matter?

We have already seen that one of the remarkable developments in Shakespeare's career involved the creation of linguistically self-aware characters possessing the full range of discursive genres, verse and prose alike. And it could be argued that Hamlet switches from prose to verse here for the same reason that Shakespeare gave Hamlet the very power of 'impromptu' decision-making where it comes to verse and prose in the first place. That is, to demonstrate ability, range, and facility in discourse. By the end of the 1590s Shakespeare had redefined aristocratic speech (and the speech of his dramatically central characters, whatever their social station) to encompass extensive use of prose as well as verse. Such redefinition likely came less out of any democratizing impulse than from a recognition, on Shakespeare's part, of the power inherent in prose and its many subgenres, including the formal, atemporal proofs evident in 5.1. Giving Hamlet the appearance of choice over verse and prose is to give him the appearance of making a significant distinction between 'Alexander' and 'Caesar' in the Shakespearean world-picture. This is far from an accidental distinction, yet it leads us to consider what distinction there was between these two figures in the Elizabethan mind. No less than Rome, of course, Caesar was important to England's myths of origins. And we have already heard John Davies call 'poësie' the '*Cæsar of speech* that monarchizeth *Ears*.' It was this very association of Caesar with power and authority that prompted Shakespeare to use the name (and character) in his most 'authoritative' medium: verse. Of the 423 times that the playwright uses a form of 'Caesar' in his works, for example, he deploys the word in verse nearly 92 per cent of the time. Forms of 'Alexander' (when used in reference to Alexander the Great) are less common in Shakespeare, but of the 31 instances over half – including these uses in *Hamlet* – come in prose.

Readers today may find it difficult to imagine a culture that could not only 'place' Caesar and Alexander so variously but that would accordingly associate their names with correspondingly higher (verse) and lower (prose) media. That such was the case, however, can be seen in the percentages of deployment across Shakespeare's works, in Hamlet's 'impromptu' switch from prose to verse when he changes examples from Alexander to Caesar, and also in Shakespeare's own, and similar, commitment to verse when writing *Julius Caesar* (1599) during a period when he was using more prose than ever when composing his plays. During the late Elizabethan era, as we have seen, London's writers, audiences, and readers had embraced prose in the service of wit and humors comedy. Shakespeare adapted his compositional practices to this development, and in the later 1590s his plays featured a much higher percentage of prose. But when composing *Julius Caesar*, he drastically limited the prose spoken in Caesar's Rome, making it a kind of formal anomaly in his career. Like Hamlet, Shakespeare exhibited with flair the ability to accommodate his media to contingent objects of representation. Like Shakespeare, Hamlet seems able consciously to switch codes when addressing subjects that may seem almost identical in nature. As we have seen with *Shrew*'s Signior and clown, however, what is being spoken can matter as much as who is speaking. More than any of the rival playwrights who pioneered the verse/prose distinction for world-picturing on the commercial stages, Shakespeare remained aware of the cultural valences of various topics, just as he was aware of the registers and varieties of speech that seemed appropriate to various speakers. Unlike most of his contemporaries in the theater, he lived to complicate the verse/prose division. That he did so by having many of his central characters learn to speak fluent prose, and to speak it frequently, testifies to his appreciation of its power and depth as a resource.

Notes

1. On the 'world-picture' as a system, see Martin Heidegger, 'The Age of the World Picture,' in *The Question Concerning Technology and Other Essays*, 115–54. Robert Weimann elaborates on this concept in *Authority and Representation in Early Modern Discourse*, 2, 193. See also Bruster and Weimann, *Prologues to Shakespeare's Theatre*, pp. 80, 117, 119.
2. See Jonas Barish, *Ben Jonson and the Language of Prose Comedy* and Brian Vickers, *The Artistry of Shakespeare's Prose*.
3. Weimann, *Authority and Representation*, p. 249.
4. See D. Allen Carroll, ed. *Greene's Groatsworth of Wit: Bought With a Million of Repentance*, p. 85, ll. 938–43.
5. Dating for Shakespeare's plays supplied in this essay come from the estimations offered in *William Shakespeare: A Textual Companion*, ed. Stanley Wells and Gary Taylor (1987). Approximate dates for non-Shakespearean plays are taken from *Annals of English Drama, 975–1700*, 3rd edition, ed. Alfred Harbage, revised by S. Schoenbaum and Sylvia Stoler Wagonheim. All quotations from Shakespeare are from *The Riverside Shakespeare*, 2nd edition, ed. G. Blakemore Evans *et al*.
6. I should point out here that what this essay addresses is prose (and verse) as spoken on stage. Stage directions are customarily written in prose.
7. See Henry Medwall, *Nature* in *The Plays Of Henry Medwall*, ed. Alan H. Nelson, p. 112, ll. 845–50.
8. For commentary from the period on the felt distinctiveness of verse over prose, see, among others, Richard Willes (sometimes 'Wills'), *De re poetica* (1573), 86, 90; George Gascoigne, *Certayne Notes of Instruction Concerning the Making of Verse or Rhyme in English* (1575), in Smith, ed. *Elizabethan Critical Essays*, vol. 1, p. 52; William Webbe, *A Discourse of English Poetry* (1582) in Smith, ed. *Elizabethan Critical*

Essays, vol. 1, pp. 267, 274; George Puttenham, *The Arte of English Poesie* (pub. 1589), ed. Gladys Doidge Willcock and Alice Walker, pp. 8–9, 23, 76.
9. On these two plays, see the discussion by G. W. Pigman III in his edition of *Gascoigne's A Hundreth Sundrie Flowres*, pp. 470–6, 509–18.
10. Christopher Marlowe, *Tamburlaine the Great*, Part 1, in *'Doctor Faustus' and Other Plays*, ed. David Bevington and Eric Rasmussen.
11. For treatment of Richard Jones's preface epistle which discusses the omission, from his text of *Tamburlaine*, of 'some fond and frivolous jestures' that 'were showed upon the stage in their graced deformities,' see Bruster and Weimann, *Prologues to Shakespeare's Theatre*, pp. 82–4, 172 n13.
12. J. F. Macdonald, 'The Use of Prose in English Drama Before Shakespeare,' p. 476. Henry Sharpe similarly noted that while in Peele's *Edward I* (1591) both the English King and nobles and the Scotch nobles speak verse, 'the Welsh nobles and gentlemen,' like the French nobles in Shakespeare's *Henry V* (1599), 'prefer prose,' 543.
13. Thomas Greene, 'The Flexibility of the Self in Renaissance Literature,' in *The Disciplines of Criticism*, pp. 241–64.
14. John Davies, *Microcosmos. The Discovery of the Little World, with the government thereof*, p. 211. I have modernized spelling and punctuation in this extract.
15. Alastair Fowler, *Kinds of Literature: An Introduction to the Theory of Genres and Modes*, p. 9.
16. George Chapman, *The Widow's Tears*, in *Plays of George Chapman: The Comedies: A Critical Edition*, Allan Holaday, gen. ed., 4.1.
17. See John Marston, *The Dutch Courtesan*, in *The Selected Plays of John Marston*, ed. MacDonald P. Jackson and Michael Neill; and Ben Jonson, George Chapman, and John Marston, *Eastward Ho!*, ed. C. G. Petter; for the assignment of 5.3 to Jonson, see p. xxi.
18. For the 'Hierarchies of Genres and Canons of Literature,' see the chapter of that same name in Fowler, *Kinds of Literature*, pp. 213–34; see also the section 'Maps of Genres,' pp. 239–46.
19. George Chapman, 'To the High Born Prince of Men, *Henrie* Thrice *Royall inheritor to the united kingdoms of Great* Brittaine, &c.' in Phyllis Brooks Bartlett, ed. *The Poems of George Chapman*, pp. 385–8.
20. Puttenham, *The Arte of English Poesie*, pp. 144–6.
21. Henry Chettle and Anthony Munday, *The Downfall of Robert, Earl of Huntingdon*, K1[v].
22. In *The Three Parnassus Plays (1598–1601)*, ed. J. B. Leishman, p. 223, ll. 56–7. Leishman notes that Defensor's subsequent speech is actually in heroic couplets.
23. John Marston, *Parasitaster, or The Fawn* (London: 1606), E3[r].
24. Frank Kermode, *Shakespeare's Language*, p. 81.
25. For a recent study of 'wit' as it related to print culture in early modern London, see Ian Munro, 'Shakespeare's Jestbook: Wit, Print, Performance,' *ELH* 71.1 (2004): 89–113.
26. Brian Vickers, *The Artistry of Shakespeare's Prose*, p. 53. See ch. 3, 'From Clown to Character,' pp. 52–88.
27. Harold Jenkins, ed. *Hamlet*, note to 5.1.191.
28. Jenkins, ed. *Hamlet*, note to 5.1.206–9.

Works cited

Barish, Jonas. *Ben Jonson and the Language of Prose Comedy*. Cambridge, MA: Harvard University Press, 1960.

Bruster, Douglas and Robert Weimann. *Prologues to Shakespeare's Theatre*. London and New York: Routledge, 2004.
Carroll, D. Allen, ed. *Greene's Groatsworth of Wit: Bought With a Million of Repentance*. Binghamton: Medieval & Renaissance Texts & Studies, 1994.
Chapman, George. *The Widow's Tears*, in *Plays of George Chapman: The Comedies: A Critical Edition*. Ed. Allan Holaday. Urbana: University of Illinois Press, 1970.
Chapman, George. *The Poems of George Chapman*. Ed. Phyllis Brooks Bartlett. New York: Russell and Russell, 1962.
Chettle, Henry and Anthony Munday, *The Downfall of Robert, Earl of Huntingdon*. London: 1601.
Davis, John. *Microcosmos. The Discovery of the Little World, with the Government Thereof*. London: 1603.
Fowler, Alastair. *Kinds of Literature: An Introduction to the Theory of Genres and Modes*. Cambridge, MA: Harvard University Press, 1982.
Gascoigne, George. *Certayne Notes of Instruction Concerning the Making of Verse or Rhyme in English*, in Smith, ed. *Elizabethan Critical Essays*, 1: 46–57.
Gascoigne, George. *Gascoigne's A Hundreth Sundrie Flowres*. Ed. G. W. Pigman III. Oxford: Clarendon Press, 2000.
Greene, Thomas. 'The Flexibility of the Self in Renaissance Literature.' *The Disciplines of Criticism: Essays in Literary Theory, Interpretation, and History*. Ed. Peter Demetz et al. New Haven: Yale University Press, 1968, pp. 241–64.
Harbage, Alfred, ed. *Annals of English Drama, 975–1700*. 3rd ed. Rev. by S. Schoenbaum and Sylvia Stoler Wagonheim. London: Routledge, 1989.
Heidegger, Martin. 'The Age of the World Picture.' *The Question Concerning Technology and Other Essays*. Trans. William Lovitt. New York: Harper and Row, 1977.
Jonson, Ben, George Chapman, and John Marston, *Eastward Ho!*. Ed. C. G. Petter. London: Ernest Benn, 1973.
Leishman, J. B., ed. *The Three Parnassus Plays (1598–1601)*. London: Ivor Nicholson & Watson Ltd, 1949.
Macdonald, J. F. 'The Use of Prose in English Drama Before Shakespeare.' *University of Toronto Quarterly* 2 (1933): 465–81.
Marlowe, Christopher. *Tamburlaine the Great, Part 1*, in *"Doctor Faustus" and Other Plays*. Ed. David Bevington and Eric Rasmussen. Oxford: Oxford University Press, 1995.
Marston, John. *The Dutch Courtesan*, in *The Selected Plays of John Marston*. ed. MacDonald P. Jackson and Michael Neill. Cambridge: Cambridge University Press, 1986.
Marston, John. *Parasitaster, or The Fawn*. London: 1606.
Medwall, Henry. *Nature* in *The Plays Of Henry Medwall*. Ed. Alan H. Nelson. Cambridge: D.S. Brewer, 1980.
Munro, Ian. 'Shakespeare's Jestbook: Wit, Print, Performance.' *ELH* 71.1 (2004): 89–113.
Owen, John Isaac, ed. *The Rare Triumphs of Love and Fortune*. New York: Garland, 1979.
Puttenham, George. *The Arte of English Poesie*. Ed. Gladys Doidge Willcock and Alice Walker. Cambridge: Cambridge University Press, 1936; repr. 1970.
Shakespeare, William. *The Riverside Shakespeare*. 2nd ed. Ed. G. Blakemore Evans *et al.* Boston: Houghton Mifflin, 1997.
Shakespeare, William. *Hamlet*. Ed. Harold Jenkins. London: Methuen, 1982.
Sharpe, Henry. 'The Prose in Shakespeare's Plays, the Rules for its Use, and the Assistance that it Gives in Understanding the Plays.' *Transactions of the New Shakespeare Society*. Series 1.10 (1880–86): 523–62.

Sidney, Philip. *The Defence of Poesy*, in *Sir Philip Sidney: Selected Prose and Poetry*. Ed. Robert Kimbrough. 2nd ed. Madison: University of Wisconsin Press, 1983.
Smith, G. G., ed. *Elizabethan Critical Essays*. 2 vols. Oxford: Clarendon Press, 1904; repr. London, 1959.
Vickers, Brian. *The Artistry of Shakespeare's Prose*. London: Methuen, 1968.
Webbe, William *A Discourse of English Poetry*. In Smith, ed. *Elizabethan Critical Essays*, 1: 226–302.
Weimann, Robert. *Authority and Representation in Early Modern Discourse*. Ed. David Hillman. Baltimore: Johns Hopkins University Press, 1996.
Wells, Stanley and Gary Taylor. *William Shakespeare: A Textual Companion*. Oxford: Clarendon Press; New York: Oxford University Press, 1987.
Willes, Richard. *De re poetica*. Ed. and trans. A. D. S. Fowler. Oxford: Blackwell, 1958.

6
Mercutio's Bad Language
William N. West

> Then every man's name, as I tell him, is that which he is called. To this he replies, "If all the world were to call you Hermogenes, that would not be your name."
>
> Plato, writing as Hermogenes, *Cratylus* (c. 360 BCE)

> There is a name and a thing, and a thing, And a name, And a name, and not the thing, And the Name and the thing both in one according to the Obedience to the thing and name.
>
> Thomas Tany, writing as Theaurau John (1650)[1]

It does not take Juliet's explicit demand 'What's in a name?' (2. 2. 43) to alert us to the importance *Romeo and Juliet* attaches to names and their relations to things. In plot as well the play is organized into dyads; the Verona it represents is composed of binaries internally defined by their mutual exclusivity, such as the strife between of 'Two households both alike in dignity' with which it opens (1. Prol. 1) – fundamentally, to be a Montague is to be the opposite of being a Capulet, and vice versa; to participate in civil and familial duties is not to be in Petrarchan love, and vice versa. Criticism often follows the play's lead. Combining a sense of its violent actions and its gorgeous language, Mark van Doren called *Romeo and Juliet* 'furiously literary,' and critics have continued to follow him in exploring the play's divisions.[2] The rift in rhetoric identified by van Doren can be translated into a generic one, for *Romeo and Juliet* is traditionally identified as one of Shakespeare's most lyrical plays, rhetorically for its use of highly marked and often static, monologic poetic language; literary-historically as part of a mid-1590s group of similar tone; and structurally and thematically in its adaptation of the conventions of sonnet sequences to the stage.[3]

Such readings of the play as internally divided have recently been rematerialized – that is, given a local habitation and a name – by Robert Weimann and Douglas Bruster, who show how what has been read as a transhistorical split between modes of discourse can also be seen as a historically particular negotiation between longstanding conventions of performance and developing ones of print and authorship.[4] The play's prologue, note Bruster and Weimann, is delivered as a sonnet, the very form of written form (its name claiming an allegiance to song that its use contradicts), and its evocation of 'lyric pathos' (113) and its setting 'in fair Verona, where we lay our scene' (1. Prol. 2) make it representational in all that word's senses, while the performance aspects and the 'traffic' with which the prologue-sonnet ends are presentational. The prologue thus provides a site for (as well as citing) different traditions with separate histories – the sonnet's form as written, Italianate, authorial, private; the Prologue's performance as enacted, native, improvisational, communal – in which their usually disjoined trajectories converge. The connotation of the sonnet as a form of writing is initially exploited to convey a sense of the tragic inevitability of the story of the 'starcross'd lovers' (6), but transcended in its final lines, which turn over the authority the sonnet claims as the play's literal pre-scription (formally, historically, thematically) to 'the two hours traffic of our stage' and the 'patient ears' of the listeners and their (possibly less patient) desire for 'what here shall miss' (13f.). In contrast to a tradition that, following Jonson in the 1610s and 1620s, would try to control the lability of performance by making it an appendix to literature, 'this,' Bruster and Weimann conclude, 'is a theatricalization of writing' (113).

Bruster and Weimann show the relation of these historical modes of production, print and voice, to be a manifestation of what Robert Weimann has described elsewhere as the 'bifold authority' of early modern performance, which drew ambidextrously on the representation of established authority, textual and social, and the individual resources of its performers to authorize itself.[5] As Frederic Jameson has suggested, Bruster and Weimann's historicizing comprehends the various formal modes of earlier critics.[6] It also, however, focuses its attention on the play's conditions of production and the particular status of the prologue as a negotiation between audience and performance. What is represented, rather than how it is represented, is thus foregrounded in their account. What would happen, however, if we took the play's representational binarism seriously in its own formal terms? As Jameson also argues, the rigor of formal criticism can flag the cultural blind spots where ideology falters, but which escape notice when plotted in a less schematic form. Structuralism's strength, as well as its limitation, is its conscientious restriction to the world of culture and ideology, a world itself produced by the ideological operation of excluding part of it from consideration as alien, whether as nature, history, idiosyncrasy, or something else. These symbolic actions of identification and exclusion impose a comprehensible order onto the undifferentiated manifold of reality, offering, as Claude Levi-Strauss put it, imaginary solutions to real problems. In a work of fiction like *Romeo and Juliet*, even the so-called real problems are imaginary, although there is real exchange between the play and the discourses of the larger social world it inhabits.[7] Because of this, though, the imaginary solutions achieved function as real within the world of the play – nothing need prevent the resolution of the problems the play sets for itself, since within the play's representation problem and solution are equally discursive. Moments in which the play's imaginary solutions themselves begin to pose real problems, then, deserve further attention.

The Verona represented in *Romeo and Juliet* is a place that prizes its names, although (or because) the most noticeable distinction, that between Montague and Capulet, is indifferent in all but name: 'alike in dignity,' 'A plague o' both your houses' (3. 1. 108). But from the brawl with which the play opens to Tybalt's apparent ability to sense the difference that names represent ('This by his voice would be a Montague,' 1. 5. 53), the names and the categories by which people are sorted – young, old, male, female, princely, civil – organize the first interactions that take place on stage. The most obvious imaginary solution is true love as articulated in the lovers, which serves the play as a kind of panacea for interfamilial violence, patriarchal oppression, and the empty protestations of Petrarchism. But in order to find a language in which their love can speak, Romeo and Juliet must reject this culture of naming.

Without question, from our perspective the discourse with which Romeo and Juliet explore love continues to be the play's dominant note.[8] As they attempt to describe their love, Romeo and Juliet seek a language of transcendence, in which names do not count. For them, love seems necessarily to be based on experience that defies expression in language: 'Thou canst not speak of that thou dost not feel,' snaps Romeo at Friar Laurence (3. 3. 64). They insist on the failure of their language to name themselves or their experience; the discourse Romeo and Juliet weave around their love asserts the inadequacy of their speech to the love that lies beyond it. The balcony scene is a crucial moment in declaring their need for a new language:

> O Romeo, Romeo, wherefore art thou Romeo?
> Deny thy father and refuse thy name.
> Or if thou wilt not, be but sworn my love
> And I'll no longer be a Capulet ...
> 'Tis but thy name that is my enemy:
> Thou art thyself, though not a Montague.
> What's Montague? It is not hand nor foot
> Nor arm nor face nor any other part
> Belonging to a man. O be some other name.
> What's in a name? That which we call a rose
> By any other word would smell as sweet.
> (2. 2. 33–6, 38–44)

Juliet's 'Wherefore ... ?' and her reasoning after it insist on the separability of name and being, of a name and the qualities it stands for, and implies the priority of an unnamed self that can provide a locus for true love.⁹ It is a claim that Romeo eagerly echoes, likewise rejecting his name and his place in the social network for an identity that promises to be more true: 'I take thee at thy word./Call me but love, and I'll be new baptis'd:/Henceforth I never will be Romeo ... ' (2. 2. 49–52).¹⁰ He reiterates his rejection of the name – as well as his still unexplained hostility towards it – as restricting or even missing the self when, banished, he asks Friar Laurence 'In what vile part of my anatomy/Doth my name lodge? Tell me that I may sack/The hateful mansion' (3. 3. 105–7).

James Calderwood identifies the linguistic theory implicit in Romeo and Juliet's speech as nominalism, the scholastic philosophical doctrine that while names usefully organized real entities, they referred to nothing real themselves; while there might be any number of individual human beings, no thing corresponded to the class Human Being.¹¹ The individual instance can thus never truly be captured in language. Love therefore must be anti-conventional in every sense – no existing discourse or other set of conventions can legitimate or guarantee it, and it actively resists circumscription within existing conventions, just as social conventions oppose it. Such a concept of love equally opposes the patriarchal ideal of profitable marriage endorsed by Capulet¹² and the overwrought misery of Petrarchism, the discourse of love associated with Romeo's wooing of Rosaline that Mercutio identifies as merely conventional: 'Now he is for the numbers Petrarch flowed in. Laura, to his lady, was a kitchen wench – marry, she had a better love to berhyme her –' (2. 4. 40–2). Romeo's Petrarchism is a way of speaking that makes no reference to reality, an empty form that Mercutio identifies and mocks with embarrassing facility:

> Romeo! Humours! Madman! Passion! Lover!
> Appear thou in the likeness of a sigh,
> Speak but one rhyme and I am satisfied.
> Cry but "Ay me!" Prounounce but "love" and "dove" ...
>
> (2. 1. 7–10)

The mannered patterns – numbers, rhymes, names – that Mercutio picks out by replicating them are, in his view, all there is to Petrarchism. The only thing real in Petrarchism, as Mercutio observes, are the endlessly iterable patterns of Petrarch's language, not the feelings or experiences to which it refers. Friar Laurence describes this vacuity as Petrarchism's open secret, apparent even to Rosaline, which is perhaps a contributing factor in Romeo's failure to move her: 'O, she knew well/Thy love did read by rote, that could not spell' (2. 3. 83f.).

This rejection of the conventional demands a novelty of expression from Romeo and Juliet. Romeo describes himself as setting sail for Juliet's love as for a new world (' ... wert thou as far/As that vast shore wash'd with the farthest sea' [2. 2. 82f.]), and Juliet responds by rejecting the old patterns of courtship, ('Fain would I dwell on form. ... /But farewell, compliment!' [2. 2. 88f.]). This sense of the incommensurability of experience to language – indeed to any kind of representation – extends to the relation of unique self to self that is love; as Juliet says, 'My bounty is as boundless as the sea,/My love as deep; the more I give to thee,/The more I have, for both are infinite' (2. 2. 133–5). There is no calculating love or the true self in love; either must be felt to be known and can only be expressed, as Romeo and Juliet continually attempt, in figures, metaphors, indirections, poetry:

> Come night, come Romeo, come thou day in night,
> For thou wilt lie upon the wings of night
> Whiter than new snow upon a raven's back.
> Come gentle night, come loving black-brow'd night,
> Give me my Romeo; and when I shall die
> Take him and cut him out in little stars,
> And he will make the face of heaven so fine
> That all the world will be in love with night,
> And pay no worship to the garish sun.
> (3. 2. 17–25)

Juliet's unexpected praise of night rather than day and her striking images of Romeo cut into starlight or as the snowy raven recall but also revise commonplace Petrarchan paradoxes, while the repetition of the word 'night' suggests a language that impoverishes itself against the all but inexpressible theme it aims at. This desire to name love in the face of its impossibility is what produces the lovers' lyric passages and the play's overall dreamlike effect of lyricism, both attentive and blurry, as if language were somehow the barrier to expression rather than the means. But ultimately even poetic innovations in language such as the lovers undertake must fail; since any language relies on conventions, true love can never be fully articulated in any ordinary language at all, but must always look beyond words for analogies, like the sweet-smelling, nameless rose.[13]

If love is an imaginary solution, though, Mercutio is its real problem. Punning, dreaming, and finally dying, Mercutio's presence disrupts the smooth running of the course of true love that Romeo and Juliet define with such effort. His close connection to the lovers appears most strikingly shortly after the balcony scene, when Mercutio provides what sounds like an answer to Juliet's more famous question 'Wherefore art thou Romeo?':

> Why, is this not better now than groaning for love? Now art thou sociable, now art thou Romeo; now art thou what thou art, by art as well as by nature. For this driveling love is like a great natural that runs lolling up and down to hide his bauble in a hole.
> (2. 4. 88–93)

The echo of words makes sense only from a dramaturgical perspective (Mercutio has not heard Juliet's question), but both speakers share the gesture towards a natural existence outside the grasp of artificial language, whether rose or bauble.[14] For Juliet, Romeo's true identity transcends what in him can be named; in contrast, Mercutio has confidence that he knows Romeo and can rightly recognize and name him. The crucial difference is the question each assumes to be at stake – *wherefore* or *what*. While Juliet asks *what it means to be Romeo*, Mercutio asks *what Romeo is*. Juliet's *why* bypasses the problematic relation of name and thing that is Romeo and goes directly to the metaphysics of final causes, leaping over the problems of *what* and the completely elided one of *how*. Mercutio's *what*, in contrast, requires him to define Romeo's nature *qua* Romeo and also provides a basis from which *how is this Romeo* can first be asked.

The answer to *how* seems to be 'tautologically.' 'Now art thou what thou art' seems incontrovertible: the thing is what it is, and in such a way that its right name is part of the thing, 'by art as well as nature.' Mercutio is as invested in the tropics of language as Romeo and Juliet, but his language is relentlessly anti-transcendent. Unlike that of the lovers, it never suggests that what it points to can elude it – 'sociable' or 'Romeo' seem fully and definitionally interchangeable with each other and with 'what thou art.' When his language refers beyond itself, it is with a knowing self-referentiality that constantly calls us back to its own texture, as later in the play: 'Ask for me tomorrow and you shall find me a grave man' (3. 1. 98f.).

With his apparently limitless verbal energy, though, it is easy to overlook how conservative, even reactionary, are the positions that Mercutio espouses. Mercutio's values conform strikingly to the interests of Verona's ruling forces of state and patriarchal power and not just against Romeo as a lover, whether the Petrarchan lover of Rosaline (which Mercutio opposes for its empty rhetoric) or the true lover of Juliet (which Mercutio opposes for how it removes Romeo from the demands of manly honor). Mercutio consistently upholds the aristocratic ideals associated with men like Prince Escalus and County Paris, his kinsmen, as we are repeatedly reminded (e.g. 3. 1. 147, 5. 3. 294) – male friendship and loyalty, scorn for women, and the code of honor that finally leads to his death. For all his much-remarked disruptive vigor onstage, it is not because of the causes he backs that he offers any resistance to the values that the play represents as dominant.

Mercutio's use of language, too, while playful and often fantastic, is likewise surprisingly conservative. With 'Now art thou Romeo,' Mercutio asserts an understanding of identity as equivalent to a name and assumes or announces a self that can be re-identified or recognized because it has all of a name's stability. These lines, and his dismay at Romeo's not behaving (as he sees it) like Romeo, recall Juliet's namesake and forerunner in Shakespeare's canon, Julia in *Two Gentlemen of Verona*, who 'would always have one play but one thing'

(4. 2. 69). In an earlier scene, Julia tears up a letter from her lover Proteus and then contritely reassembles the pieces because of the names written on them:

> Look, here is writ 'Kind Julia' – unkind Julia,
> As in revenge of thy ingratitude
> I throw thy name against the bruising stones, ...
> And here is writ 'love-wounded Proteus.'
> Poor wounded name ...
> (1. 2. 110–12, 114f.)

Romeo also offers to tear his unpleasing name for Juliet: 'Had I it written I would tear the word' (2. 2. 57). He also offers to rebaptize himself as Love for Juliet (2. 2. 51), as Mercutio actually has rebaptized him in the previous scene ('Romeo! Humours! Madman! Passion! Lover!' 2. 1. 7). But in each case, Romeo merely describes a possibility that he does not enact and which he can offer because it is indifferent to him. He can rename himself or tear up his old name because to him a name is separate from what is real. In contrast, Mercutio – like Julia – seems passionately to believe in the names of things. His discourse, as when he tries to conjure Romeo or elaborately mocks Tybalt as a nine-lived King of Cats (2. 4. 19; 3. 1. 75–79) or imagines Mab as the source of dreams, consists largely of namings and renamings the world around him; for him, names have power. Mercutio, like Julia with her concern for poor wounded names, enacts a kind of Cratylism, the belief that names were ties to essences of things and were thus real. Nominalism developed within the Aristotelian philosophy of the scholastics, while Cratylism is associated with Plato; Julia in *Two Gentlemen* precedes Juliet in the Shakespeare canon. The theory of language implied in Mercutio's discourse is thus doubly marked as outdated, as conservative as the values he is mouthpiece for. Mercutio's arty ontology of Romeo and his name thus seems both to precede and to complicate Juliet's unnaming of him.

Mercutio is thus not just thematically opposed to Romeo and Juliet's love, but formally opposed to their theory of language. Kiernan Ryan sees Romeo as a prisoner of Petrarchism and Mercutio as the agent of Petrarchism's inversion.[15] But Petrarchism as a style includes its own inversion – such poetry's perennial critique of its conventions is itself one of its conventions, from Petrarch onwards.[16] Mercutio's attitude towards Romeo's Petrarchism is indeed negative, but his own linguistic use does not invert or negate Romeo's. Instead it posits alternatives. The clearest example of this force of Mercutio's discourse is his description of Queen Mab, which is not based on the negation or rejection of another discourse but rises from and returns to 'nothing,' to 'dreams' (1. 4. 96), after suggesting that there is nothing on heaven or earth that it cannot dream:

> Her chariot is an empty hazelnut
> Made by the joiner squirrel or old grub,
> Time out o' mind the fairies' coachmakers;
> Her waggon-spokes made of long spinners' legs,
> The cover of the wings of grasshoppers,
> Her traces of the smallest spider web,
> Her collars of the moonshine's watery beams,
> Her whip of cricket's bone, the lash of film,
> Her waggoner a small grey-coated gnat ...
>
> (1. 4. 59–67)

Romeo's announcement 'I dreamt a dream tonight' (1. 4. 50) implies a set of assumptions about individual identity, personal pathos, and the tradition of the dream-poem as the locus of prophecy, all of which Mercutio deflates first by redoubling them ('And so did I,' l. 50) and then by denying them ('*Rom.* Well, what was yours? *Mer.* That dreamers often lie,' 1. 4. 51).

The imaginative and verbal power of the monologue that follows is almost unrivalled in the play, and recent performers have matched it with corresponding emotional intensity.[17] For all that, Mab and her retinue remain curiously insubstantial, as Mercutio freely acknowledges, 'the children of an idle brain/Begot of nothing but vain fantasy' (1. 4. 97f.). Their insubstantiality, though, is not only because Mab is the product of Mercutio's imagination. Contrary to Romeo's intimation of the mystery of dreams, the dreams that Mab produces are surprisingly direct, or what Mercutio calls 'straight':

> ... she gallops night by night
> Through lovers' brains, and then they dream of love;
> O'er courtiers' knees, that dream on curtsies straight;
> O'er lawyers fingers who straight dream on fees;
> O'er ladies lips, who straight on kisses dream, ...
>
> (1. 4. 70–4)

Like the tautology that lets Mercutio recognize Romeo when he is what he is, the truth that lies in the dreams that Mab brings is exactly what it appears to be in the ordinary waking lives of the dreamers – lovers dream of things that characterize lovers, and so on.[18] Whatever they reveal – and the power of the speech is such that it seems to ask some sort of revelation – it is neither the hidden desires of a quasi-Freudian unconscious nor the prophetic signs that Romeo expects. Since it shows nothing more than meets the eye, then, Romeo seems right to protest, 'Peace, peace, Mercutio, peace./Thou talks't of nothing' (1. 4. 95f.). To *be* nothing, though, is not in the terms of Mercutio's discourse to *do* nothing. The nothing of fantasy which begets the Queen Mab speech identifies what is *apparent* with what is *true*, in other words flattens the thing into its name, while simultaneously acknowledging its own non-existence, as nothing, as fantasy, as play.

Mercutio's Mab reveals not an unconscious of desire, but the consciousness of language. Like the Petrarchism it opposes, Mercutio's discourse has no referent but itself, which is why it is marked by punning as much as by tautology. Romeo and Juliet transcend Petrarchism, finding an appropriate referent for it at another level that it expresses not as linguistic paradox but as a kind of *koan*, the seemingly senseless question of Zen practice that forces one to surpass ordinary logic, designed to throw its users beyond language. Mercutio, in contrast, throws himself into language. Whereas Romeo and Juliet gesture towards a beyond of language, the discourse of Mercutio, in particular his puns, repeatedly brings language back to itself and its own status as paradoxically both unreal and powerful. Names and words, even in puns and wordplay, are powerful because they are indices to the essences of things: Mab's dreams reveals truths; knowing or not, Tybalt really is a 'rat-catcher' (3. 1. 75); when he says so, Mercutio really is a 'grave man.' But words are also unreal, 'nothing,' because they add nothing to the existing reality of the world, but only point to it: Mab's dreams reveals no secret truths, only obvious ones. The naturalizing, ideological force of this linguistic theory is clear; it insists on forever naming the *status quo*. But in its very literality Mercutio's language undermines its own efforts. Words in their naming of things indicate what might otherwise escape notice, and Mercutio's language is generous in all the essences it indicates – Tybalt does not possess only the identities he avows, as a Capulet and enemy of Montagues (1. 5. 85), or as a duelist (3. 1. 41f.), but also those other qualities that his name assigns to him, as, say, King of Cats (3. 1. 77). The conservatism of Mercutio's language undoes the values that it supports by demonstrating that an identity never resides in its name alone – that whatever is named, in other words, is not one, but both inseminated by other identities and disseminating its own outside itself. It is not that, as Romeo and Juliet suggest, there is more to anything than its name. Rather, each name reaches further than any identity associated with it imagines.

The pun, for this reason, is the enemy of love. In *Romeo and Juliet*, love is about essence ('a rose by any other name would smell as sweet'), but puns are about names without essences. While Romeo and Juliet seek ways to push beyond language to a true love that eludes it, Mercutio's discourse multifariously and relentlessly calls language back to itself, and in so doing resists the play's drive towards ineffability and stillness.[19] The transcendent discourse of Romeo and Juliet shows its antipathy to language in its reliance on imagery that is visual:

> It seems she hangs upon the cheek of night
> As a rich jewel in an Ethiope's ear –

> Beauty too rich for use, for earth too dear.
> So shows a snowy dove trooping with crows ...
>
> (1. 5. 44–7)

Such images veil the verbal artifice that constructs them in the dazzling light of a picture, converting the material signifiers of language into ideal imaginary ones, the temporal flow of speech into a static portrait. They draw tacitly on the Petrarchan tradition of paradox, expressed verbally earlier in the play (e.g. Romeo's 'O brawling love, O loving hate,/ O anything of nothing first create!' 1. 1. 174f.), but now imagined as a striking contrast of real black and white (cf. Juliet's 'Whiter than new snow upon a raven's back,' 3. 2. 19). This represented contrast, repeatedly invoked by both lovers, suggests how in their transcendent discourse, identity is expressed differentially, by emphasizing the distance between one thing and another ('Beauty too rich for use, for earth too dear'). What is invoked is not the meaning of either of the poles of light and dark, but the space between them. It might go too far to claim how Romeo and Juliet's signs are defined against the signs they are not as a kind of incipient Saussureanism, but not a great deal too far. Any discourse that imagines its referent eluding it thereby implies a theory of meaning based on difference.

Romeo's Petrarchan 'Anything of nothing first create' recalls Mercutio's description of his praise of Mab. Mercutio's discourse, however, differs from Petrarchism in its presentation of its own nothingness, the nothingness that Petrarchism only represents as it represents any other thing. Mercutio's Cratylism differs from the nominalism of Romeo and Juliet in its claim to posit or invoke what it names by naming it, imagining, as in the identity-mirroring dreams produced by Mab, no distance between what represents and what is represented, or between presentation and representation. Whereas the transcendent discourse of Romeo and Juliet is defined and authorized by the ineffable love it wants to represent, Mercutio's Cratylan discourse, tautologically, idiotically (literally – *idios* is 'the proper,' which Mercutio's discourse assumes just as that of Romeo and Juliet assumes difference) cannot imagine any other and so, necessarily, is positive rather than differential. Regardless of the 'wit of cheveril' (2. 4. 83) Mercutio credits Romeo with, that can at will advance one or the other, word and thing remain bound securely together and, more significantly, mean not univocally – Mercutio's puns demonstrate the fallaciousness of that assumption – but independently of other signifiers.[20]

The conservatism of Mercutio's stance towards language – as ridiculous from a sixteenth-century standpoint as a flat-earther from our own[21] – turns out to be differently disruptive of the social order and the constitutive logics that the play represents than is Romeo and Juliet's. And this is the real problem that Mercutio's language poses. Mercutio, I have argued, invariably supports the more traditional and conservative position of every choice the play offers, most notably in his code of honor and his misogyny. His disruptiveness within the play lies in how his use of language ultimately denies the ability to draw the distinctions that Verona's society demands, between Montague and Capulet, love and hate, male and female, citizen and prince, all of which require some kind of contrast and opposition. But Mercutio names and defines positively, irrelationally, even irrationally, and in so doing undermines the very logics that allow Montague to be that which is not Capulet. Romeo and Juliet resist and deny the values and structures of the play's Verona, but Mercutio subverts them even as he embraces them.

To take one example of the danger Mercutio's language poses to the values his character declares, his Cratylism disrupts (rather than simply opposes or negates) other systems of discourse by assuming a power of prescription otherwise associated with the authorized discourse of writing that lies outside the bounds of represented character, in, for instance, the presentational language of the Chorus. I have already discussed how Mercutio's 'Now art thou Romeo ... ' is a kind of unknowing response to Juliet's 'Wherefore art thou Romeo,' but more than once in the play Mercutio's language is uncannily canny. For instance, parodying Romeo's Petrarchism, Mercutio asks him to 'Appear but in the likeness of a sigh. ... Cry but "Ay me!" ' (2. 1. 8, 10). In the next scene, Juliet's first words on her balcony are the Petrarchan 'Ay me!' (2. 2. 24). A few scenes later Mercutio identifies Romeo again as the likeness of a sigh when Romeo appears as Romeo 'without his roe' (2. 4. 38) – that is, as 'Me, oh!' Ultimately these sighs and signs will be resolved into the Prince's anagrammatic 'more woe' (5. 3. 306). Such echoes cannot be explained in any analysis that remains at the level of individual character; they uncover the principle of iterability, which subverts the concepts of identity on which character relies.

But perhaps the most striking instance of Mercutio's prophetic strain is the gift of the play's plot to Romeo before he has seen Juliet, while he is still enraptured with Rosaline, in Mercutio's conclusion to Queen Mab. As Mercutio admits, he talks of dreams, of nothing, of fantasy,

> Which is as thin of substance as the air
> And more inconstant than the wind, who woos
> Even now the frozen bosom of the north
> And, being anger'd, puffs away from thence
> Turning his side to the dew-dropping south.
>
> (1. 5. 99–103)

His prediction of the course of the play is quite different from the official, self-aware, instrumental one expressed by the sonnet in the Prologue, but the structure is unmistakable: Romeo's inconstant wooing will leave cold Rosaline for dewy Juliet. In Mercutio's words, we can see the inscribing of futurity as drama rather than as lyric – that is, as a fate unconscious of what it means, a fate not articulated outside its own process and that can only be recognized in retrospect. Truth lies outside the represented character of Mercutio, outside even knowing itself, in the presentational medium of the words.

Along with this drift of knowledge from a represented character to presented and presenting language, the emphasis on forms, puns, and tautologies in Mercutio's bad language further leads to a dissociation of voice from character. It is prophetic in the examples I note above; it can also be daemonic. Unlike the other discourses I have noted, which are represented as 'belonging' to particular characters, Mercutio's discourse exceeds the limits of character, seemingly the basis for the stable, named identity it posits. At Mercutio's death, the punning, playful, performative language associated primarily with him suddenly passes to other characters in ways that are not easily explained mimetically or even structurally. The Nurse, coming to tell Juliet of Tybalt's death, echoes Juliet's words on the balcony: 'O Romeo, Romeo!/Who ever would have thought it? Romeo!' (3. 2. 41f.); Paris demurs to the Capulets with inexplicable homonymy, 'These times of woe afford no times to woo' (3. 4. 8); and Capulet's response to Juliet's supposed death is as indecorous as any of Mercutio's banter elsewhere ('Flower as she was, deflowered by him,' Death, 4. 5. 37). Most striking, though, a Mercutian moment transforms the transcendent language of Juliet. The news of Tybalt's death interrupts Juliet's reverie about the coming of Romeo, 'thou day in night,/For thou wilt lie upon the wings of night/Whiter than new snow upon a raven's back' (3. 2. 17–19) and momentarily changes her evaluation of her lover. She expresses her horror in an image that has just expressed her longing: 'Dove-feather'd raven' (3. 2. 76). The image with which she names Romeo remain the same even as its value inverts. What is shown to be stable, then, is not the transcendent truth of love towards which she and Romeo have pointed with images of light and dark, but the image itself, the sign rather than anything it signifies. As in Mercutio's discourse, the sign calls attention to itself and to its own nothingness, not so much productive as evocative – it calls out the divisions *within* identities rather than only those *between* them.

The self-declared nothingness and self-contained formality of Mercutio's discourse render it so mutable that it infects each of the play's other discourses. Better, it recurs in them – with its own gesture of positing words as words it reveals the Mercutio in every way of speaking. This means that there can be no reduction of these different discourses to relations to each other or to anything transcendent; rather, as Mercutio's discourse posits, each has qualities and characteristics that, while not unique to it, nonetheless remain irreducible to the qualities of any other. The binaries that structure *Romeo and Juliet* are broken by Mercutio's bad language, which opens up the play of culture to whatever lies outside it – history, language, the world? – by demonstrating the inability of culture to knowingly or definitively structure itself.

Its purely formal force undoes the mythic ordering of Verona by evoking their logical inconsistencies, that is, their reliance on or resistance to authority that is always in itself necessarily bifold. In so doing, it crosses from a merely formal trait of language to become an existential one, addressing in representation the modes of production that allow it to be represented. This is the power of language as active, positive semiosis, as self-resembled mimesis. Romeo and Juliet use discourse to express a true love that escapes signification, but Mercutio recalls us to the *how* of that transcendent moment, the work of engaging, always, in the presentation of representation and, irreducibly, the reverse.

Notes

1. *The Nations Right in Magna Charta* ([London: s.n.], 1650), [1].
2. Van Doren, *Shakespeare* (New York: Henry Holt, 1939). The play's language has been the focus of many influential studies, such as Harry Levin, 'Form and Formality in *Romeo and Juliet*,' *Shakespeare Quarterly* 4 (1960): 3–11, and Ralph Berry, 'The Sonnet World of Verona,' *The Shakespearean Metaphor* (Totowa: Rowman and Littlefield, 1978): 37–47. See also the survey of the play's criticism in Bryan Reynolds and Janna Segal, 'Fugitive Explorations in *Romeo and Juliet*: Searching for Transversality in the Goldmine of R&Jspace'; Reynolds and Segal suggest that the play's divisions are superficial representations of a common idealization of a money-economy forthcoming in Bryan Reynolds, *Transversal Enterprises in the Drama of Shakespeare and His Contemporaries: Fugitive Explorations* (London: Palgrave Macmillan). To offer anything other than a merely suggestive list of works that address the play's language would be madness, but to name only a few works that focus on one or more aspects of this division, Catherine Belsey, 'The Name of the Rose in Romeo and Juliet,' *YES* 23 (1993): 126–42; Jonathan Goldberg, '*Romeo and Juliet*'s Open Rs,' *Queering the Renaissance* (Durham: Duke University Press, 1994), on the relation of language to desire and to sexed bodies, an essay that notably resists the critical drive to distinction; James Calderwood, *Shakespearean Metadrama* (Minneapolis: Minnesota University Press, 1971), on the relation of lyric and dramatic modes; Joseph Porter, 'Eloquence and Liminality: Glossing Mercutio's Speech Acts,' *Shakespeare's Mercutio* (Chapel Hill: University of North Carolina Press, 1989), on the performative aspects of speech; Kiernan Ryan, ' "The Murdering Word," ' in *Shakespeare* (2nd ed., Hemel Hampstead: Harvester, 1995): 74–86.
3. For the play as 'lyrical' in a generalized sense that includes all three meanings I distinguish here, see, e.g. Brian Gibbons, Introduction to *The Arden Edition Romeo and Juliet*, ed. Brian Gibbons (London: Methuen, 1980), 27–31, henceforth *Arden*. All citations to the play are to this edition.
4. Douglas Bruster and Robert Weimann, *Prologues to Shakespeare's Theatre* (New York: Routledge, 2005): 112–14. See also Weimann, *Author's Pen and Actor's Voice*, eds. Helen Higbee and William N. West (Cambridge: Cambridge University Press, 2000), for a larger consideration of these two aspects of early modern drama and Gayle Whittier, 'The Sonnet's Body and the Body Sonnetized in *Romeo and Juliet*,' *Shakespeare Quarterly* 40 (1989): 27–41 for a similar project of rematerialization.
5. ' "Bifold Authority" in Reformation Discourse: Authorization, Representation, and Early Modern "Meaning," ' in Janet Levarie Smarr, ed., *Historical Criticism and the*

Challenge of Theory (Urbana: University of Illinois Press, 1993): 167–82; 'Bifold Authority in Shakespeare's Theatre,' *Shakespeare Quarterly* 39 (1988): 401–17.
6. Frederic Jameson, *The Political Unconscious* (Ithaca: Cornell University Press, 1981): 46–9.
7. Dympna C. Callaghan, 'The Ideology of Romantic Love: The Case of *Romeo and Juliet*,' in R.S. White, ed. *New Casebooks: Romeo and Juliet*; Goldberg "Open Rs."
8. See, for example, Callaghan, 'Ideology.'
9. Belsey, 'Name.'
10. Romeo's desire for unconventionality is preempted by Mercutio's earlier naming of him as a Petrarchan 'Lover' (2. 1. 7); see p. 121.
11. Calderwood, Metadrama. See also Berry, 'Sonnet World'.
12. For a fuller consideration of this position, extended to others besides Capulet, see Reynolds and Segal.
13. Belsey, 'Name.'
14. Although the outside of language Juliet imagines is beautiful and Mercutio's is grotesque, suggesting how differently they value their shared poles of nature and art.
15. Ryan, ' "Murdering Word," ' 119; for a similar view, see Levin, 'Form and Formality,' who calls Philip Sidney anti-Petrarchan because, conventionally, he critiques Petrarchan conventions.
16. Roland Greene, *Post-Petrarchism* (Princeton: Princeton University Press, 1991); Whittier, 'The Sonnet's Body'; one might speculate how this containment of its own inversion is what differentiates Petrarchism from the similar poetry written by Dante and others; see Joel Fineman, *Shakespeare's Perjured Eye* (Berkeley: University of California Press, 1986).
17. Porter, 'Mercutio's Shakespeare,' in *Shakespeare's Mercutio*.
18. I am grateful to Ali Crockett for this counterintuitive observation.
19. See Stephen Greenblatt, 'Fiction and Friction,' *Shakespearean Negotiations* (Berkeley: University of California Press, 1988), on verbal chafing as the source of desire – but as he notes, this friction makes heat, not love. On the drive to 'lyric stillness' in the play, Calderwood, *Metadrama*, 93.
20. See the discussion of Feste's cheveril wit in *Twelfth Night*, Greenblatt, 'Fiction and Friction.'
21. Margreta de Grazia, 'The Secularization of Language in the Seventeenth Century,' *Journal of the History of Ideas* 41 (1980): 319–29; Richard Waswo, *Language and Meaning in the Renaissance* (Princeton: Princeton University Press, 1987).

Works cited

Belsey, Catherine. 'The Name of the Rose in *Romeo and Juliet*.' *YES* 23 (1993): 126–42.
Berry, Ralph. 'The Sonnet World of Verona.' *The Shakespearean Metaphor*. Totowa: Rowman and Littlefield, 1978: 37–47.
Bruster, Douglas, and Robert Weimann. *Prologues to Shakespeare's Theatre: Performance and Liminality in Early Modern Drama*. New York: Routledge, 2005.
Calderwood, James. *Shakespearean Metadrama* Minneapolis: Minnesota University Press, 1971.
Callaghan, Dympna C. 'The Ideology of Romantic Love: The Case of *Romeo and Juliet*,' in R.S. White, ed. *New Casebooks: Romeo and Juliet*. Basingstoke: Palgrave, 2001.
de Grazia, Margreta. 'The Secularization of Language in the Seventeenth Century,' *Journal of the History of Ideas* 41 (1980): 319–29.

Fineman, Joel. *Shakespeare's Perjured Eye: The Invention of Subjectivity in the Sonnets.* Berkeley: University of California Press, 1986.
Gibbons, Brian. Introduction to *The Arden Edition Romeo and Juliet*, 1–77.
Goldberg, Jonathan. '*Romeo and Juliet*'s Open Rs.' In *Queering the Renaissance.* Ed. Jonathan Goldberg. Durham: Duke University Press, 1994.
Greenblatt, Stephen. 'Fiction and Friction.' *Shakespearean Negotiations: The Circulation of Social Energy in Early Modern England.* Berkeley: University of California Press, 1988.
Greene, Roland. *Post-Petrarchism: Origins and Innovations of the Western Lyric Sequence.* Princeton: Princeton University Press, 1991.
Jameson, Frederic. *The Political Unconscious: Narrative as a Socially Symbolic Act.* Ithaca: Cornell University Press, 1981.
Levin, Harry. 'Form and Formality in *Romeo and Juliet*.' *Shakespeare Quarterly* 4 (1960): 3–11.
Plato. *Cratylus.* Transl. Benjamin Jowett. Ed. Edith Hamilton and Huntington Cairns. *The Collected Dialogues of Plato.* Princeton: Princeton University Press, 1968.
Porter, James A. 'Eloquence and Liminality: Glossing Mercutio's Speech Acts,' *Shakespeare's Mercutio: His History and Drama.* Chapel Hill: University of North Carolina Press, 1989.
Reynolds, Bryan, and Janna Segal, 'Fugitive Explorations in *Romeo and Juliet*: Searching for Transversality in the Goldmine of R&Jspace,' forthcoming in Bryan Reynolds, *Transversal Enterprises in Drama of Shakespeare and His Contemporaries: Fugitive Explorations* (London: Palgrave Macmillan).
Ryan, Kiernan. *Shakespeare*, 2nd edn. Hemel Hampstead: Harvester, 1995.
Shakespeare, William. *Romeo and Juliet. The Arden Shakespeare*, 2nd edn. Ed. Brian Gibbons. London: Methuen, 1980.
——. *The Two Gentlemen of Verona. The Arden Shakespeare*, 3rd edn. Ed. William C. Carroll. London: Arden Shakespeare, 2004.
Theaurau John [Thomas Tany]. *The Nations Right in Magna Charta* [London: s.n.], 1650.
Van Doren, Mark. *Shakespeare.* New York: Henry Holt, 1939.
Waswo, Richard. *Language and Meaning in the Renaissance.* Princeton: Princeton University Press, 1987.
Weimann, Robert. *Author's Pen and Actor's Voice: Playing in Writing in Shakespeare's Theatre.* Eds. Helen Higbee and William N. West. Cambridge: Cambridge University Press, 2000.
——.' "Bifold Authority" in Reformation Discourse: Authorization, Representation, and Early Modern "Meaning." ' In *Historical Criticism and the Challenge of Theory.* Ed. Janet Levarie Smarr. Urbana: University of Illinois Press, 1993: 167–82.
——.'Bifold Authority in Shakespeare's Theatre.' *Shakespeare Quarterly* 39 (1988): 401–17.
Whittier, Gayle. 'The Sonnet's Body and the Body Sonnetized in *Romeo and Juliet*.' *Shakespeare Quarterly* 40 (1989): 27–41.

7
Nanti Everything
Terence Hawkes

Cruising

Round The Horne was a well-known BBC radio comedy series of the 1960s, with audience figures running into millions. Featuring the urbane talents of the comedian Kenneth Horne, it placed him each week at the centre of a number of bizarre and often bitingly witty sketches. Amongst the most popular were those in which he regularly encountered the dubious business enterprises of an outrageously 'gay' couple, 'Julian and Sandy', played with considerable vivacity by Hugh Paddick and Kenneth Williams. In them much is made of Julian and Sandy's use of 'the polari'.[1]

This is an 18th century actors' and coster-mongers' slang, drawing on Italian, French, Yiddish and obscure Romany or Gypsy words. Actively used to this day within a number of subcultures in Britain, it manifests itself particularly in those connected with the gay community and with show business.[2] In the polari, 'omi' means 'man', 'polone' means 'woman', 'eke' means 'face', 'lallies' means legs, etc. (see Appendix). It's frequently combined with items from rhyming slang and back-slang, and its use often involves *double-entendre* in the service of serpentine innuendo. It's possible to argue that the version of Jaques's speech from *As You Like It* (2. 7. 139–66), dubbed 'The Seven Ages of Omi' and delivered in one of the sketches by Hugh Paddick, with shrill encouragement from Kenneth Williams, achieves the kind of purchase on the original that, in recent years, only Richard Curtis's *The Skinhead Hamlet* has matched. Wholly disconcerting yet – momentarily and astonishingly – moving, it's worth consideration for what it can tell us about the nature of parody, the dynamics of comic performance, and the function of Shakespeare in a rapidly changing Britain.

Bona bard

The sketch is set in a bookshop in the King's Road, Chelsea, called, inevitably, *Bona Books*. It begins with a fairly predictable level of badinage between

Horne, in his usual guise of innocent customer, and the archly preening Julian and Sandy; 'Would you be interested in Spenser's *Fairy Queen*?' ('No, he's not interested in mine') etc. The polari is immediately deployed in reference to the book-trade, with mentions of the popular 'Every Omi's' editions, of Wilkie Collins's novel *Polone in White*, and such 'masterpieces of the macabree' as *The Telltale Heartface*, or *The Fall of Usher's Lattie* to say nothing of 'Longomi's *Hiawatha*'. Sandy mentions 'our own edition of Shakespeare' rewritten in 'up to date polari', including such titles as *Much Ado About Nanti*, *All's Bona That Ends Bona*, *Two Omis of Verona* etc. as well as the distinctive *As They Like It* (when Horne asks 'isn't that *As You Like It?*', the response is 'not really, but live and let live I say ...').

It's from this play which has 'some of the most beautiful language in your actual English tongue' that Julian agrees to recite the 'Seven Ages of Omi' speech. There follows a good deal of semi-salacious by-play about 'feeling the muse' which, when it finally alights on Julian, yields the following:

> *All the world's a stage*
> *And all the omis and polones merely players;*
> *They have their exits and their entrances*

(*Sandy*: That's true, Mr Horne ... carry on Jules, nice, nice, go on, love)
> *One omi in his time plays many parts,*
> *His act being seven ages. At first the infant,*
> *Mewling and puking in the nurse's arms*

(*Sandy*: that's lovely, we all mewl Mr. Horne ... I've mewled in my nurse's arms. I've mewled, and on her lap too. There's no stopping an infant is there? *Horne* (drily):
Well my thoughts were turning more to puking.
Sandy Oooh! 'Ere, it don't seem to be going down too well, Jules. I'd cut to the soldier bit.' They agree to the cut and Julian continues in a 'serious' tone: '*I'm being the soldier now*'):
> *Then the soldier,*
> *All butch and full of strange polari*

(*Sandy*: 'Oh he takes a good soldier: it's his own military background, he was in *Soldiers in Skirts* wasn't you?')
> *... then the Justice*

(*Sandy*: That's something else he knows about, mmm. Look at him, now he's aged, he's aged up for it, look at him – you'd swear he was twenty-seven. *Julian*: Oh, thank you!).
> *Full of wise saws and moral instances ...*
> *... The sixth age shifts*

(*Sandy*: We usually have trouble with that phrase ...
Julian: Today was no exception).
> *The sixth age shifts*
> *Into the lean and slippered pantaloon*

(*Sandy*: Look he's shifted into it, there he goes ...)
    His youthful hose well saved, a world too wide
    For his shrunk lallies ...
(*Sandy*: Aaah, look at that Mr Horne, his lallies seem to shrink before your very eyes, don't they? His lallies, seem to shrink, they do.)
    and his big manly Hobson's
    Turns again to a childish treble ...
(*Sandy*: Oooh! [indistinguishable]).
    Last scene of all
    That ends this strange eventful history
    Is second childishness and mere oblivion,
(*Sandy* 'course they do wonders with tablets now ... Now he's coming out with his flash finish, listen, listen, go on Jules, yes ...)
    ... second childhood and mere oblivion,
    Nanti hampsteads, nanti minces, nanti riah, nanti everything.
(*Sandy* Bravo, Jules!! *Applause*)

The use of the polari here obviously has the immediate aim of making its audience laugh. But it's also possible to discern in it the outline of a larger cultural process in which its words are deployed as part of a complex 'coding' strategy.[3] Homosexual acts were regarded as criminal offences in Britain at this time (Sandy's comment on 'the Justice', 'that's something else he knows about, mmm' generates a knowing laugh) and this remained the case until the law was changed by the Sexual Offences Act of 1967. The use of the polari to signify homosexuality in *Round The Horne* perhaps offers an example of one of the means by which, as Paul Baker puts it, 'tabooed gay identities were negotiated in a context of homophobia and censorship at an important cusp in the history of gay liberation'.[4] But this Shakespearean episode has some additional dimensions that also turn it – at this point in time – into an incisive ironic device.

Class act

First, Julian and Sandy's use of a lower class London accent together with associated grammatical features ('wasn't you?') and distinctively 'queer' intonation patterns, poses a challenge in respect of Shakespeare's cultural role. The prevailing perception that a 'middle-class' or 'posh' English accent is the only one appropriate for rendition of the Bard in Britain has of course latterly been successfully contested by enterprises such as the Northern Broadsides productions. But the combative stance of such projects in itself confirms the prevailing assumption, during the sixties and seventies, of the middle-class 'ownership' of Shakespeare, certainly in terms of performance. Its persistence to this day would not be difficult to demonstrate, although it has to be set against the clear affection for and involvement with Shakespeare's plays that remained a feature of British working-class culture throughout the nineteenth century and beyond. However, that culture would nonetheless also have tended to assume that, in general terms, the 'proper' way to perform the Bard's works involved 'posh' accents and 'normal' notions of the binary opposition of male and female. The sense of Shakespeare's plays as 'high art'; monumentalised and permanently sequestered in some sort of 'national park', was, and probably remains, widespread. Kenneth William's own diary entry of nearly fifty years ago reinforces the point:

> *Friday 18th February (1955)* The reason I don't want to act in Shakespeare at the moment is that I want to be associated with voicing the contemporary problems of my own age. I see the greatness of his (S.) poetic vision and its glory. But theatrically it is no longer meaningful for me. The idea of a crowd of people speaking Shakespearean verse on a greensward is somehow incongruous. I'm practically laughing. *Anyway* it won't be done properly because it *can't* be done properly. There aren't the Actors any more. The big heroics etc. can't be encompassed, and the audience has lost touch. This isn't a heroic age. There isn't *room* for heroics. It's *all* heroics now. So the real hero has passed away.'[5]

Julian and Sandy's involvement with Shakespeare thus presents itself as laughably inappropriate, the humour deriving from the sense that if the plays represent high art, their interpreters here stand for its polar opposite; low life. That the latter should presume to engage with former is central to the joke. Yet much of the situation's undeniable pathos lies, beyond our laughter, precisely in the aspiration of the outlawed outsider (whether gay, lower class, or both), not simply to be permitted 'inside' the culture, but perhaps also to regain a lost legitimacy for which Shakespeare is a symbol.

Striking camp

Inevitably, and not inappropriately, the scene also highlights the issue of sexuality. As usual, Kenneth Horne's suavely imperturbable manner signals a normality designed to throw the 'camp' demeanour of Julian and Sandy into sharp relief, though not without the occasional innuendo (sustained throughout the series) to the effect that this masks a more complex set of impulses on his part. Of course, this particular passage also concerns itself with the developing social roles of 'Man', carrying and reinforcing in that the assumption that 'maleness' constitutes the substantive template for all of human kind, including women. The cut to 'the soldier' emphasises a notion of aggressive 'manliness' but this is immediately undermined by the slyness of the *double-entendre*, hinting at Julian's seductive powers in 'he takes a good soldier', and the irony of 'I'm being the soldier now'. The reference to the famously transgressive wartime show *Soldiers in Skirts*, in which males openly (and presumably with Government approval) impersonated females, draws attention to the ironic reversal Julian apparently embodies here, as well as reinforcing a set of conventional twentieth century expectations linking 'gays' to the theatre.

Just a stage

Throughout the series, Sandy and Julian constantly refer to their 'real' status as 'actors' or 'theatricals' of a vaguer kind. Chronically unemployed in that profession, they nevertheless dismiss the various jobs in which they're discovered as forms of 'resting', and the lacing of their speech with theatrical jargon (talk of 'ageing up' and a 'flash finish') is consequently telling. With the decline of the Church, to say nothing of the shrinking of the colonial civil services and the changing nature of academe, it's arguable that the theatre in Britain had become, by the First World War if not before, one of the few acceptable 'havens' for homosexuals. The result was slightly paradoxical. Committed to secrecy, and to covert relationships that dared not speak their name, they became members of a profession whose public mode was declamatory and whose very essence involved display. An additional irony also pertains in that, at the foundational moment of professional acting in Britain, during the early modern period, females were normally represented by males. The idea of 'soldiers in skirts', of males playing female roles, would scarcely have seemed outrageous at Shakespeare's Globe.

But contradiction and irony seem always to have existed close to the heart of the gay situation in Britain. Unofficially tolerated, even institutionalised in the middle-class educational system at the height of, and perhaps in the service of Empire, homosexuality was nonetheless officially repressed with considerable savagery, particularly after the Oscar Wilde trials. It was a state of affairs that perhaps helped to generate some of the massive social and psychological tensions surfacing in novels, plays and poems during and after the First World War. In the period in which *Round the Horne* flourished, British society still remained remarkably hypocritical about homosexuality's role both in middle-class British life and its now fading imperial past. However, the pressure for change was also considerable and there's little doubt that the 'Julian and Sandy' sketches proved subtly instrumental in defusing a potentially explosive situation and helping to hasten a modification of the law.

Speaking out

With regard to language at large, the polari has a complex function. In terms both of words and the way of life they imply, it shadows its host through a reductive and occasionally lubricious pantomime of its some of its major components. In the process it mocks at and so disputes the English language's dominance over the culture it brings into being and aims to shape. Although, according to Baker, only 2.5 per cent of the words in the *Round The Horne* sketches derive from the polari, their impact proved surprisingly powerful with the result that, by the late sixties, some of them had passed into the mainstream of British English. The process offers a vivid illustration of the degree to which – far from enjoying 'stability' – all living languages exist in a permanent state of actual or potential flux in which alternative linguistic forms or competing 'registers' hover uninvited at their edges, ever ready, like inebriated gate-crashers, to invade and disrupt the dance of meaning.[6]

Of course, the systematic means by which 'slang' or 'innuendo' operate in relation to 'straightforward' reference are not easy to formulate, particularly when paralinguistic features such as accent or 'tone of voice', or extra-linguistic actions such as gesture and facial expression, reinforce them. That fact that English is a global language brings many additional factors into play. Millions of its speakers inhabit a world in which their speech signals and confirms a particular condition of subjugation. Julian and Sandy serve to remind us of the disruptive energies such a predicament can release. Systematically deprived of a native discourse in some cases, imprisoned by a degrading accent, or outlawed as 'queer' or 'foreign' in others, large numbers of English-speakers live bound to an oppressor's tongue but with no guaranteed share in its bounty. As a result, they find themselves ignominiously forced into mimicry, or required awkwardly to engage the contours of one way of life in modes and with names that remain shackled to another. In the inevitable struggle for ownership of the means of signification which such a situation breeds, parallel but distinct orders of meaning can come to inhabit the same range of linguistic structures, and when these compete, the stakes will inevitably be high.

The polari thus operates as part of a much larger pattern: one in which the day-to-day resort of underclasses to slang, patois, or deliberately mystifying words and phrases becomes the means whereby a subordinate way of life can invade and refashion the products of its dominant partner, particularly the individual words or names of the language it is forced to share. The subcultural appropriation of linguistic items may even eventually wring their 'official' range of reference out of them and substitute an opposite one (as in the case of some British and North American black English, where words such as 'bad' or 'wicked' can come to mean 'good' or 'admirable'). At the heart of all such subversive rhetorical practice lies a revolutionary principle of revision and few enterprises could be more crucial to it than that of rebellious re-naming. For, as Julian and Sandy know, to vault the fences of nomination and signification is to challenge what counts as reality.[7]

Contestation may be a permanent characteristic of all living languages, but most British speakers of English have long forgotten that their own language began its journey towards its present dominance by disputing the claims of other tongues to engage meaningfully with, or even to create, the reality of the British Isles themselves. This is not to say that Julian and Sandy could just as well have used Welsh, Irish or Scots to comic effect (although it's worth remembering that something both of comedy and pathos invests the eruption of Welsh in its memorable confrontation with English in *1 Henry IV* (3. 1. 186–215)).[8] What gives their use of the polari its considerable subversive quality is precisely its challenge, not only to English, but also to that more recent phenomenon, Englishness, of which Shakespeare has become the most potent symbol, and, here, Kenneth Horne its discomfited voice.

No doubt Julian and Sandy pander to a prejudiced and caricatured notion of homosexual 'camp' whose eccentricities sideline and infantilise its users. Yet in the event, the 'Seven Ages Of Omi' proves able to engage fruitfully with the most fundamental of human experiences by means of an engaging, suasive rhythm, in which the unabrasive 'nanti' softens and perhaps even finally domesticates the brusquer (if no less foreign) sophistication of the original 'sans'. And Williams was never in any doubt of Shakespeare's efficacy when it came to dealing with the more desperate aspects of Englishness. In his diary on 23 January 1963, he responds angrily to the charge that his own deportment is 'outrageous':

> 'The critics … simply don't understand the very thing they're supposed to be watching. They should read Shakespeare's Clowns & see the desperation there. So great that they speak what no one else dares to speak. And they call me 'outrageous'. They don't even begin to see the desperation of my own perilous position.[9]

Outlaws

Part of Williams's 'perilous position' derived of course from his 'outlaw' status as a homosexual, and the refusal of the culture in which he lived to recognise his as an acceptable alternative lifestyle. A useful point of comparison with the 'Seven Ages of Omi', and indeed an interesting measure of the social changes that distinguish pre-1967 Britain from the culture that had developed by the 1980s is provided by Richard Curtis's famous parody *The Skinhead Hamlet*.[10] Where Julian and Sandy's offering effectively proposes a baroque linguistic confection as an acceptable alternative to Shakespeare's English, Curtis's carefully invokes the opposite: a linguistic wasteland, where traditional rhetorical patterning of the sort that signals 'old, high art' has been deliberately drained away, to be replaced by conjugations of the elemental verb 'to fuck'. The language is funny as a result of what it strips out, rather than what it adds:

> Act 1 Scene IV
> Enter Horatio, Hamlet and Ghost.

Ghost: Oi! Mush, get on with it!
Hamlet: Who did it then?
Ghost: That wanker Claudius. He poured fucking poison in my fucking ear!
Hamlet: Fuck me!
(*Exeunt*)

It would be prejudicial to assert that such 'barrenness' in the 1980's (Curtis's piece dates from 1982) represents some sort of decline from the linguistic complexity of Julian and Sandy's vocabulary of ten or so years previously. In fact, both pieces employ subtly calculated rhetorical strategies, and both possess equally and ultimately the potential to tell us a great deal about our own times through a consideration of the ways in which we use Shakespeare (as we use all art) to make our experience meaningful. They reinforce the notion of parody as a powerful indicator of that changing cultural function which, in the absence of any conclusive access to an 'essential' or 'historical' Bard, must replace the quest for his plays' final significance.

At the very least, comparison with the pared down *Skinhead Hamlet* confirms the extent to which 'The Seven Ages of Omi' depends on the deployment of competing linguistic items, offered, with knowing insouciance, as 'alternatives' to Shakespeare's words. Curtis's 'outlaw' Skinheads utterly reject middle-class 'lawful' language and the cultural values for which it is presumed to stand. The more genuinely outlawed Julian and Sandy seem, on the other hand, to propose that their language be embraced in earnest of their acceptance into and recognition by the culture that has criminalised them. To that extent, it seems a more appealing option. Oblivion no doubt awaits us all, but when it dwindles to the comfiness of 'nanti everything', infantilising perhaps turns neatly against the infantilisers, and becomes – almost – acceptable.

Appendix

Selected polari vocabulary

Barnet: hair (rhyming slang)
Bods: bodies
Bona: good
Butch: masculine
Cod: awful
Cossy: costume
Cruising: looking for sex
Dolly: good
Drag: feminine clothes
Eke: face
Fab: good
Fabe: great

Fabulosa: great
Fantabulosa: wonderful
Hampsteads: teeth (rhyming slang)
Heartface: term of endearment
Hobson's: voice (rhyming slang)
Irish: wig (rhyming slang)
Lallie: leg
Lattie: house/flat
Lucoddy: Body
Luppers: fingers
Manjarie: food/eat
Mince(s): walk/eyes (rhyming slang)

Naff: tasteless
Nanti: no/without
Nish: no/don't
Omi: man
Omi-polone: male homosexual
Polone: woman
Plates: feet (rhyming slang) also oral sex
Riah: hair (back slang)
Scotches: Legs (rhyming slang)

Sheesh: classy
Strillers: piano keys
Tat: worthless
Thews: fore-arms
Treash: term of endearment
Troll: walk
Vada: see/look
(adapted from Baker (2000), p.5)

Notes

1. Also *parlary, parlyaree, palary* etc. Hardly a 'written' tongue, a number of alternative spellings are on offer for many of the words of what Eric Partridge calls 'this Cinderella among languages', see Partridge (1972) pp. 11–12. See also Partridge (1949).
2. See Baker (2002).
3. A valuable, detailed analysis is given in Baker (2000).
4. Baker (2000) p. 23.
5. Williams (1993) p. 108.
6. Baker (2000) p. 6.
7. I make the same point, in very similar terms but in a different context, in Hawkes (2002) p. 123.
8. See Hawkes (2002) pp. 30–45.
9. Williams (1993) p. 207.
10. See Brett (1984) pp. 316–20.

Works cited

Baker, Paul (2000) 'Bona To Vada Your Dolly Old Eke! Construction of Gay Identity in the Julian and Sandy Radio Sketches', Working Paper No. 114, Lancaster: Centre for Language in Social Life, Department of Linguistics and Modern English Language, Lancaster University.
—— (2002) *Polari: The Lost Language of Gay Men*, London and New York: Routledge.
Brett, Simon (1984) ed., *The Faber Book of Parodies*, London: Faber.
Hawkes, Terence (2002) *Shakespeare in the Present*, London and New York: Routledge.
Partridge, Eric (1949) *Here, There and Everywhere*, London.
—— (1972) *A Dictionary of Historical Slang*, Harmondsworth: Penguin Books.
Williams, Kenneth (1993) Russell Davies ed., *The Kenneth Williams Diaries*, London: HarperCollins.

8
Authority and the Early Modern Theatre: Representing Robert Weimann

John Drakakis

Robert Weimann's monumental *Shakespeare and The Popular Tradition in the Theatre* first appeared in German in 1967, but since its translation into English in 1978, it has been enthusiastically rediscovered in the 1980s in Britain and the United States as a seminal work of materialist criticism.[1] This is all the more remarkable at a time when from the point of view of a practical politics as well as theoretical orientation, classical Marxism with its emphasis upon the role of collectivities such as class in the making of history, is thought by some to have entered a period of terminal decline. It is also a matter of no little inconvenience to Weimann himself, who has been forced to divide his time between the recently 'unified' Germany and the west coast of the United States, where, paradoxically, the intellectual cachet of Marxism as a developing discourse continues to command serious and sustained, although, as Jacques Derrida indicated, somewhat nervous attention.[2] There has, of course, been a significant burgeoning of historical research into Renaissance culture among literary scholars during the last two decades, despite tendentious proclamations of 'the end of history',[3] all of which have forced a radical reconsideration of some of the fundamental tenets of classical Marxism. This context has proved to be more important than ever for Weimann, who, in his own writing, has continued to engage in a rigorous self-reflexivity in the face of an increasingly feverish circulation and exchange of professional intellectual capital: refusing to be swayed by fashion, but still remaining receptive to the questions which new advances in critical theory have opened up.

In an early essay that Weimann contributed to Arnold Kettle's *Shakespeare in a Changing World* (1964) he had already begun to question a critical practice that was indifferent to 'the facts of economic and social history'.[4] Moreover, some three years later, and at a time before English translations of Bakhtin had appeared, Weimann demonstrated in *Shakespeare and the Popular Tradition in the Theatre* that he was already attuned to the multi-vocal nature of theatrical representation and to an implicit politics of signification, and also to the limitations of a positivist model of the theatre as an artistic phenomenon which merely 'reflected' its environment. This has been one of his abiding concerns, and his recent book, *Author's Pen and Actor's Voice: Playing and Writing in Shakespeare's Theatre* (2000), along with a series of articles on the theme of theatrical mimesis, represent a return to these complex issues. For Weimann, and very much in keeping with his commitment to a vibrant Marxism, art is a special mode of production, an observation that has led him to insist from the outset that 'Shakespeare's theatre and his society were interrelated in the sense that the Elizabethan stage, even when it reflected the tensions and compromises of sixteenth-century England, was also a potent force that helped to create the specific character and transitional nature of that society.'[5] Indeed, he perceived in what he called 'the receptivity of the audience' and 'the consciousness and artistry of the drama ... a new historical synthesis', forming a 'dialectics of interdependence' (*Popular Tradition*, xii).

Weimann is fascinated by what he describes as the 'mingle-mangle' of late sixteenth-century society, and a corresponding mixture in the drama of the period of the styles of 'conventionalism' and 'naturalism' which, taken together, 'helped constitute the universalising pattern in Shakespeare' (*Popular Tradition*, p. 251). Nor could this be a mere formal matter, since it was in precisely that combination of tension and mutual inter-relation between these two modes of representation that a much larger, implicitly political, freedom resided.[6] Indeed, he has re-iterated this view more insistently in *Author's Pen and Actor's Voice* where, in a comment upon the tension between *locus* and *platea*, he insists upon 'intersection' and 'mutual engagement' as distinct from 'confrontation' and 'separation'.[7] His initial affirmation of a 'universalising pattern in Shakespeare', whose origin is ascribed to a security born of the dramatist's access to 'the fully developed techniques and values of a popular theatre turned into a national institution', may read, some thirty years on, as a form of special pleading. But this is perfectly consistent with an issue that by the mid-1970s had become one of Weimann's abiding concerns, and which he explored in more detail in his book, *Structure and Society in Literary History* (1976; expanded ed. 1984). Unhappy with the formalist reading practices of American New Criticism, which depended upon 'the postulate of the timelessness of reading and an a-historical conception of the reader and his responses',[8] Weimann was concerned to maintain a clear distinction between 'the reciprocal quality of the most basic historical relationship between the past significance of the work and the present meaning of its revitalised use and interpretation' (*Structure and Society*, p. 32). In the essay he contributed to *Shakespeare in a Changing World* he had already taken severely to task 'a certain critically inert type of sociological or even Marxist writing' which did not distinguish between literature as 'literature' as 'a medium of sociological reference and exemplification', and he insisted that what cannot be ignored is the contradiction between the historicity of the work and its enduring value as art (*Structure and Society*, p.18). When he came to reconsider some of these issues a decade or so later, it was against a background of crisis, both in the discipline of literary criticism, and also in Western society generally, 'in which the revolutionary idea of change, organic and dialectical concepts of evolution, and the liberal and humanist traditions of progress' (*Structure and Society*, p. 18) had all been rendered problematic.

By this time Weimann was clearly thinking of the United States, where what he called 'the most general assumptions about the practical uses of literature as an agent of social change and consciousness', and a critical practice which was characterised by 'scepticism and retreat', had been subsumed under a purely self-serving academic discourse designed to fulfil 'professional requirements' (*Structure and Society*, p. 30). He has always been stubborn in his resistance to the Leavisite notion of 'tradition', on the grounds that such a view of the literature of the past overlooks the historically complex dialectic between 'past significance and present meaning' (*Structure and Society*, p. 43). Of course, this is an issue which more recent attempts to historicize the literature of the Renaissance have attempted to address, most notably Stephen Greenblatt's dismissal of 'an aestheticized and idealized politics of the imagination' in favour of a study which had forced him 'simultaneously to feel more rooted and more estranged in my own values.'[9] If we take this, together with the contributions of Foucault to the analysis of discourse, and with Derrida's account of the durability of the text in history as the consequence of its own 'iterability', something 'which puts down roots in the unity of a context and immediately opens this non-saturable context onto a recontextualisation',[10] we can then begin to locate the complexity of the discursive field within which Weimann has been moving (with a degree of caution) over a long period of time.

We may trace the trajectory of Weimann's concern with these issues through a series of essays that he contributed to various books and journals throughout the 1980s. For example, in 1981, in an essay entitled 'Society and the Individual in Shakespeare's Conception of Character', he sought to locate in the radically transitional art of Shakespearean drama a historically significant relation between 'the self' and 'the social', but that has been for some time a consistent feature of the post-structuralist concern with subjectivity:

> It is only when these two points of reference – the self and the social – are seen as entering into a dynamic and unpredictable kind of relationship that the most original and far-reaching dimension in Shakespeare's conception of character – the dimension of growth and change – can be adequately understood.[11]

Here 'character' is something more than the human essence that art liberates, and which the spectator or reader glimpses at particular moments in the text or in performance; rather it emerges as a series of contingent identities, while at the same time aligning contingency with social process. Weimann ascribes to Shakespeare a conception of characterisation that draws upon 'that basic contradiction according to which the individual ultimately, in the course of modern history, does not achieve his particularity and individuality in isolation from, but only in connection with, the social process' ('Society and the Individual', p. 30). Moreover, and in a way that returns our attention to the vexed question of universality, he affirms that in the England of the time 'it was possible to comprehend the emerging forms of individuality not as the least, but as the most universalised dimension of character' ('Society and the Individual', p. 31). This argument hints at the proposition that, in the words of Ernesto Laclau, 'nobody can aspire to be the true consciousness of the world', and that the 'endless interaction between perspectives' renders more remote than ever the possibility of 'any totalitarian dream'.[12] Thus already by the early 1980s Weimann was beginning to wrestle with a series of political problems in his own writing which have become even more germane to the history of Marxism in the light of the receding of the Cold War and the unification of Germany.

The question of 'character' dovetails neatly into two of Weimann's abiding concerns, the relationship between mimesis and ideology, and the question of authority. Between the first appearance of *Structure and Society in Literary History* and its re-issue in 1984, he attempted to think through more systematically what he perceived to be the aporias in particular aspects of post-structuralist theory.

> Whereas the communicative functions of the spoken word will again and again establish the signifying principle *aliquid stat pro aliquo*, the textualised stratum of language as inscription can more easily be dissociated from the necessary historicity of such significations. What 'textuality' presupposes, then, is a self-generating mode of interaction within a system of *difference* to which the scriptor (and reader) can relate in response to some unbearable constraint in the socially representative function of language. In relinquishing this function, the poststructuralist critic suspends the need for continuing to confront the links as well as the contradictions between voice and utterance, life and writing, socio-individual existence and the systematic uses of language. As against the weight of these contradictions, culminating as they do in the triumphs and defeats, the possibilities and impossibilities, of representation, the Derridean textuality shields the inscribed from the historical compulsions of the author in his social acts of cultural representativity.[13]

Here Weimann raises the question of what happens when the concepts of 'production' and 'reproduction' are 'pushed beyond the limits of textuality';[14]

he perceives in what he believes to be the '(self)-repressive strategies' of the Derridean critique of metaphysics and logocentricity a privileging of certain textual strategies which occlude what he calls 'a referential and pragmatic (non-differential) definition of the links between mimesis and "production" or even theatrical "production",' and that it is here, at the point of intersection between text and historical context, that 'an opening for a radically historicizing use of "mimesis" would have to be sought' (*Structure and Society*, pp. 308–9):

> To produce is to go beyond the eternal circle of deferment, beyond the limitations of the sign and the permanent displacement of meaning; it is, even more, to break through the textualization of experience and to undermine any hierarchical relationship between writing and speech vis-à-vis discursive practice. The person who makes a watch and reads the time, who plants a tree and harvests its fruit, constitutes himself or herself as a subject; the meaning of his or her activity is not deflected by verbal language as a differential system of signification. The theatrical person who knocks at a door or embraces his or her partner may not, through the production of an object, constitute himself or herself as a subject; but neither can that person's activity be subsumed under the depersonalised modes of textualization. The production of his or her "voice" is both a premise and a product of the particular social activity that a theatrical production re-presents (*Structure and Society*, p. 309).

This distinction is seminal insofar as it focuses on precisely what Weimann wishes to retain of the classical Marxist logic of labour, production, and appropriation, that he has more recently extended to the cultural labour of Shakespeare's actors. Texts do not, he insists, *produce* themselves, and while it is perfectly legitimate to explode the mirage of its surface univocality, a post-structuralist commitment to the principle of linguistic difference as constitutive remains, he emphasises, 'blind to the essential challenge in the link between production and value, as contained in the Marxian concept of *Aneignung*' (*Structure and Society*, p. 310). In his essay 'Mimesis in *Hamlet*', which appeared a year after this Epilogue, he sought to distinguish between Marx's the theoretical limitations of 'the old mimesis', which had implied that there was a stable connection between 'language and meaning, signifier and signified',[15] and a theatre still committed to a culture which was yet to become fully literate and which could not, therefore, 'lend itself easily to those semiotic and deconstructive methods which take as their starting point a purely literary definition of the sign or some exclusively textualized concept of language' ('Mimesis in *Hamlet*', p. 276).

On the surface such an argument would appear to render impossible any *rapprochement* with post-structuralist theory. In both *Shakespeare and the Popular Tradition in the Theatre* and 'Society and the Individual in Shakespeare's Conception of Character' Weimann wrestled with the opposing demands of medieval allegory and its commitment to a harmonised relationship between the universal and the particular, on the one hand, and the new, mimetic more openly agonistic ways of figuring the relationship between these two categories which emerged during the Renaissance, on the other. Weimann perceives a critical distinction between a discursive, irreducibly textualized definition of mimesis which privileges the constitutive function of difference, and which is constructed around a pre-existing 'subject' of discourse, and a non-discursive definition in which there is an assumed 'continuity and congruity between the act of interpretation, its cultural function, and its unique object, the Shakespearean text' ('Mimesis in *Hamlet*', pp. 275–6). If it is assumed that mimesis traditionally involves 'relatively stable links between language and meaning, signifier and signified', then the linguistic self-consciousness of the Shakespearean text, by virtue of its exposure of the homogenizing practices of representation, poses a threat to the 'principles of homogeneity, "closure" and authority in representation' of ideology itself, and nowhere more so than at the very point where ideology is being represented:

> If "representation" is said to homogenize textual production, stabilize hierarchies and privileges (and so void the text of contradictions and interrogations), then, indeed, the dramatic representations of Shakespeare may well be shown not to exhaust their mimetic potential under these modes of closure and plenitude. On the contrary, although the specular reading or viewing of the plays can of course fix the reader or viewer in the plenitude of some false consciousness, there is ample evidence that, over and beyond its stabilizing functions, Shakespearean mimesis comprehends a self-conscious subversion of authority in representation ('Mimesis in *Hamlet*', pp. 276–7).

Thus Weimann can propose that 'the issue of authority in representation need not necessarily preclude its deconstruction *through* representation' ('Mimesis in *Hamlet*', p. 279). In focusing on ideology as the means by which interests are naturalised Weimann halts the slide into the Nietzschean figurations of power which would collapse absolutely his own holistic account (which he was not yet prepared to relinquish in its entirety) into the sphere of a Foucauldian micro-politics, or into a post-structuralist revision of an identity politics. The conclusion to 'Mimesis in *Hamlet*' firmly resists any move into a spiralling textuality, regarded here as both a necessary and sufficient condition of post-structuralist critical practice, insisting upon a refusal to separate representation 'from some more comprehensive idea of the connectedness of social, economic, and cultural productions' ('Mimesis in *Hamlet*', p. 289).

This ingenious compromise, however, does not fully address the question of a referential model of language that haunts Weimann's argument. The re-admission of a deconstructive turn, through a Brechtian notion of defamilarization, enables him to postulate a politics of representation. However, in choosing to privilege the discussion of mimesis, Weimann is able to bypass the question of whether or not material production precedes the linguistic sign. The general direction of his argument aligns itself with Fredric Jameson's revisionary position, whereby history is perceived *neither* as a text, nor as a narrative, but as 'an absent cause' accessible to us 'in textual form, and that our approach to it and to the Real itself necessarily passes through its prior textualization, its narrativization, in the political unconscious'.[16]

In a short essay he contributed to *Shakespeare Reproduced: The Text in History and Ideology* (1987) Weimann carried his thinking on the question of textuality a stage further, suggesting that the contradiction between mimesis and the linguistic sign requires critics to

> grapple with the actual non-identity between the referential and the signifying dimensions of the text ... far from obliterating or displacing this contradiction, we need to bring it out into the open, in order to use it with a view to stimulating a materialist and historicist understanding of the mimetic dimensions of the theatrical sign and the signifying dimensions of theatrical mimesis – 'mimesis' taken in both its discursive and non-discursive dimensions, in language as well as action. It is at the cross-roads of these two dimensions that, I think, the production and reception of theatrical texts can best be explored as to the strengths and limits of the ideological function involved in them.[17]

Here difference is perceived not as a primary structural mechanism necessary for the production of meaning, but rather as a representation 'of "difference" in both the social sense of class conflict, gender, and cultural heterogeneity *and* the linguistic sense of the discontinuity between signifier and signified' ('Literary Theory of Ideology', p. 268). It is this insistence upon 'existential needs, desires and appropriations' that he returns to as a constant *motif* throughout *Author's Pen and Actor's Voice*, and that provides the motivation for the complex mimetic art of the theatrical performer.

This negotiation and cannot easily be dismissed as a casually pragmatic gesture. Weimann's Marxism will not permit him to depart absolutely from the classical tenet that both the act of appropriation of representation itself and 'the material reproduction of life precede the problematic of the sign' ('Literary Theory of Ideology', p. 269), although there is in this a tacit acknowledgement of the materiality of representation which will allow him occasionally to be more receptive than he is here to the post-structuralist, dynamics of discourse. In 'Shakespeare (De)Canonized: Conflicting Uses of "Authority" and "Representation" ',Weimann makes explicit his own theoretical stance:

> Perhaps the best way to avoid any eclectic confusion between semiotic and sociological perspectives is to hint at my own position (which

relates to, but is not quite identical with, the current languages of [de]canonization) by saying that I propose to use these languages as a genuine pre-text, in the sense that I find it difficult to subscribe to either the traditional naturalizing mode of canonization, or, for that matter, a deconstructionist position which, beyond all considerations of the cultural uses and values of Shakespeare, presumes to re-write literary history outside the dialectic of continuity and discontinuity, tradition and revolution ('Shakespeare (De)Canonized', p. 67).

Weimann is less concerned with the archaeology of discourse itself, and the regulative functions of particular discourses, than with the negotiation and contestation that takes place for particular positions within a single discourse. His preoccupation with Shakespeare's monumental reputation, or to be more precise, his cultural authority, and its interfacing with the authority of theatrical performance, involves primarily 'both its construction and deconstruction, in terms of those modes of authorization by which differing types of critical discourse engage in the representation of a representation' ('Shakespeare (De)Canonized', p. 66).

Any suggestion that he has succumbed to a full-blown post-structuralist theory of textuality here would be to mistake Weimann's purpose. Instead he proposes an updated but recognisably Bakhtinian 'notion of discourse as appropriated language', leaning more in the direction of Habermas than towards Foucault:

> This would involve inscribed or oral utterances in the form of constative and performative speech acts and would allow us to view, as mutually related, signification *and* co-operation in the uses of language, the semiotics of the sign *and* the contingency of communication. Such a notion of discourse would link the problematic of the sign with the pursuit of social, cultural, and individual interests and legitimations as they cut through the specificities of poetic and critical uses of language.[18]

He is prepared to subscribe to a post-structuralist suspicion of any discursive stabilizing of cultural hierarchies, and attempts in the interests of canonicity to suppress discontinuity, but he stops short of a full endorsement, fearing that it is history itself, and its material overdeterminations, that might ultimately be jettisoned. In attempting to historicize what he calls 'the decanonizing gesture itself', Weimann aims to get under discourse, to explode its claim to irreducible textuality and to explore its representational properties. Once the concepts of representation and discursive practice are elided, both demand to be viewed 'as an act of either embodying or intercepting the commission, the delegation, the mediation of certain powerful or, indeed, certain underprivileged interests and activities in history' ('Shakespeare (De)Canonized', pp. 70–1). This is a bold recuperation of the Foucauldian dynamics of the structure of power for a thoroughgoing dialectical materialist model of history which preserves, however gingerly, and in conditions which are far from auspicious, a pre-existent but frustrated fundamental human social identity which demands to be emancipated. This is, in short, a vital, but fully historicised force that, even if it cannot quite hold out the promise of a quasi-Hegelian synthesis, remains nevertheless committed to writing the history of human oppression and the revolutionary efforts necessary to alleviate its negative effects.

The difficulty, however, with seeking to separate out the elements of a structural model is that it lays Weimann open to the danger, so eloquently described by Ernesto Laclau, of inscribing the identity of the forces of oppression within that which searches for emancipation.[19] Thus, having acceded to at least part of the Foucauldian structuration of the dialectics of power at the level of a micro-politics, Weimann cannot escape entirely from some of its larger consequences in relation to totalities. To attempt to recuperate discourse as an instrumental phenomenon, while at the same time conceding that it is also the *object* of struggle is to try to have it both ways. This is not to say that Weimann is committed to the concept of an absolute knowledge, rather he is a little less sanguine about what Laclau perceives as 'the exhilarating effects' of dispensing with it altogether. More than anyone, Weimann has good reason to suspect the consequences of the 'totalitarian dream', but he is unwilling to jettison the concept of totality for the still unnerving prospect of 'an endless interaction between various perspectives' (Laclau, *Emancipation(s)*, p. 17). He perceives what he calls 'the methodological alliance' and the 'contradiction' between history and language (two interconnected sites of the construction of the subject) as being currently unresolved, but also holds that attempts to resolve them are likely to be crucial to the development of Shakespeare Studies in the decades to come.

This is the methodological and theoretical context within which Weimann's *Authority and Representation in Early Modern Discourse* (1996) requires to be situated. He reprises, in this important text, those themes that have been the focus of an *oeuvre* that has been systematically developed during the last thirty years or so. In concentrating on the broader aspects of early modern culture, Weimann pushes further his insights into the liminal nature of the Elizabethan stage, and reaffirms his interest in the Renaissance as a transitional moment from the medieval to the modern world. The contours of that transformation have long fascinated historians, but Weimann eschews the nostalgia occasionally associated with it for a much more rigorous historiography which simply refuses to make of the past a site upon which the present projects its own identity. Moreover, he is cautious about monological constructions of early modern 'authority', while at the same time remaining acutely aware that certain continuities are implicit in discursive and non-discursive practices of, say, the language of 'legitimation and "possession" ', which 'extend right to our own doorstep'. At the same time, he recognises that this is a world that, 'although it made ours possible, is light years removed from the uses of power (and its opposite) in the age of electronic information'.[20] The issue, for him, is the historical difference between how early modern culture represents its own concerns to itself, and how modern critics read and interpret those problematical self-representations. In this respect he seems at one with those he labels '(post)modern critics' for whom:

> Sixteenth century culture presents itself as a language ruptured by divisions, a language whose configurations need to be read against the grain of early modern meanings. There is an irresistible (some critics would say ethical) urge to look at the Renaissance rhetoric of aggrandisement as a discourse of impoverishment, to read the fame of exploration as infamous news of colonisation, the triumphs of self-liberation as testimony to social fission, the pride in appropriation as a condoning of vast expropriations (*Authority and Representation*, p. 7).

At stake here are two different categories of 'authority': first there is the question of the authority from which the historical discourses and practices of colonisation derive their own legitimacy, and second there is the authority which particular modern readings seek in order to validate their own practices. In neither case can the appeal be made to 'assumptions of any univocal articulation of authority as a given, unitary court of appeal' (*Authority and Representation*, p. 8). As a scholar who continues to write and think within the tradition of Marxism, Weimann is always interested in those historical conjunctures in which hitherto oppressed energy finds and secures its emancipation. He is also interested in the changing relationship between 'subject' and 'object' during the Renaissance, although he remains wary of an unexamined version of the proposition that modern authority 'became a product of writing, speaking, and reading, a result rather than primarily a constituent of representation'.[21] Fictional discourses in the Renaissance carry with them the traces of a range of antecedent cultural practices, and their complexity is exacerbated by an 'interiorization and privatization of meaning' consequent upon the social, cultural, and ecclesiastical changes which took place during the Reformation (*Authority and Representation*, p. 4), along with a relatively new means of the circulation and exchange of these ideas, the printing press. Indeed, he identifies a link, which he suspects '(... is of unique cultural potency) between the decline of given, unitary, locations of authority and an unprecedented expansion of representational discourses' (*Authority and Representation*, p. 4).

Weimann is at pains to stress that Renaissance authority, and by implication Renaissance subjectivity, cannot be reduced to a simple binary opposition between 'outward power and inward spirituality' (*Authority and Representation*, p. 25). Without subscribing to the exclusively constitutive power of difference in the production of the signifier, Weimann is able to draw a crucial distinction between pre-Reformation legitimation practice in which representation was a 'delegated act of institutionalised power and homogeneity, where alterity was affirmed as something given even before the particular acts of writing, thinking, and reading began' (34) and a post-Reformation strategy that foregrounded 'incertitude, between the signifying and the signified levels of representation'; the notion of a 'strategy' here, it would seem, leaves open the possibility of a self-fashioning which retains some degree of agency in the process of rendering compatible 'political subordination and spiritual freedom' (35).

In an argument whose ramifications spread into many aspects of Renaissance culture, Weimann analyses acutely both the linguistic practices within whose aegis authority was produced and also its thematisation as a preoccupation of absolutist rulers. Indeed, what began as Reformation became in some instances revolution (the Kett rebellion of 1549, for example), as the struggle for control of the authorising of representation in ecclesiastical discourse spilled over into a contest for discourse itself and the power to legitimize meaning. Moreover, and despite the possibilities of physical coercion, the legacy of discord that this contestation bequeathed was connected, so Weimann argues, to 'the need to negotiate vital interests ideologically, to shift the medium through which power was appropriated from that of violence and tradition to that of discourse and argument' (*Authority and Representation*, p. 64). Here Weimann fleshes out the New Historicist perception of the theatricality of identity by demonstrating its imbrication in the primarily linguistic performance of a conflict in which signs were now severed from their stable anchoring points in authorised representations of the world. The public theatre becomes, in this argument, symptomatic of 'the empty signifier', of the gulf between reality and appearance induced by a new social mobility (66). And yet, he will go on to argue in *Author's Pen and Actor's Voice*, that the cultural labour of performance itself can still be glimpsed in those instances of heteroglossia, vulnerable to critical exposure, that persistently return to catch the representation in its own act of mimetic gesture, and to question its claim to authority.

The operative term here is 'differentiation', and it is worth recalling in this connection the Heideggerian roots of Weimann's preoccupation with representation. For Heidegger the notion of a 'world picture' is emphatically not a picture of the world, but 'the world conceived and grasped as picture'. Heidegger continues:

> What is, in its entirety, is now taken in such a way that it first is in being and only is in being to the extent that it is set up by man, who represents and sets forth. Wherever we have the world picture, an essential decision takes place regarding what is, in its entirety. The Being of whatever is, is sought and found in the latter.

However, everywhere that whatever is, is *not* interpreted in this way, the world cannot also enter into a picture; there can be no world picture. The fact that whatever is comes into being in and through representedness transforms the age in which this occurs into a new age in contrast with the preceding one.[22]

Weimann has no wish to pursue the anti-humanist implications of this Heideggerian position. Rather, he wishes to retain an integrated vision of the totality of the social formation, where each activity is over-determined, but cannot be reduced to the status of a text. For Weimann, the concept of a radical rupture remains a possibility, although he is perfectly well aware of the historically verifiable fact that revolutionary energy is frequently dispersed across a number of positions which may well be in conflict with each other. However, what is crucial to his thesis is the emerging notion of authorship whose definition does not hinge upon a Derridean distinction between speech and writing as 'a duplicitous attempt to justify the autonomous subject and the subjective world' (*Authority and Representation*, p. 108), or upon the Foucauldian notion of disciplinary regimes. Rather, he sees the emerging category of authorship during the period as an essentially humanist 'positioning of the writer as a creative and responsible agent between interior and exterior modes of expression [which] helped fortify the public plane and moral status of authorship' (109). This leads him to the conclusion that there existed a continuity between the verbal articulations of authority and 'the political parameters of authority' which could be viewed both 'strategically', and, in the case of the public theatres, 'ironically' (110).

It would be misleading to suggest, however, that Weimann's project is the production of a unified historical narrative. It is indeed the case that in *Authority and Representation in Early Modern Discourse* he returns regularly to a number of issues that have both a social and economic resonance. For example, linguistic indeterminacy and the impulse to reconstitute and legitimise authority occurs at a historical conjuncture marked by the displacement and volatility of commercial markets (*Authority and Representation*, p. 150ff), and he cites Jean-Christophe Agnew's neatly elliptical observation that that market 'was made meaningful at the very moment that meaning itself was becoming marketable'.[23] But anthropological concerns never become obstacles to the respect that Weimann accords the texts he discusses. In this sense he retains a firm commitment to the social value of art as an irrepressible human activity capable of undermining ideology as well as figuring forth its contours. He is doubtful about what he calls 'the inverted teleology' behind Foucault's analysis of the history of representation, but he is characteristically generous in his acknowledgement that Foucault's account is persuasive 'on the *ends* and *limits* of representation'. And yet, when all is said and done, theories of representation are, he argues, ineffective when dealing with 'the non-representable dimension of existence' (*Authority and Representation*, p. 190). For Weimann the late sixteenth-century crisis in representation derives from the growing opacity of the sign itself: 'there is no representation without taxation', and he sees what he calls 'the overtaxing' of representation as the consequence of 'exacting from it too much presence in the presentation of too many imaginary articles, actions, and relations in a new, movable order of contingency' (*Authority and Representation*, p. 197).

It is at the point of intersection between 'imagination' and 'the imaginary' that Weimann's thesis finally comes to a provisional rest. Taking his cue from Theseus's account of the characteristic features of the early modern poetic imagination in *A Midsummer Night's Dream*, he insists that this faculty, 'far from serving as the innermost source and image of subjectivity', was also a 'strong vessel for shaping and transfiguring perceptions' (*Authority and Representation*, p. 200), a species of 'radical imaginary' which can become the vehicle for emancipatory narratives. Moreover, in a bid to shake himself free from the now discredited subversion/containment debate Weimann seeks to map out briefly a site for a more wide-ranging early modern political unconscious. In a manner which is in some ways similar to Foucault's idea of the rule of the 'tactical polyvalence of discourses',[24] he wants to emphasise the *positive* opportunities within the process of representation itself for change and innovation: 'Positively speaking, the sites of conscience, choice, invention, exchange, and the imaginary, especially strong when linked, marked the broadest space for innovative practices in and through representation' (*Authority and Representation*, pp. 202–3). It is clear from this that Weimann wishes to hold on to the methodology of Marxist dialectics. And he retains a firm belief in historical materialism, hence his fascination with the Elizabethan theatre as a limit case.

In certain respects, *Author's Pen and Actor's Voice* (2000), a series of essays on the subject of 'mimesis', along with *Prologues to Shakespeare's Theatre: Performance and Liminality in Early Modern Drama* (2004), an extended account of the significance of prologues and epilogues in Renaissance plays, retraces the path of earlier concerns while at the same time extending their scope. *Author's Pen and Actor's Voice* and the later introductory chapter to a volume entitled *Symbolism: An International Annual of Critical Aesthetics* (2004) entitled 'Representation and Mimesis: Towards a New Theory', debate an issue raised, initially by Foucault, but re-iterated in Philippe Lacoue-Labarthe's re-reading of the Platonic concept of mimesis. It is Lacoue-Labarthe's contention that:

> Short of controlling rigorously the procedure of enunciation (which is the very philosophico-political task that the *Republic* essentially assigns itself), there is in language from the very beginning, from the simple fact of the position (*Stellung*) of the speaking subject, every risk of mimesis. Hidden in it and always imminent there is the risk of *disinstallation* of the 'subject'. Whether we look at it from the side of *logos* or from the side of *lexis*,

mimesis is always related to the pre-inscription of the 'subject' in language (Lacoue-Labarthe, *Typography*, p. 133).

It is precisely the distinction between what Weimann perceives as the 'materiality' of institutions, and the post-structuralist claim that language is an originary 'material practice' that he sets out to clarify in *Author's Pen and Actor's Voice*. Here he begins by accepting 'the Saussurian maxim that difference is a condition of meaning', but he resists Derridean *différance* on the grounds that it is too absolute to cater for cases where 'the discontinuity of texts and institutions is an issue', and he wants to re-establish the principle of 'agency' as a feature of collectivities rather than the contingent effects of subjectivity:

> In their materiality, institutions like the early modern theatre are subject to discursive as well as non-discursive circumstances; their workings are dominated by parameters of profit, desire, production, consumption, and power – practices that constitute, and are served by, agencies (*Author's Pen*, p. 13).

In an institution like the Elizabethan popular theatre, founded on the 'formidable compulsion [...] to become and behave like something else', *representation* is bound up with *presentation*, and it is the task of scholarship to tease out 'sites of cultural authority, sources of pleasure and knowledge that derive from the interaction, even the intersubjectivity, of several agencies engaged in acts of communication' (13). These sites involve the emergent figure of 'the author' whose future is entwined with the development of printing, and the evolution of individualism. It is not difficult to see how the 'author's pen' assumes an authority, beloved of literary biographers, whose personal experience in certain circumstances, comes to be regarded as the *fons et origo* of his representations. At the other extreme is the presentational 'actor's voice', deploying a complexly over-determined art that produces an alternative 'authority'. The Elizabethan actor's commitment to the spoken word discloses the tendency of representation to conceal what Weimann calls 'the hardness of things, the irreducible and the inexpressible, in short the non- representable dimension of existence'.[25] Following first Benjamin, and Adorno, Weimann observes that "[t]he mimetic substratum of most representational practices goes hand in hand with a move of going outside of ourselves', a move that 'constitutes a "non-conceptual affinity between what is individually brought forth [in the text or art work] and its Other"' ('Representation and Mimesis', pp. 2–3). It is precisely this 'doubleness' that Weimann seeks to explore in the institution of the Elizabethan and early Jacobean theatre, what he identifies as 'a duplication (and in female roles, triplication) of disguise' that 'foregrounds its ultimate agency in the work of the actor ... the depth of the resulting ambivalence, the vibrant display of doubleness betwixt word and show, can best be conceived on the threshold of, and through the interplay between 'textual authority and performative agency' (*Author's Pen*, p. 65). The *heteroglossia* that he reconstructs active beneath the surface of represented 'character' also owes something to Bakhtin's economies of discourse, to Benjamin's account of Brecht's *Verfremdungseffekt* as an interruption of 'the gest', and, through that, to Brecht's own admiration for the self-consciousness of the Elizabethan theatre.

To some extent this is a re-visitation of the question of the spatial division of the popular stage into *locus* and *platea*, although the context within which that division operates is now considerably enlarged. It would be a mistake, however, to accuse Weimann of a knee-jerk capitulation to vitalism, or to perceive in his enterprise a nostalgia for the professional 'player'. Indeed he declares that 'there is no need, in vindicating a centuries-old, lost tradition of playing, to minimise the achievements of the "personating" method that, forcefully or otherwise, prevailed'. Rather, for him, 'the task is to recover, to make visible again on our stages and in our studies, the mode of presentation, not to privilege it over any successful rival tradition', and it is the 'diversity' and 'contingency' of early modern performances that he seeks to reconstruct (*Author's Pen and Actor's Voice*, p. 136). In the case of a play like *Hamlet* where the business of 'playing' is paramount, 'two different projections of theatrical space: one – the antic – with an open, *platea*-like use of the stage-as-stage; the other – the representational – with a more or less localised scene dominated by the symbolic use of theatrical space'. Rather than formulate this in terms of a simple binary opposition, Weimann perceives the protagonist as 'the product of a new, brilliant mode of characterisation, but he is also deeply tinged by the theatrical process of both advancing and resisting the new self-contained mode of impersonation' (*Author's Pen and Actor's Voice*, pp. 169–70). This intricate interweaving of residual, dominant and emerging forms probes the presentational skills of the actor at the same time as it charts the representation itself, and the exposure of the resultant *heteroglossia* permits us to glimpse the various thresholds that the play persistently traverses. Whereas for representation, and particularly written representation, cultural authority resides within the author as agent, the final authority of performance is achieved 'in the exchange of cultural labour with the audience' (*Author's Pen and Actor's Voice*, p. 224). In Weimann's most recent book, *Prologues to Shakespeare* (2005), jointly authored with Douglas Bruster, detailed attention is turned to prologues and epilogues as modes of entry and exit from the stage representation that serve to bridge this gap, and that raises important questions about the beginnings and endings of theatrical performance.

No overview can do full justice to the intricacy, and the inclusiveness of Weimann's arguments, nor to the density of his references. His style is characterised by an exponential but painstaking scholarly uncovering of the conditions of oral narrative, the labour of 'playing' and the techniques of characterisation, in short, the 'interplay between language and history, text and theatre' all of which open themselves to 'the all-important "part" of the audience' with the result that 'the authority of the text, as well as that of performance practice explodes in an acute crisis when, between them, the ultimate voice of authorisation, the cheering, hissing, clapping audience, finally declares itself' (*Author's Pen and Actor's Voice*, p. 225). Weimann's manner is not to confront what he calls 'the deconstructionist *dis*linkage between the signifier and the world', but to suggest that 'the early modern commercial playhouse is apt to refer beyond itself' in such a way as to undermine the Derridean conception of *différance*. In this way Weimann both recognises the operations of language and the generation of meanings, while at the same time respecting the material world whose complex agencies texts mediate. It is no accident that Weimann's enquiries should continually return, time after time, to the vexed question of *mimesis* and to the intractable problems that they pose for the theatre historian, the textual scholar, and the literary theoretician. It is also no accident that his arguments persistently cross the theoretical gaps between post-structuralist conceptions of subjectivity and their installation in the mechanisms of language on the one hand, and the complex material overdeterminations of human agency that inform language and particular fields of discourse. Weimann's careful uncovering and assembly of the institutional intricacies of the Elizabethan and early Jacobean public theatre, his congenial engagements with some of the most pressing theoretical issues of our time, and his exemplary intellectual generosity evident in his productive debates and collaborations with younger scholars, continues to demonstrate that a vibrant, supple, unapologetically Marxist epistemology, remains a formidably effective intellectual lens through which to scrutinise the most important challenges facing the discipline of English Studies in the twenty-first century.

Notes

1. I wish to thank Professor Catherine Belsey of the Centre for Critical and Cultural Theory at the University of Cardiff for having read and commented on an earlier version of this eassay, which appeared in *Shakespeare Studies* 26 (1998). I wish to thank the editors, Leeds Barroll and Susan Zimmerman for permission to reprint material that first appeared in this journal.
2. Jacques Derrida, *Specters of Marx* (New York and London, 1994), p. 50.
3. Cf. Francis Fukuyama, *The End of History and the Last Man* (London, 1992), pp. 44–51.
4. Robert Weimann, 'The Soul of the Age: Towards a Historical Approach to Shakespeare', *Shakespeare in a Changing World*, ed. Arnold Kettle (London, 1964), p. 17.
5. Robert Weimann, *Shakespeare and the Popular Tradition in the Theater: Studies in the Social Dimension of Dramatic Form and Function*, ed., Robert Schwartz (Baltimore and London, 1978), p. xii.

6. *Popular Tradition*: 'these techniques helped to define and achieve a social and artistic position more comprehensive and more vital in the areas of both its independence and its relatedness, its skepticism and its freedom'.
7. Robert Weimann, *Author's Pen and Actor's Voice: Playing and Writing in Shakespeare's Theatre*, ed. Helen Higbee and William West (Cambridge, 2000), p. 208.
8. Robert Weimann, *Structure and Society in Literary History: Studies in the History and Theory of Historical Criticism* (London, 1976), p. 23.
9. Stephen Greenblatt, *Learning to Curse: Essays in Early Modern Culture* (New York and London, 1990), p. 167.
10. Jacques Derrida, *Acts of Literature*, ed. Derek Attridge (New York and London, 1992), p. 63.
11. Robert Weimann, 'Society and the Individual in Shakespeare's Conception of Character', *Shakespeare Survey*, 34 (Cambridge, 1981), ed. Stanley Wells, p. 25. Cf. Jonathan Dollimore, *Radical Tragedy: Religion, Ideology and Power in the Drama of Shakespeare and His Contemporaries*, 2nd edition (New York and London, 1989), pp. 70–1ff.
12. Ernesto Laclau, *Emancipation(s)* (London and New York, 1996), pp. 16–17.
13. Robert Weimann, *Structure and Society in Literary History*, Expanded edition (Baltimore and London, 1984), p. 287.
14. Robert Weimann, *Structure and Society in Literary History: Studies in the History and Theory of Historical Criticism*, Expanded edition (Baltimore and London, 1984), p. 309.
15. Robert Weimann, 'Mimesis in *Hamlet*', *Shakespeare and the Question of Theory*, ed. Patricia Parker and Geoffrey Hartman (New York and London, 1985), pp. 275–6.
16. Fredric Jameson, *The Political Unconscious: Narrative as a Socially Symbolic Act* (London, 1981), p. 35.
17. Robert Weimann, 'Towards a Literary Theory of Ideology: Mimesis, Representation, Authority', *Shakespeare Reproduced: The Text in History and Ideology*, ed. Jean E. Howard and Marion F. O'Connor (New York and London, 1987), p. 266.
18. 'Shakespeare (De)Canonizedm', p. 67. Cf. Jurgen Habermas, *The Theory of Communicative Action: The Critique of Functionalist Reason*, trans., Thomas Mc Carthy (Cambridge, 1987), Vol. 2, pp. 68–70.
19. Ernesto Laclau, *Emancipation(s)*, p. 17.
20. Robert Weimann, *Authority and Representation in Early Modern Discourse*, ed. David Hillman (Baltimore and London, 1996), p. 7.
21. *Authority and Representation*, p. 5. But cf. also, *Subject and Object in Renaissance Culture*, ed. Margreta de Grazia, Maureen Quilligan, and Peter Stallybrass (Cambridge, 1996), p. 5: 'The very ambiguity of the word "ob-ject", that which is *thrown before*, suggests a more dynamic status for the object. Reading "ob" as "before" allows us to assign the object a prior status, suggesting its temporal, spatial, and even causal *coming before*. The word could thus be made to designate the potential priority of the object. So defined, the term renders more apparent the way material things – land clothes, tools – might constitute subjects who in turn own, use and transform them. The form/matter relation of Aristotelian metaphysics is thereby provisionally reversed: it is the material object that impresses its texture and contour upon the noumenal subject. And this reversal is curiously upheld by the ambiguity of the word "sub-ject", that which is *thrown under*, in this case- in order to receive an imprint." This argument attempts to explode the connection between "the subject" and the Foucauldian "sovereignty of consciousness"

at the expense of the object. What is not clear in the Introduction to this volume is the extent to which objects here designated are what Bataille would call "raw phenomena". (Georges Bataille, 'Materialism', *Visions of Excess: Selected Writings 1927–1939*, ed. Alan Stoekl (Manchester, 1985), pp. 15–16. See also Martin Heidegger 'The Age of the World Picture', *The Question Concerning Technology and Other Essays*, trans. William Lovitt (New York, 1977), p. 128 for a gloss on the term 'subject' which is diametrically opposed to that of de Grazia, Quilligan, and Stallybrass. In concerning himself primarily with the process of *representation* Weimann neatly circumvents this complex issue, although it is one of which he is very much aware.

22. 'The Age of the World Picture', pp. 129–30. For Heidegger, to represent (*vorstellen*) 'means to bring what is present at hand [das *Vorhandene*] before oneself as standing over against, to relate it to oneself, to the one representing it, and to force it back into this relationship to oneself as the normative realm. Wherever this happens, man 'gets himself into the picture' in precedence over what is. But in that man puts himself into the picture in this way, he puts himself into the scene, i.e. into the open sphere of that which is generally and publicly represented. Therewith man sets himself up as the setting in which whatever is must henceforth set itself forth, must present itself [*sich ... prasentieren*], i.e. be picture. Man becomes the representative [*der Reprasentant*] of that which is, in the sense of that which has the character of object' (pp. 131–2).
23. *Authority and Representation*, 131–2, citing Agnew, p. 179.
24. Michel Foucault, *History of Sexuality Vol. 1*, trans. Robert Hurley (Harmondsworth, 1981), pp. 100ff.
25. 'Introduction: Representation and Mimesis: Towards a New Theory', pp. 1–2.

Works cited

Agnew, Jean Christophe. *Worlds Apart: the Market and the Theater in Anglo-American Thought*. Cambridge: Cambridge University Press, 1986.

Anderson, Perry. *In the Tracks of Historical Materialism: The Wellek Library Lectures*. London, 1983.

Battaille, Georges. 'Materialism', *Visions of Excess: Selected Writings 1927–1939*. Ed. Alan Stoekl. Manchester, 1985.

de Grazia, Margreta, Maureen Quilligan, and Peter Stallybrass, eds. *Subject and Object in Renaissance Culture*. Cambridge: Cambridge University Press, 1996.

Derrida, Jacques. *Acts of Literature*. Ed. Derek Attridge. New York and London, 1992.

———. *Specters of Marx: The State of the Debt, the Work of Mourning, and the New International*. Trans. Peggy Kamuf. New York and London, 1994.

Dollimore, Jonathan. *Radical Tragedy: Religion, Ideology and Power in the Drama of Shakespeare and His Contemporaries*, 2nd edition. New York and London, 1989.

Foucault, Michel. *The Archaeology of Knowledge*. Trans. A.M. Sheridan Smith. London, 1972.

———. *History of Sexuality*, Vol. 1. Trans. Robert Hurley. Harmondsworth, 1981.

Fukuyama, Francis. *The End of History and the Last Man*. London, 1992.

Greenblatt, Stephen. *Learning to Curse: Essays in Early Modern Culture*. New York and London, 1990.

Habermas, Jürgen. *The Theory of Communicative Action: The Critique of Functionalist Reason*. Vol. 2. Trans. Thomas McCarthy. Cambridge, 1987.

Heidegger, Martin. 'The Age of the World Picture'. *The Question Concerning Technology and Other Essays*. Trans. William Lovitt. New York, 1977.
Jameson, Fredric. *The Political Unconscious: Narrative as a Socially Symbolic Act*. London, 1981.
Laclau, Ernesto. *Emancipation(s)*. London and New York, 1996.
Lacoue-Labarthe, Philippe. *Typography: Mimesis, Philosophy, Politics*. Trans. Christopher Fynsk. Stanford, 1998.
Weimann, Robert. *Authority and Representation in Early Modern Discourse*. Ed. David Hillman. Baltimore and London, 1996.
——. *Author's Pen and Actor's Voice: Playing and Writing in Shakespeare's Theatre*. Ed. Helen Higbee and William West. Cambridge: Cambridge University Press, 2000.
——. 'Introduction: Representation and Mimesis: Towards a New Theory'. *Symbolism: An International Annual of Critical Aesthetics* 6 (2004): 1–33.
——. 'Mimesis in *Hamlet*'. In *Shakespeare and the Question of Theory*. Ed. Patricia Parker and Geoffrey Hartman. New York and London, 1985.
——. ' "Moralize Two Meanings" in One Play: Divided Authority on the Medieval Stage'. *Medievalia* 18 (1995): 427–50.
——. *Shakespeare and the Popular Tradition in the Theater: Studies in the Social Dimension of Dramatic Form and Function*. Ed. Robert Schwartz. Baltimore and London, 1978.
——. 'Shakespeare (De)Canonized: Conflicting Uses of "Authority" and "Representation." ' *New Literary History* 20 (1988–89): 65–81.
——. 'Society and the Individual in Shakespeare's Conception of Character', *Shakespeare Survey* 34 (1981): 23–31.
——. 'The Soul of the Age: Towards a Historical Approach to Shakespeare'. *Shakespeare in a Changing World*. Ed. Arnold Kettle. London, 1964.
——. *Structure and Society in Literary History: Studies in the History and Theory of Historical Criticism*. London, 1976.
——. *Structure and Society in Literary History*, Expanded edition. Baltimore and London, 1984.
——. 'Textual Authority and Performative Agency: The Uses of Disguise in Shakespeare's Theatre'. *New Literary History* 25 (1994): 789–808.
——. 'Thresholds to Memory and Commodity in Shakespeare's Endings', *Representations* 53 (1996): 1–20.
——. 'Towards a Literary Theory of Ideology: Mimesis, Representation, Authority'. In *Shakespeare Reproduced: The Text in History and Ideology*. Eds Jean E. Howard and Marion F. O'Connor. New York and London, 1987.

Part III
Creatures Sitting at a Play: The Authority and Representation of Audiences

9
Homo Clausus at the Theatre
David Hillman

Among the many far-reaching changes European culture underwent in the course of the sixteenth and seventeenth centuries, one of the most fundamental was the shift in the way in which the human body was understood: one predominant notion of human embodiment, in which the body was thought of as open in a positive manner, was gradually being displaced by a radically different one, which involved a significantly more closed ideal of the body – more bounded, more deeply separated from its surroundings and from other people. In conceptualising this shift it may be difficult for us fully to imagine the first view, since our post-Enlightenment assumptions are so dominated by the second: we tend to take for granted the notion that the human body constitutes a more or less sealed unit (orifices notwithstanding). After Harvey and Descartes and Locke, we tend to treat the body, in the words of the philosopher John Sutton, as 'a solid container, only rarely breached, in principle autonomous from culture and environment, tampered with only by diseases and experts.'[1] I want to point out, first, some places where this shift from the first to the second construction of embodiment can be seen; I then want to suggest that this collision, and the emergence of what Norbert Elias has termed *homo clausus*, were essential to the rise of early modern drama.

The period during which this drama flourished was marked, as numerous scholars have argued, by multiple social, economic and epistemological crises – a widespread sense of radical instability born of being on the cusp of the monumental shifts that marked the transition to modernity.[2] Faultlines of doubt had opened up in almost every sphere of life, inducing what Stephen Mullaney has described as 'a collective vertigo' in early modern England.[3] One can imagine this vertigo to have been, among other things, quite literal – which is to say, corporeal: these faultlines in notions of faith and identity, and the associated feelings of perplexity and confusion, may not have been divorced from a loss of somatic bearings, and concomitantly from significantly changing attitudes to the notion of embodiment – attitudes about the relation of mind and body, affect and body, body and world.

Elaine Scarry argues that 'when there is within a society a crisis of belief, that is, when some central idea or ideology or cultural construct has ceased to elicit a population's belief [...] the sheer material factualness of the human body will be borrowed to lend that cultural construct the aura of "realness" and "certainty."'[4] But what happens when that construct has itself everything to do with the human body, when the old ideology is centrally about the aura of the body itself? The very word, 'crisis,' like so many others during this period, was undergoing a crisis of its own, a process of metaphorisation from its specific sixteenth-century medical sense, 'the turning-point of a disease for better or worse,' to its more abstract modern meaning, a little less than a century later.[5] Words and their users were going through a crisis *of* disembodiment, so that 'the sheer material factualness of the human body' could no longer be counted on, in and of itself, to lend a grounding to new ideologies. The body was losing its ontological standing of primacy and having to struggle, as it were, in the realms of epistemology – a position from which it has never recovered. One could almost say that, gradually forfeiting its aura of presence or givenness, the body now had to defend *itself*, and – in the case of early modern England – what was turned to in these circumstances was the fantasy of a clearly defined boundary between the 'inside' and the 'outside.' In such a context we might amend Scarry's formula and say that during periods of extreme instability in a society's (as in a person's) self-identity, a regression often takes place to a defensive insistence on an absolute inner – outer gap – and the insistence will be strident in proportion to the depth of the crisis; indeed, such stridency could be seen to be a sure symptom of a profound crisis in a belief system. The extreme sense of vulnerability inherent to such periods tends to bring with it an urgent desire for reaffirmation of one's own boundaries, of the imagined original contours of the self. As Jean Starobinski argues: 'Endangered by the hidden design he suspects before him, the individual seeks to protect his own frontiers; he sees to it that the barriers under his control are closed – barriers within which his life remains safe.'[6] It is as if at the most acute transitional periods (in our lives, in history), faced with the fear of the unknown, what we tend to focus on are the transitional areas of our own (personal, national, symbolic) bodies.

Early modern medical explanations of the effect of fear on the body make clear this sense of the vulnerability of the borders of the body. In almost all Renaissance physiological theory, fear and extreme grief were thought to cause the vital spirits to rush from the extremities back to 'the labouring heart' (*2 Henry VI*, 3.2.162); this was what caused one to look pale at such times. The following excerpt – to take just one example – is about the effects of the plague, but its description of the body's reaction to a crisis could be referring to a reaction to any feared external threat:

> From the heart proceed [...] vitall spirits, whereby man is made active and courageous. If they by feare be inforced to retire inward, the outward parts

be left infirme [...] so that as enemies easily scale the walles of a towne abandonned by souldiers; so the Plague [...] doth find readie passage into the outward parts of a man [...] feare (adversarie to faith) pulleth to the wicked the evill which he feareth.[7]

There is nothing unusual about this passage – similar descriptions of physiological symptoms associated with fear (and diametrically opposite descriptions of the physiological effects of joy as flooding the extremities with spirits or blood) are commonplace in this period. Evident here is an understanding of the emotions as intimately linked not only to the body but more specifically to the movement of bodily fluids inward and outward, in particular when an external agent – an other – threatens some form of invasion (or, conversely, a promise of containment). A picture of the bodily contours of scepticism '(adversarie to faith)' is concretely illustrated here – the way a focus on the purported distance and difference between the interior and the exterior ends up, in trying to protect the self, leaving the 'barriers within which [...] life remains safe' peculiarly vulnerable; as if the body of the sceptic, through a kind of somatic irony, is destined to bring upon itself 'the evill which he feareth.'

In terms of what Louis Montrose calls 'the historical specificity of psychological processes,' the English Renaissance was a period during which the never less than anxious relation between inside and outside was especially fraught, and, side by side with this, recourse to the body's visceral or symbolic interior evident everywhere.[8] Anne Ferry has traced the rise of a new vocabulary of 'inwardness' in the language of early modern England, as well as a development of literary genres particularly apt for the expression of the emergent forms of interiority.[9] 'In late sixteenth- and early seventeenth-century England,' Katharine Maus has written, 'the sense of discrepancy between "inward disposition" and "outward appearance" seems unusually urgent and consequential for a very large number of people.'[10] If the period ushered in a shift away from the notion of the embodied nature of the self, it was a move that paradoxically could not do without the body as the essential other of this new self, for modern interiority depends heavily on the perceived gap between the 'spiritual' inner and 'corporeal' outer; as Anthony Dawson puts it, 'the body is instrumental in delivering a sense of interiority, one that is constructed in and *through* the separation between inner and outer, self and body.'[11]

The transformations involved in these separations have a long, complex and uneven progress, proceeding (as in all such matters) by fits and starts; but that a transition from a more open or 'ecological' mode of inhabiting the body to a more bounded or closed one was taking place during the sixteenth and seventeenth centuries in Northern Europe seems to me indisputable. We might think of the earlier modality as depending on a notion of the human body as just one more layering in the multiple concentric forms of nature;

of the later one as relying on an idea of the body as far more individuated, monadic, defined over against the outside world.¹² This is what, for example, Jorge Arditi seems to imply in speaking of a medieval reality 'of interwoven selves and bodies and of a more immediate relation between self and nature [...] a reality, that is, of selves and bodies embedded in one another and in nature.'¹³ Arditi describes a relative 'absence of corporeal boundaries in medieval societies,' and characterises 'the collective self of ecclesias' during the Middle Ages as existing in 'a fundamental condition of fusion.'¹⁴ His argument relies in part on the work of Mikhail Bakhtin, who has described the pre-sixteenth-century body as conforming to a grotesque, open, non-individuated image, one which was gradually replaced by a new bodily canon which 'carefully removed [...] all the signs of [the body's] inner life' – a process which culminated in an image of the body as insular, based on 'the individual, strictly limited mass, the impenetrable façade.'¹⁵

In Elias' formulation, *homo clausus* is a being 'severed from all other people and things "outside" by the "wall" of the body.'¹⁶ Through the course of the sixteenth and seventeenth centuries, in a wide variety of fields, there is an increasingly strict demarcation of the interior of the human body as separate from and problematically related to the exterior world. When, therefore, we find early moderns referring to the porousness of bodies and the accessibility of various kinds of interiors, we need to consider whether the emphasis is on an embracing of the osmosis of self and environment or a far more problematic attitude – whether nostalgic or repudiatory. Are, for example, 'the natural gates and alleys of the body' (*Hamlet*, 1.5.67) – its orifices and pores – spoken of as valuable points of passage or dangerous loci of vulnerability? One might similarly interrogate the manner in which the body's containment is characterised: is the skin a positive, protective element – as for example the flesh-like wall surrounding Spenser's Castle of Alma, 'all so faire, and sensible withal' (*Faerie Queene*, 2.9.21.3) – or does it create a sense of imprisonment or claustrophobia creep in? Generally speaking, the more clamorous the declarations of openness, the less we can believe that it is in fact taken for granted, and the more closed the body-*ideal* may therefore be. Too much protestation upon the accessibility of the interior can thus be understood as evidence of the pressure under which we find the 'environmental' notion of the self.

Elias – following Bakhtin – describes the ways in which the 'civilising' and 'disciplining' of the body during the sixteenth century – the new norms of self-control, non-tactile interaction, and politeness – led to an inhibition of external manifestations of the interior. These disciplines, he writes, 'interpose[d] themselves more sternly than ever before between spontaneous and emotional impulses, on the one hand, and the skeletal muscles, on the other'; thus arose 'the notion of the individual "ego" in its locked case, the "self" divided by an invisible wall from what happens "outside." '¹⁷ Peter Stallybrass's seminal analysis of 'the body enclosed' and Gail Kern Paster's detailed work on the mobile thresholds of embarrassment in early modern England emphasise the fact that it was first and foremost the female body that was constructed as needing greater closure; but the perception of the dangers of somatic openness gradually came to encompass everybody.[18] Such (non-linear but nonetheless inexorable) transformations in the socio-cultural body were paralleled by changes in religious, national, architectural, philosophical, and, especially, medical-physiological spheres. Above all, this involved the transition from a humoral model of the body to the circulatory one which gradually displaced and indeed finally eviscerated it. I believe that Harvey's 'discovery' of the circulation of the blood should be understood as at once symptom and cause of the new ideology of somatic closure – the 'discovery' comes from and contributes to what we could almost refer to as an emergent 'claustrophilic' world-view. Harvey's circulatory body represents a radically new image of the body as a closed system – more self-contained, less permeable than its Galenic predecessor: the body, so to speak, has been taken out of circulation. Alongside this, the old physiological understanding of sensory activity (such as sight and hearing) as based upon something (eye-beams, rays) entering and leaving the interior of the body was changing to fit in with a much less permeable model of the way the body naturally works.

The new post-environmental notion increasingly defined health not in terms of positive osmosis with the outside world but rather in terms of control over the relations between that world and the interior. We could give 1546 as a symbolic inaugural date for this new concept – the year Girolamo Fracastoro published his revolutionary thesis *On Contagion*;[19] coming just three years after the publication of Andreas Vesalius' *De Humanis Corporis Fabrica*, this text could be ranked alongside the more famous anatomical treatise as breaking radical ground in the move towards a new notion of human embodiment. Indeed, the astonishing prominence of anatomical dissection (and its attendant discourses) in the sixteenth and seventeenth centuries may be viewed as an index of the prevalence of the newfound idea of somatic closure: the intrusive appropriation implicit in anatomy conceptualises knowledge as lying beyond a boundary, within a closed body. From the mid-sixteenth century onwards, the medicalised body was opened up primarily in order to achieve access from without, rather than to allow egress (of harmful substances or excess humours) from within. Still, through much of the Renaissance the body's openness tends to be spoken of as a positively-inflected concept. As Michael Schoenfeldt has written, 'most illness in the [early modern] period is imagined to derive from the body's inability to rid itself of excess humours'; he cites, for instance, the sixteenth-century Dutch physician Levinus Lemnius, who writes approvingly that God created 'many wayes and passages to purge forth the humours, and to wash away the excrements, lest a man might be oppressed by the abundance of them.'[20] Similarly, the English doctor Tobias Venner writes that 'they that have their belly naturally loose and open [...] are not easily affected with sicknesse: whereas of the contrary, they that have the same bound up [...] have for the most part often conflicts with sicknesse.'[21] The idea of being 'naturally loose and open' has affinities with a sense of trust or faith in the environment, as the need to be 'bound up' literally embodies a more sceptical relation.[22] Gradually through the course of the early modern period trust in the environment seems to have diminished, and, correspondingly, disease became increasingly construed as originating outside the body.[23] Through the course of the early modern period, death became less and less a matter of what Phillipe Ariés describes as '[an eruption] out of the bodily envelope of the rottenness within,' and increasingly something which penetrated the body, attacking from without;[24] the body's permeability was thought of more often now as the source of danger, the threat as emanating from external agents: as James I's physician, Helkiah Crooke, put it, 'to death and diseases *we lie open on every side*.'[25] Jonathan Gil Harris argues that the period around the turn of the seventeenth century was marked by a heightened stress on 'the body's margins and orifices [...] as potential sites of infiltration':[26] the emphasis in medical theories on the importance of protection from external threat, rather than on the restoration of internal balance, played a major part in the emergence of ideas of hospitalisation and quarantine – indeed, of a whole practical and psychic structure of notions of discipline and control (of body *and* body politic) in the later Renaissance.

One may be tempted to understand such infiltration-anxieties as a matter of a gradual draining of confidence in the efficacy of the bodily container which had in earlier times felt more securely bordered. Margaret Healy has recently argued that 'by the late sixteenth century [...] the body's fleshy envelope was imagined to be so fragile and permeable that it seemed to provide very little protection against incursion by a panoply of "evil" enemy agents.'[27] I think, however, that this lack of confidence in the somatic container derives not so much from a sense of its fragility or loss of solidity as such as from a vastly increased sense of urgency regarding the *need* for inner and outer to be kept separate. That is to say: prior to this, things coming into and out of the body were generally accepted, *embraced* even, as part of our porous human nature – our being part of nature. By the late sixteenth century the inevitable permeability of the body had become a matter of high anxiety, a vulnerability to the invasions of 'evil agents' which, we could add – from the point of view of subjective embodiment – might be taken to include the objectifying, prying eyes of scientific knowledge.

Recent scholarship examining historical transformations in the role and understanding of skin from early modern times to the present lends support to this view, portraying 'an intensifying ideal of continence, in which the skin functions as the body's principle of self-possession' – a gradual move from a pre-Enlightenment way of thinking of the skin as 'an organ of interchange, or permeable membrane, traversable in two directions,'[28] 'a porous layer with a multitude of possible openings'[29] – to an idea of the skin as barrier, 'a two-dimensional and linear boundary surface';[30] these scholars perceive 'a general defensive closing of the pores [...] from the end of the medieval period until the nineteenth century' – a radical shift which did away with idea of the skin as a therapeutic organ and aimed instead 'to achieve a static condition of closure rather than a "multidimensional" traffic of substances and qualities.'[31]

The drive to achieve such stasis or closure can be discerned in other areas of the early modern world. Demarcating the boundaries between the 'inner' and the 'outer' became a significant impulse in, for example, the increased emphasis on national boundaries, on the borders of the body politic, as well as the massive growth in practices of land enclosure and the new penal arrangements in what Foucault calls the 'carceral society.'[32] Similarly, one cannot separate the emergence of new kinds of private spaces – 'closets,' 'privies,' inner 'cabinets,' and other sanctuaries for the sequestration of the self[33] – from the somatic trend I have been highlighting (call it a move towards home clausus); the emergence of new notions of privacy and intimacy is the flipside of the anxiety associated with the attempt to keep inside and outside strictly apart.[34] These new spaces are architectural concomitants (even perhaps reinscriptions) of the closure of the body (and the commonplace Renaissance analogy between the body and the house lends support to this idea). These, I would contend, are all connected in the cultural imagination of the time: the loci of the emergence of early modern subjectivity, like the subject him or herself, grow steadily more and more enclosed.

This loss of transparency, the perception of an 'invisible wall' between the inside and the outside of the body – 'as if this flesh which walls about our life / Were brass impregnable' (*Richard II*, 3.2.167–8) – is in good measure an invention of the Renaissance, one without which it is hard to imagine the concept of the disciplined, privatised individual. It is by the same token inseparable from the interiorising movement of Protestantism, with its emphasis on inner conviction and private prayer. As several critics have recently argued, the Reformation highlighted the gap between material sign and invisible reality, inculcating a distrust of externals and a corresponding turn away from physical signs towards inner conviction.[35] The links between the Reformation and *homo clausus*, though complex and elusive, are undeniable. Faith, no longer as communal – or as physical – an act as it had been, now increasingly came to be based on a direct communication between the spiritualised human interior and the divine. What the Reformation dispensed with can be described, from this perspective, as somatic transitionality or bodily openness. The rejection of the sacrament of the Eucharist, the denial of Purgatory (the very word derives of course from an idea of somatic openness), the suppression of relics, the virulent debates regarding possession and exorcism, the arguments about the reality of stigmata, even the abandonment of Catholic sacraments of anointing with holy unguent – all these may perhaps be seen, from a corporeal point of view, as being in part disputes about notions of the openness of human bodies.[36] The wounded or otherwise open corpus of Christ now became a near-obsessional topic of sermons, religious poetry, and visual iconography, as if Doubting Thomases everywhere suddenly needed confirmation of his divinity. This lavish attention to Christ's permeability may be taken as a sign of a *loss* of certainty about access to the divine interior. No longer could this access be taken for granted. If Christ's offering of himself as bread and wine, to be incorporated literally into the bodies of the believers, is the central symbol in Christianity of the mutuality of access to the interior of the body of the other, one could say that part of the quarrel between Catholicism and Protestantism is around this problem of the material availability of the human interior to the divine or demonic Other. And one could generalise that after the Reformation, the accessibility of the interior of the believer's body could no longer be taken for granted. From this perspective, Protestantism may be said to resituate faith from a relation between the inside and the outside to the interior self.

If we accept this idea, we might briefly reconsider the much-debated issue of the precise location of Martin Luther's great moment of illumination – the moment which brought him the fundamental understanding of the doctrine of justification by faith: 'This knowledge the Holy Spirit gave me on the privy in the tower,' he famously declared.[37] Generations of commentators have strenuously denied that this statement should be allowed to bear any weight in the history of the Reformation. The psychoanalyst Norman O. Brown was perhaps the first to accord Luther's placement of the event any deep significance, arguing that 'it is Luther's grossly concrete image of the anal character of the devil that made the privy the appropriate scene for his critical religious experience. [...] Protestantism was born in the temple of the Devil, and it found God again in extremest alienation from God.'[38] But we can add to this, or vary this, in light of what I am suggesting about the link between Protestantism and the problematisation of the body's openness. If indeed Protestantism defined itself in part in opposition to the somatic transitionality of the Catholic faith, then Luther's enlightenment-in-the-privy is neither insignificant nor a personal obsession or pathology, but intimately tied to a historically-conditioned sensibility inseparable from the emergence of homo clausus.

The loss of faith-based access to the interior of the body went hand in hand with the growth of a new, more intrusive kind of access – the empirical access of the anatomist; and this practice, in turn, was one of the major contributing factors to the waning of an analogy-based view of the world. Science (and above all in this period, anatomy) was rapidly putting paid to the notion of a concrete correspondence between the cosmos and the 'little world of man'; now no longer could the microcosmic body be imagined to be materially continuous with the macrocosmic world; no longer did each part of the body reflect the elements, the signs of the zodiac, the planets, the hierarchy of the entire cosmos. While science, the microscope and the telescope were opening new vistas on the cosmos, and the Renaissance idea of 'man' as infinite possibility gained widespread credence, this same 'man' became increasingly cut off – both from a powerful sense of access to and by God, and from the surrounding cosmos. Somatically and ontologically more isolated than ever before, the human being was becoming an increasingly closed system.

* * *

Elizabethan drama can in part be understood to be an outgrowth of and an ambivalent reaction to these changing modes of embodiment in the early modern world. We can see the rise of the theatre as profoundly linked both to the ongoing processes of corporeal enclosure (and the corresponding creation of a new sense of interiority) *and* to a resistance to these processes (and a vital restitution of corporeal openness). The new drama seems to have thrived upon the contest between open and closed notions of embodiment; it worked both with and against the complex process of corporeal closure which gave 'form and pressure' to 'the very age and body of the time,' reconnecting – *even as it separated* – inner and outer. The purpose of playing cannot be unconnected to this somato-cultural context. To be more precise: it is the *transitionality*, the extreme instability, of the notion of embodiment that seems to me crucial to the existence of this theatre – the *tension* between a closed and an open idea of the body. Nietzsche claimed that tragic drama is born at the meeting-place of the Apollonian and the Dionysian, the principles of individuation and of unity. 'The Birth of Tragedy' occurs where the Apollonian imperative – 'the delimiting of the boundaries of the individual' – comes up against the Dionysian – 'a surrender [...or] shattering of individuality.'[39] Of course, the two are always in some sort of dialectic or equipoise, in any individual or culture, but there are moments in (individual and cultural) history where the tension is particularly marked, and particularly acute in relation to the body – when the clash between the two, and their somatic associations of openness and closure, creates a new cultural form.[40]

By way of digression, it is interesting to note a certain parallel which can be drawn between classical Greece and early modern England – two salient periods and locations for the thriving of drama in European history. It could be argued that the transitions in the sense of embodiment in Greece, circa the fifth century BC were comparable (though of course not in any precise way) to those of England, circa 1600; and that the emergent Renaissance humanistic ideal of the classical body harks back to the earlier culture's somatic ideals and values, glimpsed in, for example, ancient Greek sculpture. 'Classical Greece,' writes Steven Connor, 'seems to have maintained a strong conception of the inviolability of the body, as guaranteed by the smooth and immaculate skin.'[41] Is it no more than coincidence that both cultures can be imagined as growing 'thick-skinned' in the periods leading up to the efflorescence of the stage? And that it was at around the same period in classical Greece that notions of catharsis and of mimesis – and indeed of selfhood – were apparently beginning to shift away from the body and towards more disembodied ideals?[42]

Early modern theatre played with the idea of trying to construct seamless somatic enclosure through the medium of bodily re-opening. While at the *representational* level we find repeatedly on the early modern stage characters attempting – and, crucially, failing – to keep inner and outer strictly separate, at the level of *presentation* (of the activity of the theatre itself, and at a meta-theatrical level) what is enacted is a (necessarily limited) crossing of bodily (and other) thresholds. The exhibition – the performative or presentational dimension – keeps undoing the inhibition that is represented and is associated with the characters' interiority. At the same time there are powerful complicities between the two, and it is worth remembering both that the presentational level demands somatic closure in order for any mimesis to exist, and that the audience's empathy with the represented characters relies upon some degree of openness to them.[43] The fictional striving towards somatic closure involves the depiction of the extravagantly opened bodies of the early modern stage – 'out of joint,' dismembered, tortured, pierced, raped, flayed; in general: spectacularly destroyed. These can be understood as signifiers of the pressure (to be closed) under which the body was placed during this period. The bodies here are not open bodies, they are open*ed*, like bodies in anatomy theatres; the analogy is hardly new – but it is important to recognise that what takes place in the anatomy theatre at the presentational level is re-enacted at the representational level in the theatre. The end-point of this pressure is depicted most starkly by the 'monumental alablaster' of Desdemona's suffocated body, or by the 'marmorialisation' of Hermione; but it is visible everywhere on the Renaissance stage, coupling a profound loss of transparency – a sense of the inaccessibility of other people – with a new kind of corporeal isolation. The Ghost of Old Hamlet may be taken as the father-figure, the pattern, of this closure, his death-throes symbolically the birth-pangs of *homo clausus*: his formerly open body, which is described as having easily and rapidly let in the poison, is now enclosed in a tetter, 'barked about,' even his returning spirit encased in 'complete steel.' This instantiates the moment when the more positive spin on the body's openness becomes negatively valorised: *ecce homo clausus*. It is striking that it is the closing of the paternal body that institutes the commencement of the regime of interiority – the founding moment of modern subjectivity, so often associated with *Hamlet* – is the moment the body is shut up, confined in solitude; when the subject can declare that he has 'that within which passes show.' Similarly, *Othello* can be said to *stage* (and simultaneously diagnose) the transition from (call it) *homo agoricus* to *homo clausus* ('my unhoused free condition / Put into circumscription and confine' – 1.2.26–27). It is partly for this reason that the play has become such a central test-case for many of the recent studies of early modern subjectivity. The disembodied inwardness of the future, along with the depth-effects of the new interiorised subject, depend upon the arrival onstage of *homo clausus* – which is to say, of a new kind of solitary confinement in the body.

But this drama is of course far more than a didactic tool in the service of the new decorum, holding the flat surface of the mirror up to nature: its vitality relies crucially upon the re-opening as well as the closing of the body. Indeed, the enclosure is always in a dialectic relation to the disclosure: *homo clausus* and *homo ludens* are closely linked. This is in part a matter – at the representational level – of showing either the consequences or the failure of closure; that is to say, in the tragic vein: death, isolation, a rejection of empathy and indeed of any true human connection; or in the comic key: either festive release (where, as C.L. Barber puts it, 'the body and its environment interpenetrate'[44]) or a more exclusionary type of comedy, in which the desire for closure – Malvolio's, Duke Vincentio's, etc. – is mocked. In so much Renaissance drama, as in the anatomy theatres, the body is fully substantiated only in its aperture – its destruction or its embarrassment. The period's tragedies tear apart the flesh of their protagonists; its comedies make merciless fun of the ways in which characters aspire in vain to a classical, decorous body. In either case, pride in the body's imagined closure and self-sufficiency precedes a fall. It is as if the historical closure of the body – a crucial step on the path towards the Cartesian separation from 'mind' or 'soul' – has gone *too far*; as if theatre, while at one level pushing this separation further than it had ever been, at another level provides a kind of safety-valve to relieve the pressure placed upon the body to be shut. One might say, without wanting to adhere too strictly to generic categories, that if the tragic muse's *thanatos* attempts (in vain) to suppress the body's incapacity to respect boundaries, the comic spirit of *eros* depends upon an embracing of the body's desire to go beyond itself; the latter is, we could say, a kind of 'anti-enclosure riot' (a frequent enough occurrence in England in the 1590s). This is loosely correlated with an emphasis in comedy on the grotesque or 'orificial' body's natural openings, in tragedy on a 'carnal, bloody, and unnatural' (*Hamlet*, 5.2.387) forcing open of the 'artificially' classicised body – in the former it is the shamefully *open* body, in the latter of the violently *opened* body, that is being staged. One can view this from a comic point of view – how ridiculous our desire for closure can seem, how pleasurable aperture can be; or from a tragic one – how much suffering is involved in learning that we are anything but enclosed. They are surely not that different ['*Exit, pursued by a bear* ...'].

But it is above all through its medium (rather than its content) that early modern theatre reinstates somatic transitionality. For theatrical mimesis takes for granted the subject's openness to the external world – it presupposes that the actor can enter into another's character and body (though not fully), and that the audience can be corporeally affected by what is happening onstage (though not irrevocably). The 'faulty' or damaged bodies onstage are to be taken as mirrors of the audience's own potentially permeable bodies, and we can take as one kind of evidence of this the very fact of our interest in and capacity to be moved by what is happening onstage. Actor and spectator alike must be both inside the order of representation and outside it simultaneously, balancing their belief and scepticism through, among other things, the potential openness and closure of their own bodies.[45] Elin Diamond has described theatrical mimesis as 'impossibly double' – 'simultaneously the stake and shifting sands, order and disorder': theatre may be 'understood as a symptomatic cultural site that ruthlessly maps out normative spectatorial positions by occluding its own means of production'; at the same time, it is utterly reliant on 'drama's unruly body, its material other.'[46] This dual purpose of theatre is related to a duality in the use of theatrical space – to the different uses of *locus* and *platea*, as Robert Weimann has done more than anyone to show. One could say that the shifting relations between *locus* and *platea* mirrored to a great extent changing conceptions of the closure of the body. These kinds of space are correlated, on the one hand, with relatively closed and symbolic staging (houses, courts, chambers, and so on) and, on the other, with more open and playful uses of the stage in direct communication with the audience.[47] They are also in good measure aligned – as, again, Weimann has demonstrated – with a more learned and exclusive ideal of theatricality associated with the 'author's pen' – a text-based, literate, 'antihistrionic'[48] dimension, and an older, more 'vulgar' or 'common' tradition of playing inseparable from the 'actor's voice' – a body-based practice which was increasingly being placed under pressure during the course of the later sixteenth and early seventeenth centuries. To put it in corporeal (and rather over-generalising) terms: where the former tends to idealise the classical body, the latter – what Marlowe refers to as the 'jigging veins of rhyming mother wits' (*Tamburlaine the Great*, Prologue, 1) – is repeatedly associated in the texts of the period with the less savoury, more grotesque or open, aspects of the body. A particularly striking exemplification of this can be found in John Marston's *Histriomastix, Or The Player Whip't* (1598/99). Here, the 'common' actors – with names such as 'Gutt,' 'Belch,' and 'Gulch' – are, as Weimann points out, 'represented as obtrusively concerned with bodily matters': 'there is a venomous focus on a gross and quite distasteful tenor of corporeality and sensuality throughout their dealings.'[49] From the neoclassical perspective of the new literati, they are fit only 'to fill the paunch of Esquiline:'[50] they refuse to conform to the new standards of bodily enclosure, to the emergent ideal of *homo clausus*, forcing upon the spectators' attention the life of the internal body in the face of its growing repression or disciplining by 'the more judicious sort'. In 'the long drawn-out cultural landslide [...] from body-oriented playing to text-oriented acting,'[51] this mixture of closed and open spaces, and more and less somatic acting traditions, mirrors the balance between closed and open bodies in the theatre.

What Weimann wonderfully calls, in relation to theatrical space, 'the thrill of liminality'[52] could be applied equally to the body. This is one reason, I believe, why key dramatic moments such as the knocking on the gate in *Macbeth*, the shutting of the doors in *King Lear*, or the opening of the posterns in *The Winter's Tale*, have such potent symbolic and emotional force: their power is in good part derived from the corporeal subtext. The associative register in these – and many other – instances is that of an opening or closing of the body.

What we could call the new poetics of bodily enclosure was eventually matched by a dramaturgy and architecture that worked not only as a correlative but almost literally as a mirror for the confinement of the actors' bodies: in a manner not unlike the development of cordoned-off spaces in homes and palaces, created to facilitate the privacy of the self, theatres too became increasingly circumscribed, epitomising the move to a more somatically contained style of acting. The 'external circumscription of theatrical space,' writes Weimann, 'went hand in hand with closure in representation': the growing influence of humanist ideology 'came to institute itself in and through the closing of a sharply demarcated space.'[53] The trajectory of the drama – from the popular forms to the literate stage – was, broadly speaking, simultaneously a move from open playing-spaces to increasingly closed ones. George Puttenham's description of the development of 'poemes drammaticke' in *The Arte of English Poesie* lays out just such a path. The earliest dramas were first enacted 'within the woods where they honoured their gods under the open heaven'; then 'the old comedies were plaid in the broad streets upon wagons or carts uncovered'; later, these moved into 'open pavilions or tents of linnen cloth or lether, halfe displayed that the people might see'; these were followed by 'scaffolds or stages of timber, shadowed with linen or lether [...] in the forme of a *Semicircle*' and with a tiring-room. Finally, writes Puttenham, 'as civilitie and withal wealth encreased [...] they came to be by the great magnificence of the Romain princes and people somptuously built with marble and square stone in forme all round, and were called *Amphitheaters*'.[54] The imagined trajectory of classical drama – ever more internal, ever more closed or thick-skinned – foreshadows that of the early modern stage and interestingly echoes that of the early modern body. From this perspective, the eventual transformation into closet drama seems a logical end-point to the processes described above: the closure of theatrical space not only echoed but also reinforced the closure of the body, confining the actor's voice and gesture to a greater containment than ever before. It may be added that the location of the theatres in the transitional space of the Liberties of London – 'an ambiguous territory that was at once internal and external to the city' – must have contributed to its equivocal relation to increasingly authoritarian ideas of embodiment; it was a position that allowed the taking of certain liberties with the enclosed body – a position which, as Stephen Mullaney has argued, encouraged 'commentary upon and even contradiction of [...] the body politic itself.'⁵⁵

'To expect therefore, that *Plays* should be altogether without *obscene* Passages, were it not to expect, that *Nature* should make *Bodies* altogether without *Privy parts*? [...] Have not the neatest Cities their Sinks, and Chanels?' This is from Sir Richard Baker's defence of the stage, *Theatrum Redivivium, Or the Theatre Vindicated*.⁵⁶ Early modern apologists for the theatre often portray playgoing as an opening the body, a disruption of inner-outer boundaries. Whether through tragic catharsis or through a kind of Jonsonian comic purge, the effect is (supposedly) a re-balancing of the body's internal 'complexion.'⁵⁷ This is the point of catharsis, according to many interpreters of Aristotle's notoriously opaque formulation.⁵⁸ Robert Burton recommends 'scenical shews, plays, [and] games' as a kind of purge to those who suffer from an overabundance of melancholy humours.⁵⁹ Sidney, in *The Defence of Poesy*, speaks famously of 'the high and excellent tragedy, that openeth the greatest wounds and showeth forth the ulcers that are covered with tissue; that maketh kings fear to be tyrants, and tyrants manifest their tyrannical humours.'⁶⁰ The notion of re-opening or exposing a bodily interior that has been sealed off, 'covered with tissue,' is explicit here; but 'the sweet violence of a tragedy' not only 'openeth' the bodies and makes 'manifest [the ...] humours' of the protagonists, it also draws forth from the watchers 'abundance of tears' – its 'sweetness' equally affecting the bodies of the audience.⁶¹ The spectator at a tragedy, adds Sidney, 'hearken[s] to that which might mollify [i.e., soften] his hardened heart.'⁶² Tragedies, as the anonymous *A Warning for Fair Women* puts it, 'Make the heart heavy and throb within the bosome, / Extorting tears out of the strictest eyes'; they thereby 'rap the senses from their course'⁶³ – meaning, presumably, 'knock the senses off their course, transport them.' In this vision, we go to the theatre to change course, to allow our hearts and our senses to take a different direction. 'So bewitching a thing is lively and well-spirited [dramatic] action, that it hath power to new-mold the hearts of the spectators,' writes Thomas Heywood in his *Apology for Actors*.⁶⁴ Plays thus offer what Baker calls 'a *bodily recreation*'⁶⁵ – literally. As Thomas Dekker puts it: 'Of what stamp soever you be, current or counterfeit, the stage, like time, will bring you to most perfect light, and lay you open.'⁶⁶

The basis of much of the anti-theatrical condemnation of early modern England was, similarly, that plays affect bodies; that theatre destabilises corporeal (and other) boundaries – it can transform the very interiors of both actors' and audiences' bodies.⁶⁷ William Prynne, for example, rails against the activities of the play-house as being 'sufficient to excite a very hell of noysome lusts in the most mortified Actors and Spectators bowels.'⁶⁸ 'Theatre-haunters' (to use Prynne's term) are subject to a destabilisation of corporeal boundaries; the central figure in anti-theatrical tracts of the period, as Jonas Barish has argued, is the shapeshifter Proteus.⁶⁹ It is the fact that actors can apparently 'change shapes with Proteus for advantage' (*3 Henry VI*, 3.2.192), and that audiences may be contaminated by this changeability, that frightens the anti-theatricalists. Specifically, in these tracts, the theatregoing experience is 'noisome to the body'[70] in its wilful destruction of necessary corporeal boundaries: the 'carnall solace' of the stage is, according to Prynne, 'sinfull in regard of its excess, it being altogether boundlesse'; 'Theatricall laughter knowes neither bounds nor measure; men wholly resigne and let loose the reines of their hearts unto it, glutting, nay tyring their sides and spirits with it.'[71] The stage lays the body *open*: 'The fomentations of uncleanesse in the Play-house,' writes Prynne, are 'as so many Conduit-pipes, or Chariots, to usher concupiscence into our hearts, thorow the doores, the portals of our eyes and ears' (375). (In this context, it is noteworthy that in both Old Hamlet's and Othello's cases, the inception of modernity described above is associated with a poisoning through the unprotected ear.) Anthony Munday repeatedly fulminates against the 'open shameless behaviour' of the actors; 'they commit that filthiness openlie'; the audience, for their part, 'have received at those spectacles such filthie infections, as have [...] turned their bodies into sicknes.'[72] Thus the 'poisonous Stage-plays' – these 'inveterate gangrend ulcers' – are associated over and over (not entirely without reason) with the plague or other forms of contagion.[73] In early modern England, we could say, just as the flourishing of the drama was closely connected to the closure of the body, the closing of theatres had everything to do with the perception of bodies being too open.

Early modern writers thus portray the experience of going to the theatre as a kind of somatic opening – for good or ill. All sorts of things can get into or out of the bodies of those who attend the theatre: 'A Christian woman [...] going to see a Stage-play acted, returned from it possessed with a Devill,' warns Prynne;[74] on the other hand, as C.L. Barber puts it, 'dramatic art can provide a civilized equivalent for exorcism.'[75] One important reason for going to the theatre is precisely the promise of a relinquishing of corporeal self-possession. The theatregoing experience is founded upon our willingness to be open to one another (to enter into the experience of the other) – and certainly in the early modern context this means physiological quite as much as emotional openness. As purging and blood-letting were slowly becoming a thing of the past, playgoing might be said to be enacting something like a vicarious version of these. For as I've been arguing throughout this paper, it is at this period that the (previously more or less obvious) notion of being humorally, physically, part of or open to the world can no longer be taken for granted – it becomes something that needs to be achieved against the odds.

'He that will understand Shakespeare must not be content to study him in the closet,' wrote Samuel Johnson.[76] Perhaps one of the purposes of this early modern theatre (and above all of Shakespeare's plays) was – alongside the propagation of new forms of interiority – to provide some relief from the inexorable historical process of confining the body within its own borders; from the anxiety inherent in the attempt to keep inner and outer so separate. Theatre reminds us in several ways that 'we have our exits and our entrances'; it satisfies what Thoreau called '[our] need to witness our own limits transgressed,'[77] allowing us to remember that we are not altogether *clausus*, shaking our presumptuous inviolability. As Theodor Adorno put it, 'It is part of morality not to be at home in one's home.'[78] We all inhabit the modern regime of *homo clausus*; perhaps the centrality of Shakespeare to our culture has something to do with the way his plays equivocally show the arrival of this character onstage – even as they allow a glimpse, and an experience, of other ways of being embodied, which is to say other ways of relating to one another, and hence to ourselves.[79]

Notes

1. John Sutton, *Philosophy and Memory Traces: Descartes to Connectionism* (Cambridge: Cambridge University Press, 1998), 41.
2. Numerous scholars have pointed to different aspects of this crisis; see, e.g. Jean-Christophe Agnew, *Worlds Apart: The Market and the Theater in Anglo-American thought, 1550–1750* (Cambridge: Cambridge University Press, 1986), 97, on a 'crisis of representation' in the early modern period; Thomas Docherty (*On Modern Authority: The Theory and Conditioning of Writing, 1500 to the Present Day* [New York: St. Martin's Press, 1987]) and Robert Weimann (*Authority and Representation in Early Modern England*, ed. David Hillman [Baltimore: Johns Hopkins University Press, 1996]), both have extended discussions of the period's 'crisis of authority'; Stanley Cavell (*Cities of Words: Pedagogical Letters on a Register of the Moral Life* (Cambridge, Mass.: Harvard University Press, 2004), 424) emphasises the deep 'crises of knowledge' associated with 'the religious and scientific revolutions of the sixteenth and early seventeenth centuries.'
3. The term is taken from his talk, 'Affective Irony,' at a conference entitled 'Inhabiting the Body/Inhabiting the World,' at the University of North Carolina, April 2004.
4. Elaine Scarry, *The Body in Pain: The Making and Unmaking of the World* (New York: Oxford University Press, 1985), 14. Cf. Mary Douglas's suggestion that 'cultures which frankly develop bodily symbolism may be seen to use it to confront experience with its inevitable pains and losses.' *Purity and Danger: An Analysis of the Concepts of Pollution and Taboo* (1966; rpt. London: Ark, 1984), 120.
5. *OED* records its first use in English in 1543 – the year of the publication of Vesalius' *Fabrica* – in the medical sense; its first use in the latter sense as 1627.
6. Jean Starobinski, *Blessings in Disguise, Or The Morality of Evil*, trans. Arthur Goldhammer (Cambridge, Mass.: Harvard University Press, 1993), 201.
7. James Balmford, *A Short Dialogue Concerning the Plague's Infection* (London, 1603), 15, cited in Margaret Healy, 'Anxious and Fatal Contacts: Taming the Contagious Touch,' in *Sensible Flesh: On Touch in Early Modern Culture*, ed. Elizabeth D. Harvey (Philadelphia: University of Pennsylvania Press, 2003), 27.
8. Louis Adrian Montrose, '*A Midsummer Night's Dream* and the Shaping Fantasies of Elizabethan Culture: Gender, Power, Form' in *Rewriting the Renaissance: The Discourses of Sexual Difference in Early Modern Europe*, ed. Margaret W. Ferguson,

Maureen Quilligan, and Nancy J. Vickers (Chicago: University of Chicago Press, 1986), 65–87; 66.
9. Anne Ferry, *The 'Inward' Language: Sonnets of Wyatt, Sidney, Shakespeare, Donne* (Chicago: University of Chicago Press, 1983), 1–70. These genres include the Montaignean essay, the dramatic soliloquy the sonnet, and autobiographical writing.
10. Maus, *Inwardness and Theatre*, 13.
11. Anthony Dawson, 'Performance and Participation,' in Dawson and Paul Yachnin, *The Culture of Playgoing in Early Modern England* (Cambridge: Cambridge University Press, 1999), 21. See also Huston Diehl, *Staging Reform, Reforming the Stage: Protestantism and Popular Theater in Early Modern England* (Ithaca: Cornell University Press, 1997), esp. 38; Katharine Eisaman Maus, *Inwardness and Theater in the English Renaissance* (Chicago: University of Chicago Press, 1995), 8–12, and Michael Neill, *Issues of Death: Mortality and Identity in English Renaissance Tragedy* (Oxford: Clarendon, 1997), 156–8.
12. On the idea of the body as partaking in a series of nested enclosures, see Marie-Christine Pouchelle, *The Body and Surgery in the Middle Ages*, trans. Rosemary Morris (Cambridge: Cambridge University Press 1990), 125–59.
13. Jorge Arditi, *A Genealogy of Manners: Transformations of Social Relations in France and England from the Fourteenth to the Eighteenth Centuries* (Chicago: University of Chicago Press, 1998), 43. Cf. Phillipe Ariès and Georges Duby, eds. *A History of Private Life*, vol. 2: *Revelations of the Medieval World* (Cambridge: Harvard University Press, 1988).
14. Arditi, *A Genealogy of Manners*, 45; 53; 40. See also Caroline Thomas Bynum's *Jesus as Mother: Studies in the Spirituality of the High Middle Ages* (Berkeley: University of California Press, 1984), 82–109, which describes a transition from a medieval balance between the 'self' and the group to the increasing idea of individuation after the Lateran council of 1215.
15. Mikhail Bakhtin, *Rabelais and His World*, trans. Hélène Iswolsky [Bloomington: Indiana University Press, 1984], 320. See also Jean Starobinski, 'The Body's Moment,' in *Montaigne: Essays in Reading*, ed. Gérard Defaux, *Yale French Studies* 64 (1983), 273–305 (esp. 274–7) & 'The Natural and Literary History of Bodily Sensation,' in *Fragments for a History of the Human Body*, II: 350–405 (esp. 353–5).
16. Norbert Elias, *The History of Manners*, Vol. 1 of *The Civilizing Process*, trans. Edmund Jephcott (New York: Pantheon Books, 1978), 257–8. On the idea of *homo clausus*, see also Michael Neill, *Issues of Death: Morality and Identity in English Renaissance Tragedy* (Oxford: Clarendon Press, 1997), 156–8.
17. Ibid., 257.
18. Peter Stallybrass, 'Patriarchal Territories: The Body Enclosed,' in *Rewriting the Renaissance*, 123–44; Gail Kern Paster, *The Body Embarrassed: Drama and the Disciplines of Shame in Early Modern England* (Ithaca: Cornell University Press, 1993), 16.
19. Girolamo Fracastoro, *De contagione et contagionis morbis et eorum curatione* (1546), ed. William Cave Wright (New York: Putman's Sons, 1930).
20. Michael C. Schoenfeldt, *Bodies and Selves in Early Modern England: Physiology and Inwardness in Spenser, Shakespeare, Herbert, and Milton* (Cambridge: University of Cambridge Press, 1999), 31, 13. Levinus Lemnius, *The Secret Miracles of Nature* (London, 1658), 343.
21. Tobias Venner, *Via Recta ad Vitam Longam. Or, A Treatise wherein the right way and best manner of living for attaining a long and healthfull life, is clearly demonstrated* (London, 1623; 1650), 321–2, cited in Schoenfeldt, 14.

22. On the corporeal contours of scepticism, see my 'The Inside Story,' in *Historicism, Psychoanalysis, and Early Modern Culture*, ed. Carla Mazzio and Douglas Trevor (New York: Routledge, 2000), as well as my forthcoming *Shakespeare's Entrails: Belief, Scepticism and the Interior of the Body* (London: Palgrave Macmillan, 2006).
23. Andrew Wear, whose compendious *Knowledge and Practice in English Medicine, 1550–1680* (Cambridge: Cambridge University Press, 2000) lays great emphasis on the unchanging '*histoire immobile*' (155) of medical practice through the course of the Renaissance, emphasizes that in terms of the conceptualization of disease, the increasing distance between subjective sensations and objective diagnoses made it more and more 'difficult to see disease as being caused by an imbalance of the four qualities, as now they were merely subjective, and it was easier to conceive disease as coming from the outside, objective world' (452).
24. Phillipe Ariés, *The Hour of our Death*, trans. Helen Weaver (London: Allen Lane, 1981), 121.
25. Helkiah Crooke, *Microcosmographia: A Description of the Body of Man* (London, 1615), 60; my emphasis.
26. Jonathan Gil Harris, *Foreign Bodies and the Body Politic: Discourses of Pathology in Early Modern England* (Cambridge: Cambridge University Press, 1998), 30.
27. Healy, 'Anxious and Fatal Contacts,' 22.
28. Both these quotations are from Steven Connor, *The Book of Skin* (London: Reaktion Books, 2004), 21–2.
29. Claudia Benthien, *Skin: On the Cultural Border Between the Self and the World*, trans. Thomas Dunlap (New York: Columbia University Press, 2002), 39. See also Barbara Duden, *The Woman Beneath the Skin: A Doctor's Patients in Eighteenth-Century Germany*, trans. Thomas Dunlap (Cambridge, Mass.: Harvard University Press, 1991), esp. 120–3.
30. Benthien, *Skin*, 38.
31. These last two quotations are from Connor, *The Book of Skin*, 22.
32. On land enclosure, see especially Raymond Williams, *The Country and the City*, 96–107 & 136–41.
33. For a reading of 'the specific role of the closet in the social and architectural schema of the early modern house,' see Alan Stewart, *Close Readers: Humanism and Sodomy in Early Modern England* (Princeton: Princeton University Press, 1997), 161–87 (the quotation is on p. 166). See also Anne Ferry, *The 'Inward' Language: Sonnets of Wyatt, Sidney, Shakespeare, Donne* (Chicago: University of Chicago Press, 1983), 47; and Orest Ranum, 'The Refuges of Intimacy,' in *A History of Private Life, Volume III: Passions of the Renaissance*, ed. Roger Chartier, trans. Arthur Goldhammer (Cambridge: Harvard University Press, 1989), 217–29.
34. On these new notions of privacy, see, e.g. Lawrence Stone, *The Family, Sex and Marriage in England 1500–1800* (New York: Harper Torchbooks, 1977), 169–72, 223–4, 245–6, and Ranum, 'The Refuges of Intimacy,' 207–63.
35. Dawson, *The Culture of Plaything*, 21. See also note 11.
36. Many of these breaks with tradition were institutionalised in the second Edwardian *Book of Common Prayer*, authorised in 1552. On the move away from the Catholic Mass, see especially Eamon Duffy, *The Stripping of the Altars: Traditional Religion in England c. 1400–c. 1580* (New Haven and London: Yale University Press, 1992), 91–130. On the abolishment of unction between the 1549 Book of Common Prayer, which includes anointing as part of the ceremony of Baptism, and the 1552 version, see especially Steven Connor's commentary (*The Book of Skin*, 203–5). As Connor argues, unctuary actions work to soften the skin,

the boundary between the inside and the outside (cf. Sartre on the disgust elicited by this 'epidermal in-betweenness' [cited by Connor, 205]). 'Liturgical forms for anointing in the Christian church often stress the symbolism and enactment of a partaking in the divine nature, parallel to the assimilation of the host' (Connor, 182). On stigmata, it is particularly interesting to note Luther's dismissal of St Francis' stigmata as nothing more than 'a pure fiction and a joke' (Martin Luther, *Luther's Works*, ed. Jaroslav Pelikan [Saint Louis, 1964], vol. 27, 142.; cited in Lowell Gallagher, 'The place of the stigmata in Christological poetics,' in *Religion and Culture in Renaissance England*, ed. Claire McEachern and Debora Shuger [Cambridge: Cambridge University Press, 1997], 99); even Paul's stigmata, as Gallagher shows, are treated by Luther 'not as literal, or even metonymic, marks but as metaphorical ones' ('The place of the stigmata,' 101). One way of reading this dismissal is through the new Protestant sensibility which partakes of the idealisation of the closed body.
37. Hartmann Grisar, *Luther*, trans. E.M. Lamond, ed. Luigi Cappadelta, 6 vols. (London: Kegan Paul, 1913–17), VI:506; cited in Norman O. Brown, *Life Against Death: The Psychoanalytic Meaning of History* (Middletown, CT.: Wesleyan University Press, 1959), 202. As Luther's biographer Grisar somewhat euphemistically explains, 'In olden times it was very usual to establish this adjunct on the city walls and its towers, the sewage having egress outside the town boundaries' (*Luther*, I:396). This location of the privy was symbolically as well as practically overdetermined, its relation to transitional spaces evident. On the Catholic Mass and somatic transitionality, compare Milton: '[T]he Mass brings down Christ's body from its supreme exaltation at the right hand of God. It drags it back to the earth, though it has suffered every pain and hardship already, to a state of humiliation even more wretched and degrading than before: to be broken once more and crushed and ground, even by the fangs of brutes. Then, when it has been driven through all the stomach's filthy channels it shoots it out – one shudders even to mention it – into the latrine' (*On Christian Doctrine*, in *The Complete Prose Works of John Milton*, ed. William Alfred *et al*. (New Haven: Yale University Press, 1973), 6.560.
38. Brown, *Life Against Death*, 209.
39. Friedrich Nietzsche, *The Birth of Tragedy*, 46; 65.
40. The psychoanalyst Herbert Rosenfeld has discussed the distinction between 'thick-skinned' and 'thin-skinned' patients, and the kinds of object-relations each type of individual tends to construct. I believe one can equally speak of 'thick-' and 'thin-skinned' cultures, or socio-cultural contexts, and discuss the kinds of subjects and objects constructed by such societies; Rosenfeld's insights have been helpful to me in thinking about issues of culturally-conditioned corporeal openness and closure – and the transitional points between them. See Rosenfeld, *Impasse and Interpretation* (London: Routledge, 1987); and Ronald Britton, *Belief and Imagination: Explorations in Psychoanalysis* (London: Routledge, 1998), 41–58.
41. Connor, *The Book of Skin*, 10.
42. See Richard Broxton Onians, *The Origins of European Thought about the Body, the Mind, the Soul, the World, Time, and Fate* (Cambridge: Cambridge University Press, 1954), 86; Bruno Snell, *The Discovery of the Mind in Greek Philosophy and Literature*, trans. T. G. Rosenmeyer (New York: Dover, 1982), 1–22; Ruth Padel, *In and Out of the Mind: Greek Images of the Tragic Self* (Princeton: Princeton University Press, 1992), esp. 9–14; Sheila Murnaghan, 'Body and Voice in Greek Tragedy,' *Yale Journal of Criticism* 1 (Spring 1988), 23–43; Jean-Pierre Vernant, 'Dim Body,

Dazzling Body,' in *Fragments for a History of the Human Body*, Part One, ed. Michel Feher (Cambridge, Mass.: MIT Press, 1989), 18–47, esp. 29–30.
43. As Dawson and Yachnin point out, there is also a kind of closure taking place at the presentational level – through, especially, the actor's control of his passions and his body. On the 'dual consciousness' of theatricality, see Dawson and Yachnin, *The Culture of Playgoing*, 16–23.
44. C.L. Barber, *Shakespeare's Festive Comedy: A Study of Dramatic Form and its Relation to Social Custom* (Princeton, NJ: Princeton University Press, 1959), 135.
45. From a psychoanalytic (Lacanian) perspective, one might say that what is being held in balance here is the imaginary body and the real ... (elaborate).
46. Elin Diamond, *Unmaking Mimesis: Essays on Feminism and Theater* (London: Routledge 1997), v; iii; and cf. Peggy Phelan, *Unmarked: The Politics of Performance* (London: Routledge, 1993) 148–50.
47. The former, as Weimann points out, 'dominated by a symbolic use of theatrical space as, for example, a house, a court, a chamber, and so forth,' the latter associated with the stage itself, 'an open stage gestus.' Robert Weimann, *Author's Pen and Actor's Voice: Playing and Writing in Shakespeare's Theatre*, ed. Helen Higbee and William West (Cambridge: Cambridge University Press, 2000), 169. See also his *Shakespeare and the Popular Tradition in the Theater: Studies in the Social Dimension of Dramatic Form and Function*, ed. Robert Schwartz (Baltimore: Johns Hopkins University Press, 1978).
48. Weimann, *Author's Pen*, 124.
49. Ibid., 124–5.
50. John Marston, *Histriomastix, Or The Player Whip't* (London, 1598/99), D4r.
51. Weimann, *Author's Pen*, 132–3.
52. Ibid., 52.
53. Ibid., 186.
54. George Puttenham, *The Arte of English Poesie* (1589), intr. Baxter Hathaway (Kent State University Press, 1970), 51–2.
55. Stephen Mullaney, *The Place of the Stage: Licence, Play, and Power in Renaissance England* (Chicago: University of Chicago Press, 1987), 21; ix.
56. Sir Richard Baker, *Theatrum Redivivium, Or the Theatre Vindicated* (London, 1662), ed. Arthur Freeman (New York and London: Garland Publishing, 1973), 133.
57. The association of actors and healers (whether charlatans or doctors) is not uncommon in the period. See, e.g. Piero Camporesi, *The Incorruptible Flesh: Bodily Mutilation and Mortification in Religion and Folklore*, trans. Tania Croft-Murray (Cambridge: Cambridge University Press, 1988), on 'the dual function of traveling actors and healers': 'Actor and purger in one – two sides of the same mask. All workers in the industry of dissimulation and of its opposite: simulation' (125). On Jonson and purging, see, e.g. James Bednarz, *Shakespeare and the Poet's War* (New York: Columbia University Press, 2001), 33–5.
58. For an exceptionally judicious discussion of the corporeal aspects of Aristotle's notion of catharsis, see A.D. Nuttall, *Why Does Tragedy Give Pleasure?* (Oxford: Clarendon Press, 1996), 1–28.
59. Robert Burton, *Anatomy of Melancholy*, Vol. 2, ed. A.R. Shilleto (London: George Bell, 1893), 142.
60. Sir Philip Sidney, *The Defence of Poesy*, in *Sidney's The Defence of Poesy and Selected Renaissance Literary Criticism*, ed. Gavin Alexander (London: Penguin, 2004), 27.
61. Ibid. In more contemporary terms, we might say that playgoing involves a heightening of projective and introjective processes.
62. Sidney, *Defence*, 28.

63. *A Warning for Fair Women* (London, 1599), ed. Charles Dale Cannon (The Hague: Mouton, 1975), Induction, 44–7.
64. Thomas Heywood, *An Apology for Actors*, in E.K. Chambers, *The Elizabethan Stage* (Oxford: Clarendon Press, 1923), Volume IV, 251.
65. Baker, *Theatrum Redivivium*, 133; emphasis in the original.
66. Thomas Dekker, *The Gull's Hornbook* (London, 1609), in Chambers, *The Elizabethan Stage*, IV, 367.
67. On this topic, see Jonas Barish, *The Anti-Theatrical Prejudice* (Berkeley: University of California Press, 1981); Laura Levine, *Men in Women's Clothing: Anti-Theatricality and Effeminization, 1579–1642* (Cambridge: Cambridge University Press, 1994); Carla Mazzio, 'Acting with Tact: Touch and Theater in the Renaissance,' in *Sensible Flesh*, 159–86, esp. 178–81; and Tanya Pollard, *Drugs and Theatre in Early Modern England* (Oxford: Oxford University Press, 2005).
68. William Prynne, *Histrio-Mastix, The Players Scovrge, or Actors Tragœdie* (London, 1633), Part I, Act 5, Scene 7.
69. Barish, *The Anti-Theatrical Prejudice*, 80–131.
70. Stephen Gosson, *The Schoole of Abuse, Containing a pleasant inuective against Poets, Pipers, Plaiers, Iesters and such like Caterpillers of a Commonwelth* (London, 1579), in Chambers, *The Elizabethan Stage*, IV, 205.
71. Prynne, *Histrio-Mastix*, 291–2.
72. Anthony Munday, *A second and third blastoff retrait from plaies and Theatres* (London, 1580), in Chambers, *The Elizabethan Stage*, IV, 211; 209.
73. Prynne, *Histrio-Mastix*, 2b ('To the Christian Reader'); 2. See also J. Leeds Barroll, *Politics, Plague, and Shakespeare's Theater* (Ithaca: Cornell University Press, 1991).
74. Prynne, *Histrio-Mastix*, 11.
75. Barber, *Shakespeare's Festive Comedy*, 139.
76. *Dr Johnson on Shakespeare*, ed. W.K. Wimsatt (Harmondsworth: Penguin, 1969), 33–34.
77. Henry David Thoreau, *Walden*, cited in Cavell, *Disowning Knowledge*, 218.
78. Theodor Adorno, *Minima Moralia* (London: New Left Books, 1974), 36.
79. Versions of this chapter were delivered at a conference entitled 'Inhabiting the Body/Inhabiting the World' at the University of North Carolina, at a lecture at Williams College, and in a workshop arranged by Michael C. Schoenfeldt at the Shakespeare Association of America in New Orleans, during March and April 2004, as well as the Cambridge Renaissance Graduate Seminar. I would like to thank the audiences at these venues – and especially John Kerrigan, Cynthia Marshall, Christopher Pye, Mike Schoenfeldt, Anita Sokolsky, Peter Stallybrass and Steve Tifft – for their generous and valuable comments on these earlier versions. I would also like to thank the Arts and Humanities Research Board (UK) for its support, which allowed me to complete some of the research for this topic. Jessa Leff has helped me immeasurably throughout.

Works cited

Theodor Adorno, *Minima Moralia* (London: New Left Books, 1974).
Jean-Christophe Agnew, *Worlds Apart: The Market and the Theater in Anglo-American Thought, 1550–1750* (Cambridge: Cambridge University Press, 1986).
Anon., *A Warning for Fair Women* (London, 1599), ed. Charles Dale Cannon (The Hague: Mouton, 1975).
Jorge Arditi, *A Genealogy of Manners: Transformations of Social Relations in France and England from the Fourteenth to the Eighteenth Centuries* (Chicago: University of Chicago Press, 1998).

Phillipe Ariès, *The Hour of our Death*, trans. Helen Weaver (London: Allen Lane, 1981).
Phillipe Ariès and Georges Duby, eds. *A History of Private Life*, vol. 2: *Revelations of the Medieval World* (Cambridge: Harvard University Press, 1988).
Sir Richard Baker, *Theatrum Redivivium, Or the Theatre Vindicated* (London, 1662), ed. Arthur Freeman (New York and London: Garland Publishing, 1973).
Mikhail Bakhtin, *Rabelais and His World*, trans. Hélène Iswolsky (Bloomington: Indiana University Press, 1984).
James Balmford, *A Short Dialogue Concerning the Plague's Infection* (London, 1603).
C.L. Barber, *Shakespeare's Festive Comedy: A Study of Dramatic Form and Its Relation to Social Custom* (Princeton, NJ: Princeton University Press, 1959).
Jonas Barish, *The Anti-Theatrical Prejudice* (Berkeley: University of California Press, 1981).
J. Leeds Barroll, *Politics, Plague, and Shakespeare's Theater* (Ithaca: Cornell University Press, 1991).
James Bednarz, *Shakespeare and the Poet's War* (New York: Columbia University Press, 2001).
Ronald Britton, *Belief and Imagination: Explorations in Psychoanalysis* (London: Routledge, 1998).
Norman O. Brown, *Life Against Death: The Psychoanalytic Meaning of History* (Middletown, CT.: Wesleyan University Press, 1959).
Robert Burton, *Anatomy of Melancholy*, Vol. 2, ed. A.R. Shilleto (London: George Bell, 1893).
Caroline Thomas Bynum, *Jesus as Mother: Studies in the Spirituality of the High Middle Ages* (Berkeley: University of California Press, 1984).
Piero Camporesi, *The Incorruptible Flesh: Bodily Mutilation and Mortification in Religion and Folklore*, trans. Tania Croft-Murray (Cambridge: Cambridge University Press, 1988).
Stanley Cavell, *Cities of Words: Pedagogical Letters on a Register of the Moral Life* (Cambridge, Mass.: Harvard University Press, 2004).
Steven Connor, *The Book of Skin* (London: Reaktion Books, 2004).
Helkiah Crooke, *Microcosmographia: A Description of the Body of Man* (London, 1615).
Anthony Dawson and Paul Yachnin, *The Culture of Playgoing in Early Modern England* (Cambridge: Cambridge University Press, 1999).
Thomas Dekker, *The Gull's Hornbook* (London, 1609).
Elin Diamond, *Unmaking Mimesis: Essays on Feminism and Theater* (London: Routledge 1997).
Huston Diehl, *Staging Reform, Reforming the Stage: Protestantism and Popular Theater in Early Modern England* (Ithaca: Cornell University Press, 1997).
Thomas Docherty, *On Modern Authority: The Theory and Conditioning of Writing, 1500 to the Present Day* (New York: St. Martin's Press, 1987).
Mary Douglas, *Purity and Danger: An Analysis of the Concepts of Pollution and Taboo* (1966; rpt. London: Ark, 1984).
Barbara Duden, *The Woman Beneath the Skin: A Doctor's Patients in Eighteenth-Century Germany*, trans. Thomas Dunlap (Cambridge, Mass.: Harvard University Press, 1991).
Eamon Duffy, *The Stripping of the Altars: Traditional Religion in England c. 1400–c. 1580* (New Haven and London: Yale University Press, 1992).
Norbert Elias, *The History of Manners*, Vol. 1 of *The Civilizing Process*, trans. Edmund Jephcott (New York: Pantheon Books, 1978).
Anne Ferry, *The 'Inward' Language: Sonnets of Wyatt, Sidney, Shakespeare, Donne* (Chicago: University of Chicago Press, 1983).

Girolamo Fracastoro, *De contagione et contagionis morbis et eorum curatione* (1546), ed. William Cave Wright (New York: Putman's Sons, 1930).
Lowell Gallagher, 'The place of the stigmata in Christological poetics,' in *Religion and Culture in Renaissance England*, ed. Claire McEachern and Debora Shuger (Cambridge: Cambridge University Press, 1997).
Stephen Gosson, *The Schoole of Abuse, Containing a pleasant inuective against Poets, Pipers, Plaiers, Iesters and such like Caterpillers of a Commonwelth* (London, 1579).
Hartmann Grisar, *Luther*, trans. E.M. Lamond, ed. Luigi Cappadelta, 6 vols (London: Kegan Paul, 1913–17).
Jonathan Gil Harris, *Foreign Bodies and the Body Politic: Discourses of Pathology in Early Modern England* (Cambridge: Cambridge University Press, 1998).
Margaret Healy, 'Anxious and Fatal Contacts: Taming the Contagious Touch,' in *Sensible Flesh: On Touch in Early Modern Culture*, ed. Elizabeth D. Harvey (Philadelphia: University of Pennsylvania Press, 2003).
Thomas Heywood, *An Apology for Actors*, in E.K. Chambers, *The Elizabethan Stage* (Oxford: Clarendon Press, 1923).
David Hillman, 'The Inside Story,' in *Historicism, Psychoanalysis, and Early Modern Culture*, ed. Carla Mazzio and Douglas Trevor (New York: Routledge, 2000).
David Hillman, *Shakespeare's Entrails: Belief, Scepticism and the Interior of the Body* (London: Palgrave Macmillan 2006).
Samuel Johnson, *Dr Johnson on Shakespeare*, ed. W.K. Wimsatt (Harmondsworth: Penguin, 1969).
Levinus Lemnius, *The Secret Miracles of Nature* (London, 1658).
Laura Levine, *Men in Women's Clothing: Anti-Theatricality and Effeminization, 1579–1642* (Cambridge: Cambridge University Press, 1994).
Martin Luther, *Luther's Works*, ed. Jaroslav Pelikan (Saint Louis, 1964).
John Marston, *Histriomastix, Or The Player Whip't* (London, 1598/99).
Katharine Eisaman Maus, *Inwardness and Theater in the English Renaissance* (Chicago: University of Chicago Press, 1995).
Carla Mazzio, 'Acting with Tact: Touch and Theater in the Renaissance,' in *Sensible Flesh: On Touch in Early Modern Culture*, ed. Elizabeth D. Harvey (Pennsylvania: University of Pennsylvania Press, 2003), 159–86.
Louis Adrian Montrose, '*A Midsummer Night's Dream* and the Shaping Fantasies of Elizabethan Culture: Gender, Power, Form' in *Rewriting the Renaissance: The Discourses of Sexual Difference in Early Modern Europe*, ed. Margaret W. Ferguson, Maureen Quilligan, and Nancy J. Vickers (Chicago: University of Chicago Press, 1986), 65–87.
Stephen Mullaney, *The Place of the Stage: Licence, Play, and Power in Renaissance England* (Chicago: University of Chicago Press, 1987).
Anthony Munday, *A Second and Third Blastoff Retrait from Plaies and Theatres* (London, 1580).
Sheila Murnaghan, 'Body and Voice in Greek Tragedy,' *Yale Journal of Criticism* 1 (Spring 1988).
Michael Neill, *Issues of Death: Morality and Identity in English Renaissance Tragedy* (Oxford: Clarendon Press, 1997).
Friedrich Nietzsche, *The Birth of Tragedy*, trans. Walter Kaufmann (New York: Vintage Books, 1967).
A.D. Nuttall, *Why Does Tragedy Give Pleasure?* (Oxford: Clarendon Press, 1996).
Richard Broxton Onians, *The Origins of European Thought about the Body, the Mind, the Soul, the World, Time, and Fate* (Cambridge: Cambridge University Press, 1954).

Ruth Padel, *In and Out of the Mind: Greek Images of the Tragic Self* (Princeton: Princeton University Press, 1992).
Gail Kern Paster, *The Body Embarrassed: Drama and the Disciplines of Shame in Early Modern England* (Ithaca: Cornell University Press, 1993).
Peggy Phelan, *Unmarked: The Politics of Performance* (London: Routledge, 1993).
Tanya Pollard, *Drugs and Theatre in Early Modern England* (Oxford: Oxford University Press, 2005).
Marie-Christine Pouchelle, *The Body and Surgery in the Middle Ages*, trans. Rosemary Morris (Cambridge: Cambridge University Press 1990).
William Prynne, *Histrio-Mastix, The Players Scovrge, or Actors Tragœdie* (London, 1633).
George Puttenham, *The Arte of English Poesie* (1589), intr. Baxter Hathaway (Kent State University Press, 1970).
Orest Ranum, 'The Refuges of Intimacy,' in *A History of Private Life, Volume III: Passions of the Renaissance*, ed. Roger Chartier, trans. Arthur Goldhammer (Cambridge: Harvard University Press, 1989).
Herbert Rosenfeld, *Impasse and Interpretation* (London: Routledge, 1987).
Elaine Scarry, *The Body in Pain: The Making and Unmaking of the World* (New York: Oxford University .Press, 1985).
Michael C. Schoenfeldt, *Bodies and Selves in Early Modern England: Physiology and Inwardness in Spenser, Shakespeare, Herbert, and Milton* (Cambridge: University of Cambridge Press, 1999).
Sir Philip Sidney, *The Defence of Poesy*, in *Sidney's 'The Defence of Poesy and Selected Renaissance Literary Criticism*, ed. Gavin Alexander (London: Penguin, 2004).
Bruno Snell, *The Discovery of the Mind in Greek Philosophy and Literature*, trans. T.G. Rosenmeyer (New York: Dover, 1982), 1–22.
Peter Stallybrass, 'Patriarchal Territories: The Body Enclosed,' in *Rewriting the Renaissance: The Discourses of Sexual Difference in Early Modern Europe*, ed. Margaret W. Ferguson, Maureen Quilligan, and Nancy J. Vickers (Chicago: University of Chicago Press, 1986).
Jean Starobinski, *Blessings in Disguise, Or The Morality of Evil*, trans. Arthur Goldhammer (Cambridge, Mass.: Harvard University Press, 1993).
Jean Starobinski, 'The Body's Moment,' in *Montaigne: Essays in Reading*, ed. Gérard Defaux, *Yale French Studies* 64 (1983).
Jean Starobinski, 'The Natural and Literary History of Bodily Sensation,' in *Fragments for a History of the Human Body*, vol. II, ed. Michel Feher (Cambridge, Mass.: MIT Press, 1989).
Alan Stewart, *Close Readers: Humanism and Sodomy in Early Modern England* (Princeton: Princeton University Press, 1997).
Lawrence Stone, *The Family, Sex and Marriage in England 1500–1800* (New York: Harper Torchbooks, 1977).
John Sutton, *Philosophy and Memory Traces: Descartes to Connectionism* (Cambridge: Cambridge University Press, 1998).
Tobias Venner, *Via Recta ad Vitam Longam. Or, A Treatise wherein the right way and best manner of living for attaining a long and healthfull life, is clearly demonstrated* (London, 1623; 1650).
Jean-Pierre Vernant, 'Dim Body, Dazzling Body,' in *Fragments for a History of the Human Body*, Part One, ed. Michel Feher (Cambridge, Mass.: MIT Press, 1989).
Henry David Thoreau, *Walden*, ed. Stephen Fender (Oxford: Oxford University Press, 1999).
Andrew Wear, *Knowledge and Practice in English Medicine, 1550–1680* (Cambridge: Cambridge University Press, 2000).

Robert Weimann, *Shakespeare and the Popular Tradition in the Theater: Studies in the Social Dimension of Dramatic Form and Function*, ed. Robert Schwartz (Baltimore: Johns Hopkins University Press, 1978).

Robert Weimann, *Authority and Representation in Early Modern England*, ed. David Hillman (Baltimore: Johns Hopkins University Press, 1996).

Robert Weimann, *Author's Pen and Actor's Voice: Playing and Writing in Shakespeare's Theatre*, ed. Helen Higbee and William West (Cambridge: Cambridge University Press, 2000).

Raymond Williams, *The Country and the City* (Oxford: Oxford University Press, 1973).

10
Figuring the Consumer for Early Modern Drama

Kathleen McLuskie

In the text of Thomas Goffe's *The Careless Shepherdess* (printed 1656), immediately preceding the text of the play, there is a short dialogue, called a 'Praeludium' between Thrift, a citizen, Spruce, a courtier, Spark an Inns of Court man and Landlord, a country gentleman. Each figure enters the scene separately: Thrift attempts to bargain with Bolt, the door-keeper who is charging a shilling to see the play, offering him 'a groat' on the grounds that 'I always use to ask just twice as much/As a thing's worth.' When Bolt insists that a shilling is the set price, Thrift argues 'I have known some Aldermen that did begin with twelve pence: and for half so much/I saw six motions last Bartholomew Fair.' Bolt insists that he can't and won't bargain: 'This is no market or exchange.' Thrift concedes the price, indicating that he can, in any case, make good his spending by cheating his own customers: 'I'll go unto my book/And set a figure to each single Cipher; I'll cheat a shilling in a penny, and a pound in twelve pence.' When Spruce, the courtier enters, Thrift asks 'if you go on tick here too, /what did it cost you to come in'. He also tells Spruce that 'There is a Courtier Sir that owes to me/Two thousand pound for Garters and for Roses' and offers to sell him some 'Ribboning round your hat'.

Spark, the Inns of Court man is astonished to find a courtier speaking to a citizen and Spruce concedes that such condescension is unusual. When Spruce asks him why he is at the theatre (in much more high flown terms), Spark replies: 'Faith sir 'tis fasting night, and I did chuse/Rather to spend my money at a Play/ Then at the Ordnary.' The Landlord, who enters last, has other reasons for coming to the theatre. He has chosen the 'twelve penny room' as a place from which to pass judgement, citing his experience 'with Judges on the Bench' and the fact that he has 'found fault with very good sermons/In my daies'.

The Landlord's remarks turn the conversation to questions of judgement. Spark is contemptuous that Landlord's knowledge of the law should allow him to presume to 'know/The Laws of Comedy and Tragedy':

> Alas you're ignorant of any stile
> But what stands in a hedge; you never heard
> Of more than the four humours of the body;
> Nor did you every understand a plot,
> Unless that grand one of the *Powder-Treason*

Spruce also turns on Thrift and denounces his effrontery in daring to 'usurp Apollo's chair':

> Cause you sell Phansies, and can cast account,
> Do y'think your brain conceives Poetique numbers?
> You cannot tell, if you were asked the question,
> Whether a Metaphor be flesh or fish;
> You may perchance have judgement to discern
> What Puppet dances well or understand
> Which Juglers mouth is best at the Bay-leafe,
> But who deserves the Lawrell wreath, you know
> No more, then you do know, which Land I'th'field
> Bears Barley and which Wheat, which Rye, which Oats.

Landlord is asked what he thinks essential for a play and answers 'I would have the Fool in every act' remembering how 'I heard a fellow/Once on this Stage cry *Doodle Doodle Dooe*,/Beyond compare; Ide give the other shilling/To see him act the Changeling once again' (pp. 4–5). Thrift agrees. However their eager reminiscences of experiences in the theatre are contemptuously dismissed by Spark:

> 'your judgements are ridiculous and vain
> As your forefathers, whose dull intellect
> Did nothing understand but fools and fighting;
> 'Twill hardly enter into my belief
> That ye are of this age, sure ye are ghosts'.

Spark then offers a eulogy to the innovations of modern stage, its preference for wit over weapons, and its attention to refined sentiments. That new refinement is associated with the entry of gentlemen to the task of writing for the stage. The gentlemen poets' work has superceded that of lazy theatre-poets, who only offer revivals 'Mouldy and stale, as was the Usurers pye.' The professional dramatists' roles have sunk back into being no more than an adjunct to the playhouse operations. Spark imagines that

> Now their trade
> Must needs go down, when so many set up.

> I do not think but I shall shortly see
> One Poet sue to keep the door, another
> To be a prompter, a third to snuff the candles.

In a final metatheatrical moment, two successive actors enter to speak the prologue and are laughed off the stage by the 'audience' of critics, *'at which an Actor plac't in the pit laughs'* and the Prologue on stage challenges him 'to speak the prologue for me'. Spark then suggests that

> some poor Hackney Poet
> Has hir'd the Players to be out upon
> Suspicion, that they are abus'd in the prologue'.

The 'real' prologue enters and the play can begin.

This Praeludium offers an unusually complex vignette of theatre-goers in the seventeenth century. However the difficulties of dating the Praeludium, and its relationship to the play it precedes, vitiate any attempts to read it as mimesis or reportage. The play was attributed to Thomas Goffe in the Stationers Register entry in 1655 and appeared on the title page of the printed text in 1656. Goffe had died a quarter of a century earlier in 1629 and G.E. Bentley concludes that 'there is nothing in the text of the play proper or the epilogue to suggest commercial production or a date'.[1] In his reprint of the Praeludium, Bentley further insists 'The theatrically allusive Praeludium and the prologues ... were written about 1638, much later than the rest of the play, and by another author, possibly Richard Brome.'[2] Bentley's evidence for Brome's involvement rests on Brome's known objections to courtier playwrights but the Praeludium seems rather to be approving their engagement with the theatre as a source of refinement that will improve its artistic standards and protect it from the old fashioned tastes of an unsuitable audience represented by Thrift and the landlord.

The Praeludium seems to me to be less driven by particular interests in a local debate than a representation of the cross currents in a theatrical culture that was coming to terms with the tensions between received artistic values and the realities of commercial theatre production. The figures represented here are too familiar from satire and city comedy to be anything more than social types but the detail with which they are presented provides a special insight into the terms in which consumers for drama could be configured. They are categorised by wealth, social standing and the location of their activity in the court, country, city and Inns of Court. These familiar social differences are used as the basis for differentiations of taste but standing and judgement (social capital and cultural capital) are complexly mapped one onto another. Spark's remarks condemn Thrift and the Landlord as the least discerning of the quartet of characters but the dialogue makes clear that this division between Spark and Spruce on the one hand and Thrift and the Landlord on the other is not simply a matter of wealth. Thrift is comically preoccupied with value for money but he is certainly not poor: to be owed 'Two thousand pound for Garters and for Roses' might create a cash-flow problem for his business but it suggests a significant turnover for the activity as a whole. Spark, on the other hand, in spite of his authoritative grasp of aesthetic judgement is poor enough to have to choose between play-going and eating out. The landlord's role on the provincial bench suggests a figure of significant standing and wealth in his county and his charming reminiscences of the actor, Reade[3] 'crying *Doodle Doodle Dooe*,/Beyond compare' or his performance as the Changeling in Middleton and Rowley's play show an experienced theatre-goer.

The Praeludium, in other words, complicates assumptions about any simple connection between social standing, wealth and artistic judgement. It also reconfigures the nature of artistic judgement by contrasting knowledge and judgement of the arts with knowledge and judgement exercised in other social spheres. The Landlords' knowledge of the law of the land does not equip him with a knowledge of the 'Laws of Comedy and Tragedy' and Thrift's canny understanding of commercial relations excludes him from the world of artistic judgement. Spark's contempt for Thrift's presumption to judge the theatre plays on the different metaphorical meanings of 'numbers':

> Cause you sell Phansies, and can cast account,
> Do y'think your brain conceives Poetique numbers?

The numerical calculations that Thrift makes about how much he can be charged or the relative value for money of different forms of entertainment cannot equip him to judge poetry.

The *Praeludium* in effect proposes a special arena for artistic judgement: one that is free from commercial considerations and one that can only be entered through aesthetic judgements and knowledge of the rules of art. The artistic knowledge necessary for judgement in this special artistic world is presented as quite different from knowledge of earlier theatre traditions and can only be created through the work of gentlemen poets whose relationship to the theatre is not commercial at all. The professional poets, whose work for the commercial theatre is commodified by its repetition, are being pushed back into commercial roles as house keepers and prompters, while the gentlemen poets bring to the theatre the 'free and well meant charity' with which they 'Devote their vacant minutes to the Muses'.

Spruce and Spark's discursive construction of a special, non-commercial, world for poetry is further complicated by the way in which the *Praeludium* also articulates a conflict between price and value within the commercial theatre. When Thrift tries to negotiate the cost of entry to the theatre, Bolt insists that the prices are not for barter and makes a distinction between the commerce of the theatre and the 'market or exchange'. His position opens up the recurring social question of the relationship between price and value, one that vexed official attempts to establish the 'just price' in commodity markets. Thrift, on the other hand, is aware of the role that competitive pressure plays in controlling value for money. He compares the theatre's value for money unfavourably with other forms of popular entertainment – 'the six motions at Bartholomew Fair'. He is able to do so because he comes from an emerging commercial world in which commodity exchange was being replaced by a market in money. He reflects that the shilling being charged for entry could provide working capital for an Alderman and is also aware that he could himself off-set his expenditure at the theatre by inflating the prices of his own wares at the expense of his creditors and customers. Competition among theatres also allows him to buy the pleasures that he expects from the theatre at a cheaper rate. He decides to

> Hasten to the Money-Box
> And take my shilling out again, for now
> I have considered that it is too much
> I'le go to the Bull or Fortune, and there to see
> A play for two pense with a Jig to boot.

On the artistic side the distinction lay between the demands of art and the familiar pleasures of performance. The landlord wants to 'see the Fool in every act/Be't comedy or tragedy' and Thrift agrees: 'I'd rather see him leap, laugh or cry,/Than hear the gravest speech in all the play.' The city and the country, regardless of wealth or standing, share the taste for performance over language, but those old and well established pleasures are available across the whole spectrum of commercial theatre and Thrift decides to take them at the cheapest rate.

This interweaving of the discourses of economic, moral and artistic value complicates our sense of the nature of the relationship between consumers of theatre and its development as a form of commercial entertainment. Classic accounts of the development of consumer behaviour have emphasised the force of the two driving forces of emulation and substitution. This model has been complicated and contested in recent accounts of consumption[4] but it is possible to perceive both of those forces at work in the motivation of the figures in Goffe's Praeludium: Spruce, the courtier could be described as being engaged in emulation in his taste for high fashion and his rejection of Thrift's offer of Ribbons round his hat as 'too pedlar like' and Spark clearly describes the substitution effect of choosing between one consumer activity (theatre going) and another (eating out). However these simple, and satirically effective, representations of emulation and substitution are clearly placed in a hierarchy of values that are quite different from those assumed by modern economists. For the modern economist, substitution is a more complex kind of choice that has at its basis, not the value of particular activities but their relative utility in their use of time. Earning time is the constant that balances the ratio between prices and wages and affects consumer choice. As Oates and Baumol explained in their 1970 essay 'On the Economics of the theatre in Renaissance London',[5]

> rising real wages increase the economic value of time. Hence they raise the relative real cost of activities like theatrical attendance whose consumption time is high relative to their price. Low real wages will always produce a substitution effect that favours this type of activity.[6]

Oates and Baumol are assuming that decisions about time take place in a wage economy that clearly does not apply across the whole spectrum of early modern society. Nevertheless, their assumption about the relative value of time helpfully identifies the key distinction between Thrift, on the one hand and Spruce, Spark and Landlord, on the other.

When Thrift observes that he will not stay at the theatre, but get his money and 'go to the Bull or the Fortune and there to see/A play for two pence with a Jig to boot', he is making calculations about relative value for money as much as about taste for a particular form of theatre. Alone of all the playgoers, he exists in a fully modern commercial environment where different theatrical offerings can be computed against money spent. His distinction from the other playgoers does not rest in low status or relative poverty but in calculation. His companions, like the gentlemen poets that they admire, need to make no calculation about the relative value of their time. Their wealth affords them not merely the price of the entrance to the theatre but the 'vacant minutes' that they can devote in 'free and constant charity' to the muses. Thrift's commercial calculations in fact disqualify him from engaging with the world of poetic drama. He is excluded from the audience and although he appears to make his calculation freely, the very fact of this calculation is felt to exclude him from the arena of aesthetic judgements.

The particular modernity of Thrift's pre-occupation with calculation or the transitory nature of the courtier poets' freedom with their time is only dimly glimpsed in the *Praeludium*. The emerging sense of an economy of time is overlaid by more familiar, satiric objects and confused by the contrasts between different aesthetic values. However this important locus of distinction between commercial calculation and the 'free' engagement with the muses is historically more significant than the often repeated distinction between public and private theatres, or between courtier poets and commercial theatre employees. The distinctions between different kinds of theatre that are made to map so neatly onto different social types remained tied to the discourses of aesthetics, to the nature of theatre that was produced and were essentially those of the pre-commercial world.

Even when commentary surrounding a plays seems self-consciously to acknowledge its commercial conditions of production, it does so only to exclude commercial considerations from the true appreciation of its art. The prologue to the Blackfriars performance of Habington's *Queen of Aragon*, for example, identifies members of the audience who might calculate the time and money spent at a play against their appreciation of it, and invites them simply to leave:

> Ere we begin, that no man may repent
> Two shillings and his time, the Author sent
> The Prologue, with the errors of his Play,
> That who will, may take his money and away.

The implied joke of this address separates the actual audience from those who would be so crass as actually to calculate the value of money and time. There is a comic double bluff involved that flatters the audience who stays by associating them with a free engagement with the play's artistic value. In the case of this play, the joke is compounded by the fact that this play was an exclusive production by a courtier poet. It had been performed at court in 1640 by the Lord Chamberlain's own servants and at 'his charge in the cloathes and sceanes, which were very riche and curious'. It was also licensed to the Kings Men by the Master of the Revels.[7]

The court connection might have been expected to commend the play to its Kings Men audience. However, the 'Prologue at the Friars' makes no mention of it and, after its rejection of the calculating audience (quoted above) reverts to discussing the play's aesthetic qualities, each of which is discussed as the negation of inappropriate taste:

> Its no way intricate
> By cross deceits in love, nor so high in state,
> That we might have given out in our playbill,
> This day's 'The Prince' writ by Nick Machiavil.[8]

The language of the Prologue flatters the audience as those who do not calculate money and time and thus do not have a taste for stories of love or politics, language that is 'Big with mysterious words', cross dressing, passionate ladies or bawdy mirth, 'the wit of bottle-ale and double-beer'. The 'bawdy mirth' is particularly associated with the taste of 'the wife of a citizen' and a 'country justice' but the explicitly socially based exclusion is not emphasised. This is the arena where taste and judgement effect their own exclusions by their implicit dismissal of those who 'repent/Two shillings and his time.'

Clearly this prologue, like Goffe's Praeludium, is working through rather laboured tropes of self-effacement rather than making assertions about a perceived social reality. Nevertheless, the distinctions made by those tropes reveal the construction of taste in which judgement is the primary desired relationship between the play and its audience . In the prologue at Court, the actors ask for mercy before the King and Queen's judgement and the Epilogue at Blackfriars equally affects to fear 'Stern judges, (who) a pardon never give;/For only merit with you makes things live.'

This construction of a judging audience, above the fray of commercial calculation and clearly differentiated from the citizen and the country justice, is most explicitly articulated in these two examples from the middle years of the seventeenth century. However these discursive distinctions had been found in the commercial theatre long before the courtier poets became involved with theatrical production. In the *locus classicus* of the debate over the value of theatre as art, Ben Jonson's *Bartholomew Fair*, the prologue sets up a comically direct relationship between the paying consumer and the right to judgement. In the Induction, Ben Jonson has his scrivener draw up a contract between the poet and the audience in which the spectators agree that they will only judge the play according to the price they have paid for their seats: they are invited, 'for themselves and severally' to covenant and agree to remain in the places their money and friends have put them in:

> ... every person here, have his or their free-will of censure, to like or dislike at their owne charge, the *Author* having now departed with his right: It shall bee lawfull for any man to judge his six pen'orth, his twelve pen'orth, so to his eighteene pence, 2. shillings, halfe a crowne, to the value of his place: Provided alwaies his place get not above his wit. And if he pay for halfe a dozen, hee may censure for them all too, so that he will undertake that they shall bee silent ... if he drop but six pence at the doore, and will censure a crownes worth, it is thought there is no conscience, or justice in that.[9]

Jonson is comically satirising the commercialised relations that might evolve between audience and writer. His reductive account of a commodified artistic product and its deformation of aesthetic judgement is for Jonson a matter for regret, however comically presented. The *reductio ad absurdum* of taste to commerce is obvious and the audience is addressed as the knowing spectators who can see the joke, and thus place themselves above this purely commercial relationship.

The contract is part of address that also mocks the judgement of oldfashioned audiences who

> will swear Jeronimo and Andronicus are the best plays yet ... as a man whose judgement shews it is constant, and hath stood still these five and twenty or thirty years ... next to truth, a confirmed error does well.

By connecting taste to economics, Jonson in fact disentangles the two, implying that the truly tasteful audience, the audience who can join him in understanding the satire, will recognise the separate arenas of commerce and taste and will also have the judgement to appreciate innovation.

For Jonson, the preferred social relations of artistic production involved the freedom from commercial constraints provided by aristocratic patronage. When the *Bartholomew Fair* was presented, on the day following its opening at the Hope, to the King, the prologue offered his majesty, 'for a fairing, true delight'. A fairing was, of course, what was brought home from a market but that old fashioned market, the locus of a direct exchange of goods for money is quite different from the market calculations made by Thrift or the incommensurate relationship between the value of a play and the precise price paid by different categories of consumers. Jonson distinguishes between a fairing, bought at a market but a sign of a personal relationship, and the contractual relations in which the individuals involved negotiate their relations in terms of value for money.

These exclusions of commercial consumers from the true relations of theatre may seem curious in a context where the theatre was dependent on paying customers for its economic survival. In 'London and the Country Carbonadoed' (1632), Lupton notes that the players 'pray the company that's in to heare them patiently, yet they would not suffer them to come in without payment' (Lupton, 179) Lupton's satiric comment indicates an awareness of the negotiations between producers and consumers that obfuscated the real relations between them. Writers sought to engage their audiences in a shared world of artistic judgement. They mocked or excluded those who might see themselves as merely buying a product and implied that the actual audience (whatever its social composition and in spite of the fact that they too had paid) was fit to be the judge of art simply because they were not identified with the excluded group.

The creation of a separate, non-commercial arena for an audience's judgement was necessary because of the variety of prices that were charged for the same activity of seeing a play. The theatre-goers in the Praeludium paid twelve pence; Habington's Prologue asks for two shillings; Jonson's Induction refers to 'his sixpen'worth, his twelvepen'worth, so to his eighteen pence, two shillings, half a crown'. Thrift can go to the Bull or the Fortune for two pence and the sums recorded by actual consumers varied from the three pence paid for William Cavendish's servant when he accompanied his master to St Paul's in 1601 to the sums of 18 pence, 12 pence, 11 pence and 4 shillings and 6 pence that Sir William paid on different visits.[10] Gurr suggests that 'the variable sums paid suggest that on some visits he may have taken guests with him' but this evidence also shows that item costs cannot be a reliable way of defining consumers for particular theatres or indentifying the value that the consumers placed on their attendance.

These complexity of these discussions of paying and judging, cost and value, was compounded by the way that they played wittily on the language both of official market regulation and of the long philosophical tradition of anti-consumerism.[11] When Dekker notes that 'the Muses are turned to merchants' in *The Gull's Horn Book*, he adds that the theatre is paradoxically

> free in entertainment, allowing a stool as well to the farmers son as to your Templar, that your stinkard has the self same liberty to be there in his tobacco fumes which your sweet courtier has.

Dekker plays on the terms 'free' and 'liberty' to connect both their economic and their legal senses. The theatre was not free in that it cost money but its consumption was free in that it could be bought by anyone who had the money and allowed them access that was free from legal and customary constraints. However that freedom to participate in the market for plays could not ensure that the audience would like what it bought and made the negotiation over judgement the more pressing. Again and again prologues to plays attempted to ensure that consumers understood what they were getting but the heterogeneity of the paying audience made a simple solution impossible. The Prologue to Day's *Isle of Gulls* despairs of meeting the demands of all the playgoers in his audience:

> Alas Gentlemen, how ist possible to content you? You will have railing and invectives, which our Author neither dares not affects: you baudy and scurrill jests, which neither becomes his modestie to write, nor the eare of a generous Auditory to heare: you must ha swelling comparisons, and bumbast Epithetes, which are as fit for the body of a Comedie, as *Hercules* shooe for the foote of a Pygmey ...
>
>> Neither quick mirth, invective, nor high state,
>> Can content all: such is the boundless hate
>> Of a confused audience. (Gurr: 228)

Faced with the potential for consumer-driven chaos, theatre writers had to managed their audience discursively. They did so by constructing categories out of social types and intellectual dispositions, insisting on differentiations of genre – as in the debate between Comedy, History and Tragedy in *A Warning for Fair Women* – or in dramatising the comic disorder that ensues when, for example, in *The Knight of the Burning Pestle*, the citizen consumers attempt to intervene in the play and force the players to perform one that better suits their taste.

In the process of this negotiation, the consumer came to be constructed by the product even though the rhetoric of liberty suggested the opposite. In *The Knight of the Burning Pestle*, the interfering Grocer is told that 'you should have told us your minde a moneth since, our play is ready to begin now' (Induction, 31–2).[12] The play in other words is not a bespoke product that can suit the needs of the consumer but a commodity, like an object, that is taken ready made. The Grocer's resistance to innovation is comically marginalised in the ensuing pastiche. As in Goffe's Praeludium and *Bartholomew Fair*, the desired customer for the *Knight of the Burning Pestle* is identified as one with a taste for the new. However, in the process, the consumer is defined more broadly as the most appropriate for the play on offer.

The particular nature of this appropriate judgement that defined the idealised consumer could vary. When the playing companies began to re-purpose their backlist of plays in the revivals mocked by Goffe's Praeludium, they insisted on the virtue of tradition. The consistency of judgement mocked in *Bartholomew Fair* was positively invoked in the Prologue to revival of *The Custom of the Country* which claimed 'It were injustice to decry this now … being like'd before' and *The Coxcomb* prologue notes that 'when it first came forth/In the opinion of men of worth/Was well received and favoured'. Revivals from the past age could be admired as representing 'the best of Poets in that age' and 'by the best of Actors play'd' as Heywood claimed for the 1633 revival of *The Jew of Malta*.

In constructing their consumers as those best suited to the play on offer, the prologue-writers were both producing a culture of consumption and creating the conditions of its reproduction. Innovation and tradition could equally be the markers of value, the prices paid for entry could vary even in the same theatre and the process of calculating the value for money offered in paying for entertainment could be marginalized as unfitting for 'men of worth'. One of the most significant effects of this construction of consumers was that it created the illusion that consumption was a matter of taste and individual choice. Jonson may have mocked the idea that price could be a determination of taste but his Scrivener contracted with individual paying customers and marginalised a generalised group whose taste was incapable of being renewed by artistic innovation. Above all, the new consumer could be certain that he was not part of the 'multitude', the excluded portion of the community who had none of these characteristics.

This 'multitude' could be variously configured as the opposite of any targeted group. Douglas Brooks's account of the emergence of a print culture for drama offers numerous examples of the term being used to describe the theatrical as opposed to the literary consumer.[13] Within the theatre itself, the term was used to oppose the judging individual to the 'multitude' who did not understand the conventions of the stage and did not recognise the differences between discrete artistic productions and the traditions of communal performance. In his defence of his contribution to the Royal Entry for James VI and I, Dekker acknowledged that 'the multitude is now to be our audience, whose heads would miserably runne a wool-gathering, if we doo but offer to break them with hard words'. His denigration of the multitude's lack of learning is commonplace but behind it lies a professional recognition of the different nature of the consumer for his different kinds of writing. That differentiation between the individual consumer and the generalised multitude was articulated in terms of a hierarchy of taste but it also constructed a difference between the selective (and he would say 'free') purchase of cultural consumption in the theatre and the participation in a communal public event such as the civic celebration of James's Royal entry.

That distinction between individual consumption and participation in communal festivities or membership of group was also evident in the treatment of the Grocer and his family in the Induction to *The Knight of the Burning Pestle*. The exchange between the Grocer and the prologue is startling because the Grocer appears to breaks the contract of consumption that requires him to accept the play on offer and insists on a more direct relationship between the audience and the players. For him, plays are not only to be consumed in the theatre but can be put to other uses. They can be raided for amateur performance of set speeches, like the one from *1 Henry IV* that Rafe presents in a 'huffing part' (Induction 72–9); they can be accompanied by other performers such as the Waits of Southwark and they can become part of the familiar repeated culture of the city like the favourite titles that he suggests as an alternative to the play proposed. His sense that the theatre could celebrate the ideals of a communal culture militated against the direction of the commercial theatre in which plays were repeatable commodities offered to an audience of individuals whose payment gave them only the right to judge the play on offer or reject it in favour of a different product offered elsewhere.

The arena of judgement in which plays were to be appreciated was carefully circumscribed so as to exclude inappropriately direct engagement with the events represented on stage. The construction of the theatre consumer as a discriminating judge assumed that the object of judgement, the play, was a discrete artistic entity, able to be judged in aesthetic terms because it was different from the life world of the discriminating audience. In cases where the boundary between the play-world and the life-world was more permeable, it seems to have required both official intervention and vigorous assertion on the part of the surrounding commentary on the play-events themselves.

In 1625, accompanied by much scandal, Dekker, Ford, Rowley and Webster were involved in presenting a play based on the true story of Anne Elsdon who had been abducted and forcibly married by a fortune hunter. The story was one of legalised rape and it clearly deeply offended Anne Elsdon's family who sought redress against the players in Star Chamber. The play is not extant but a ballad recounting the story is and it indicates that the play was performed at the Red Bull. In spite of the seriousness of the charges (and the distress caused to Anne Elsdon), the ballad concludes, cheerfully enough:

> Therefore lett yong men that are poore
> Come take example heere,
> And you who faine would heare the full
> Discourse of this match makeing,
> The play will teach you at the Bull,
> To keepe the widdow wakeing.[14]

These lines suggest that Dekker and Webster may have been trying to turn the story into they kind of city comedy they had written in the early years of the century. On this occasion, however, though the address to 'yong men that are poore' links the potential consumers to the performance the relationship between the audience who might have enjoyed this comedy and the actual individuals whose life was presented on stage was dangerously unstable. In the view of Anne Elsdon's family, this was not a commodity to be judged by paying individuals but an outrageous attack on her privacy and a threat to their standing in the community.

The Red Bull theatre was also the venue for another performance that attracted official attention, the case of *The Whore New Vamp'd*. Described as 'scandalous and libellous' the play apparently 'scandalised and defamed the whole profession of proctors belonging to the court of the civil law'. As with so many censorship cases, the defamatory lines in question seem pretty innocuous: Andrew Cane the actor was charged with having described an alderman as a 'base drunken sottish knave'. The real offence was that these general remarks, that could be found in numerous other plays, were attached to a particular individual, identified as 'the blacksmith in Holborn' and a vintner.[15] In this case the address to differentiated consumers that was commonplace in other contexts was *too* particular. It crossed the line between the engagement of particular categories – the creation of special markets in which consumers could see themselves – and the personal application that Ben Jonson warned against in the Induction to *Bartholomew Fair*. Having welcomed all who have the wit or the honesty to think well of themselves, Jonson's scrivener's final agreement with the hearers and spectators is that 'they neither in themselves conceal, nor suffer by them to be concealed, any state-decipherer, or politic pick-lock of the scene, so solemnly ridiculous as to search out who was meant by the ginger-bread woman, who by the hobby-horse man, who by the costermonger, nay, who by their wares'.

These cases, where the writers and the companies misjudged the relationship between product and consumer, demonstrate the residual instability of the process of constructing the consumer for early-modern theatre. Since neither play is extant, they can be regarded as aberrations in a theatre culture that presented plays as discrete literary works able to be presented in different houses, at court or in revivals and indeed, in some cases, reproduced in modern times.

It is probably no accident that both of them were preformed at the Red Bull, a venue that recurs in prologues from other theatres as the locus of the inappropriate consumer. As we have seen, Thrift sees the Bull as the value-for money option in offering a play for two pence and a jig to boot, Webster complained about the reception of *The White Devil* at the Red Bull, commendatory verses on Randolph's *Poems* contrasted them with plays 'Acted (more was the pity) by the Red Bull' and Jonson was admired because he did *not* write of 'Pitched fields, as Red Bull wars'.[16]

This discursive polarisation between the Red Bull audience and the consumers of more artistically satisfying plays has been accepted as a fact of theatre history ever since James Wright in *Historia Histrionica* wrote that the Fortune and the Red Bull 'were mostly frequented by Citizens and the meaner sort of people.'[17] However it represents the success with which the prologue writers for other theatre companies managed the construction of the consumer for early modern theatre. They elided the social categories of the audience with the repertory and style of the plays, creating arenas of taste that mapped easily onto social stratification. Nevertheless, when constructed by writers who practiced across the whole spectrum of theatres, the address to consumers of Red Bull plays was much the same as that of more exclusive venues. Dekker's prologue to *If This be not a Good Play the Devil is in it*, addresses the audience as the judges, asking

> Would 'twere a Custom that all New-playes
> The Makers sat o'th'stage, either with Bays
> To have their works crownd, or beaten in with hissing.

In the same prologue, judging audience is distinguished from the undiscriminating crowd who are defined only by their ability to pay:

> Ift fill the house with Fishwives, Rare they all roare
> Is it not praise is sought for now, but pence.[18]

The eclectic variety of entertainment on offer at the Red Bull may have demanded a more active construction of an appropriate response from its audience. In the prologue to another Red Bull play, *The Two Merry Milkmaids*, the audience is told it that should

> Expect no noyse of Guns, Trumpets nor Drum
> No sword and target, but to hear sense and words
> Fitting the matter that the scene affords.

The familiar opposition between noisy spectacle and a verbal theatre of sense and words once again defines the audience in terms of its capacity for judgement and an understanding of the higher value accorded to words than action. The audience is reassured that the play will include 'a conjurer, a devil and a clowne too' but the venue associated with noise and fighting could also present itself as appropriate for a new kind of theatrical pleasure:

> the stage being reformed and free
> From the loud clamours it was wont to be
> Turmoiled with battles, you, I hope, will cease
> Your daily tumults and with us, wish peace.

In the Red Bull, as in other venues that offered plays ready made for consumption, writers invoked the same set of recurring values. Judgement was set against payment and words against spectacle. It was the capacity for judgement and discrimination that defined the ideal spectator, not the nature of the actual repertory or even the venue in which it was performed. Repertory and venue were used as counters in the set of oppositions that defined the spectator's judgement but the same oppositions were used in different venues and for different kinds of plays. The commercial viability of the Red Bull as a playhouse depended as much on non-dramatic events as on drama, and its plays occasionally crossed the boundary between the autonomous, repeatable work of art and the local community. These features of its repertory may have contributed to its reputation as a special venue that could be constructed as the opposite of the one where its detractors were offering their wares or were bestowing their custom.

In the absence of any systematic or consistent records of theatre attendance it is impossible to test the model of the ideal consumer against the actual consumption of early modern drama. Even if this data did exist, it is unlikely that it would be able satisfactorily to close the gap between the rhetorical figuring that constructed appropriate consumers for the drama and the demographic definitions of play-going types that it might configure. The significance of the construction of the consumer for drama lay rather in its implications for the definition of plays as a special kind of commodity with particular utility for the development of the commercial theatre.

As David Hawkes has shown, the anti-theatrical protest against commercial theatre turned on the extent to which it could be shown as an abuse of poetry: 'to "abuse" poetry was to transform it into a commodity to be traded on the market' (Hawkes: 79). This abuse was contrasted with the proper use of objects that was connected to their function or 'end'. While this distinction was clear in the case of a physical commodities, it was rather harder to define a proper use of playing. Various attempts were made to create analogies between the pleasures of playing and other forms of objectless consumption. In the final lines of *Westward Ho*, Iustiano, connects the experience of the play with the purchase of health as a general good:

> Gold that buyes health, can never be ill spent,
> Nor howres laid out in harmlesse meryment (V, iv 307–8)

However the purchase of 'howres laid out in harmless merryment' could not be specifically associated with the costs or value of play-going. As we have seen, the money spent in attending the performance of a play seems to have varied considerably and the same play could be experienced in different settings for different amounts of money. Moreover, as the practice of revivals shows, a play, unlike a shoe or a loaf of bread, was not used up by its purchase.

This fluidity in the cost:price ratio of individual plays presented the playing companies with the classic economic opportunity both to cover their costs by increasing sales or by increasing the unit price paid by each customer constrained only by the availability of suitable spaces for playing. The opening up of new playing places in the precincts of the former religious houses of Blackfriars and St Pauls in which companies of boys performed new plays and the move of the Kings Men into the Blackfriars theatre, providing a winter house for the company's repertory, showed the companies making the most of these opportunities by shifting to provide more expensive venues.

It is unlikely that these commercial moves were the result of a particularly thought out commercial strategy. Investment in playing in the period seems rather to have been driven by a mixture of opportunism and emulation and alongside successful figures such as Henslowe, Alleyn and Christopher Beeston, there were disastrous failures such as Francis Langley and Thomas Woodford.[19] Nevertheless, the commercial implications of constructing a consumer as a 'man of worth' whose judgement allowed him to transcend mere commercial considerations worked with this tendency to move up the value scale in the developing market for entertainment. In order to sustain the move up-scale, it was also important to ensure that the plays were free of any particular reference to local events or circumstances. This was a protection against the potential disasters of censorship that might close the theatres down but it also ensured that plays, even when their first performances had caused controversy, could be repeated to produce new income. However it was precisely this absence of any connection between plays and dangerous and contingent real events that constructed a special arena of the aesthetic in which plays could continue to function as commerce.

None of these commercial considerations depended on the existence of discriminating and differentiated consumers: an ability to pay enough in sufficiently large numbers was all that was required for commercial success. However the theatre traded in the cultural currency that was available to it. These elements of this currency included a volatile and contradictory mix of neo-classical poetic theory, a habit of differentiation between social categories and a philosophical and religious tradition of anti-consumerism. What is so extraordinary is that a not dissimilar set of categories, setting popular against elite entertainment, and free (or subsidised) art against commercial entertainment, continue to inform the construction of cultural consumers to this day.

Coda

It is tempting to leave the consumer for early-modern theatre in this limbo of discursive categories. However actual consumers also existed as social beings and the social implications of their discursive construction is also at issue. When we turn to the evidence for actual playgoing, as with all documentary evidence, the records are skewed towards those that cluster around events that required some official intervention. They over-represent the literate, the diary keeping and the letter-writing sections of the population. Andrew Gurr's invaluable list in the Appendix to *Playgoing in Shakesperean London* (Gurr, 197–212) could be subdivided into those who appeared in connection with affrays – of both low life and more upper-class altercations; those who came with the frequent Mildmay and Dering theatre parties; those involved in particular celebrated productions such as *A Game at Chess* or the Essex command performance of *Richard II*; tourists, and those in the business. Reading this list of consumers, it is tempting to treat them as a sort of 'fiction in the archives': to extrapolate conclusions about taste or demography from them or even to see their case as a shifting paradigm for the whole culture of play-going. Taken as a whole, the list includes people from all social classes: it includes some Catholics (Gurr:197) some who supported the Parliamentarian side in the English Civil War (Butler: 100–40), some, not all of them citizens, who made a careful note of the costs of their play-going (Gurr: 198–9) some who saw themselves represented on stage (Gurr: 201) and even a rare few who left behind some indication of what they saw and (rarer still) what they thought of it (Gurr: 201, 207, 210).

However as soon as any pressure is brought to bear on individual cases, the evidence for theatre-going that brings them into this list is overwhelmed by the sheer idiosyncracy of their personal circumstances. Joan Drake, for example, assumed to be a theatre-goer because of an apparent reference to *The Alchemist* in her spiritual biography, was suffering from suicidal thoughts and attempts following a very difficult child-birth. Her mockery of her devout spiritual advisor John Dod, as like '*Ananias*, one whom at a play in the Blackfriars she saw scoft at for a holy brother of Amsterdam' tells us that she may have seen Jonson's play but that knowledge seems one of the least interesting aspect of her life and the story that tells it.[20]

The case of 'Browne, a serving man in a blew coat' is similarly puzzling. What was he doing quarrelling with poor boys at the door of the Theatre in 1584 and why should wounding one of the boys have brought together a crowd of a thousand people. Did he '(colour) all his doynges here about this towne with a sute that he haithe in the lawe ... in Staffordshire' because he was mad with the law like Arthur of Bradley in *Bartholomew Fair* or did Chambers record the story because he responded to the buried (and chronologically impossible) literary connection?

Figuring the Consumer for Early Modern Drama 203

These individuals cannot be defined by their consumption of theatre and their particular circumstances offer something of a reproach to our efforts to define them as such. Those efforts are coloured by what David Hawkes has described as 'the current economic orthodoxy (that) ... views human beings as consumers by nature' but they are of a piece with the process of defining consumers that was an effect of the commercialisation of theatre in the early modern period. As we have seen, those definitions of consumers were a necessary part of production, creating both a sense that the theatre was available to all, and that the action of consuming literary theatre, in contrast to other forms of entertainment or luxury goods, conferred a special status on the individuals who did so.

This discursive conflation of the effects of production and consumption has important implications for the ways that we interpret the impact of commercial theatre in the seventeenth century. Since evidence from those in the business of playing – whether in the form of play texts or in their surrounding commentary – is the most extensive and the most coherent, it creates a closed, if virtuous, circle that runs from play production to play consumption and back via consumer demand to further play production. That cycle is driven almost entirely by the supply side whose address to consumers is part of a validation of the value of their products. The assumption, understandable enough, is that producers knew their markets and consumption could be read off from the existence of production. Even when the nature of that market is the primary consideration, the focus returns again and again either to a 'poetics of the market', the terms in which markets were imagined in the early modern period (Bruster: 7) or the terms in which consumer demand might have structured production.

When social historians turn their attention to the theatre, they too construct an audience that is receiving the messages of culture in ways that are readily understood. In his monumental work on early modern 'popular' culture, *The Anti-Christ's Lewd Hat*, Peter Lake offers an image of an audience that participated equally in theatrical as well as other forms of cultural display. Accepting, as well he might, a scholarly consensus 'that access to the drama was available to relatively humble Londoners and that audiences at the theatres were socially mixed', he concludes that 'the market being aimed at was a large and socially heterogeneous one; a crowd, similar, in fact, to the socially mixed surging and swaying mass that might have attended one of the executions described in the (murder) pamphlets'.[21]

Lake carefully distances himself from those historians in search of the 'authentic expressions of the culture of the "people" but his aim as a social historian is nonetheless to identify the way that 'contemporaries made sense of their world' (pp. xx–xxi), 'were able to articulate, exploit and allay the anxieties felt by contemporaries in the face of political, religious and social change' (p. xxv). He finds evidence of these popular mentalities in a series of subtle and well informed readings of a huge range of polemical, socially descriptive and theatrical texts. Unsurprisingly to literary scholars, he also finds that 'Jonson and Shakespeare identify with uncanny precision many of the issues, tensions and conflicts that lie ... at the heart of the culture and politics of post-reformation England.' (p. xxxiv). The early modern consumer, supposedly addressed by these texts and events, steps aside and allows direct communication between the texts of the time and the modern scholar. The occlusion of the consumer from the cultural process is in part because commercial consumption is seen only as a neutral means of circulating of cultural goods: the experience of consumption is assumed to be homogeneous and to be easily equated to non-commercial forms of cultural interaction. But 'the swaying surging mass at a hanging', though its personnel may overlap with the audience at the theatre, has a different relationship to the events on the scaffold than the consumer of theatre has to those on the stage. In his analysis, Lake elides the 'fictive and festive form of the drama' (Lake: xxx) and in doing so ignores the cultural work that was done as writers helped the playing companies negotiate their way past assumptions about a communal culture and the commercial realities of their means of production.

In the event, as I have argued, the commercialised consumption of cultural goods achieved a higher status than more communal forms of entertainment. It was able to do so because it addressed the consumers as individuals, marginalized the commercial realities of their relationship to their culture and created a special arena of aesthetic judgement in which literary drama could be consumed. However, contemporary writers remained clear about this distinction between the world of the play and the life world. In a poem that seems a direct riposte to Lake's conflation of the audience for hangings and the audience for plays, Walter Raleigh sets up a series of analogies between life and the stage. However, he concludes

> Thus march we playing to our latest rest
> Only we die in earnest that's no jest.

That welcome reminder of the difference between consumption and the business of living and dying is echoed in Jean Christophe Agnew's account of 'Consumer culture in historical perspective'. Arguing against the turn to culture in recent social analysis and in particular against those who overemphasise the social utility of the symbolic power of consumption, he asks 'Were goods that good to think?'. In his own answer, he questions the limited utility of commerce and consumption to enhance our appreciation of the remote consequences of our acts or (to) clarify our responsibilities for them. (Agnew: 33) In taking this position, Agnew is aligning himself with the anti-theatricalists' fears about the damaging ethical effects of commodified culture.

This essay has shown how the construction of a consumer for drama both facilitated the emergence of commercial theatre and restricted the kinds of communal and social experience that it allowed. Placing it beside Agnew's fears for a world articulated only in commercial terms as well as brief and puzzling glimpses of the lives of individual consumers is intended as a reminder that the process described was only one side of a dialectic that remains with us and over which we still have some control.

Notes

1. G.E. Bentley, *Jacobean and Caroline Stage*, IV, Oxford: Clarendon Press, 1956, p. 302.
2. G.E. Bentley, *The Seventeenth Century Stage*, Chicago:University of Chicago Press, 1964, 28.
3. For Reade's connection with the Salisbury Court Theatre, see Bentley, *Jacobean and Caroline Stage*, II, 1941, p. 540.
4. See Lorna Wetherill, 'The Meaning of consumer behaviour in late seventeenth and early eighteenth century England,' in John Brewer and Roy Porter, *Consumption and the World of Goods*, London: Routledge 1993, 206–27.
5. Mary I. Oates and William J. Baumol, 'On the Economics of the Theatre in Renaissance London', *Swedish Journal of Economics*, 74, 1972, 136–61.
6. Oates and Baumol, p. 152.
7. N.W. Bawcutt, ed., *The Control and Censorship of Caroline Drama*, Oxford: Clarendon Press, 1996, p. 207.
8. In W. Carew Hazlitt, ed., *A Select Collection of Old English Plays*, volume 13, London: Reeves and Turner 1875, p. 327.
9. Induction, 85–96, *Ben Jonson*, Edited by C.H. Herford and Percy and Evelyn Simpson, Oxford: Clarendon Press 1938.
10. See Appendix 1 of Andrew Gurr, *Playgoing in Shakespearean London*, p. 199.
11. David Hawkes, *Idols of the Marketplace. Idolatry and Commodity Fetishism in English Literature 1580–1680*, Basingstoke: Palgrave, 2001, ch. 3, 77–94.
12. *The Dramatic Works in the Beaumont and Fletcher Canon*, Vol. 1, General Editor Fredson Bowers, Cambridge: Cambridge University Press, 1966.
13. Douglas A. Brooks, *From Playhouse to Printing House: Drama and Authorship in Early Modern England*. Cambridge: Cambridge University Press, 2000.
14. Quoted in C.J. Sisson, *The Lost Plays of Shakespeare's Age*, Cambridge: Cambridge University Press, 1936, p. 110.
15. (Wickham, Ingram and Berry: 585–6.)
16. John Webster, *The White Devil*, 1613. 'Epistle to the reader'; Randolph, *Poems, with the Muses Looking Glass* (1638); Jasper Mayne, in *Jonsonus Virbius* (1638), sig E4.
17. G.E. Bentley, *The Jacobean and Caroline Stage*, Oxford: Clarendon Press, 1956, vol. 2, 693.
18. Thomas Dekker, *If This be not a Good Play the Devil is in it*, in Fredson Bowers, ed., *The Dramatic Works of Thomas Dekker*, Cambridge: Cambridge University Press, 1953, vol. 2.
19. See William Ingram, *The Business of Playing*, Ithaca and London: Cornell University Press, 1992; Rebecca Rogers and Kathleen McLuskie 'Who invested in the Early Modern Theatre', *Research Opportunities in Renaissance Drama*, XLI, 2002, 29–61.
20. See Alan Pritchard, 'Puritans and the Blackfriar's theatre: The cases of Mistresses Duck and Drake', *Shakespeare Quarterly*, 45, 1994, 92–5.

21. Peter Lake, *The Antichrist's Lewd Hat Protestants, Papists and Players in Post-Reformation England*, New Haven and London: Yale University Press (2002), p. 377.

Works cited

Bawcutt, N. W., ed. *The Control and Censorship of Caroline Drama*. Oxford: Clarendon Press, 1996.
Beaumont, Francis, and John Fletcher. *The Dramatic Works in the Beaumont and Fletcher Canon*. 10 vols. General Editor, Fredson Bowers. Cambridge University Press, 1966.
Bentley, G. E. *Jacobean and Caroline Stage*. 7 vols. Oxford: Clarendon Press, 1956.
———. *The Seventeenth Century Stage*. Chicago: University of Chicago Press, 1964.
Brooks, Douglas A. *From Playhouse to Printing House: Drama and Authorship in Early Modern England*. Cambridge: Cambridge University Press, 2000.
Dekker, Thomas. *If This be not a Good Play the Devil is in it*. In *The Dramatic Works of Thomas Dekker*. Ed. Fredson Bowers. Cambridge: Cambridge University Press, 1953.
Gurr, Andrew, *Playgoing in Shakespearean London*. Cambridge: Cambridge University Press, 1987.
Hawkes, David. *Idols of the Marketplace. Idolatry and Commodity Fetishism in English Literature 1580–1680*. Basingstoke: Palgrave, 2001.
Hazlitt, W. Carew, ed. *A Select Collection of Old English Plays*. Vol. 13, London: Reeves and Turner 1875.
Ingram, William. *The Business of Playing*. Ithaca and London: Cornell University Press, 1992.
Jonson, Ben. *Ben Jonson*, Edited by C.H. Herford and Percy and Evelyn Simpson, Oxford: Clarendon Press, 1938.
Lake, Peter. *The Antichrist's Lewd Hat Protestants, Papists and Players in Post-Reformation England*. New Haven and London: Yale University Press, 2002.
Lupton, 'London and the Country Carbonadoed' (1632).
Jasper Mayne, in *Jonsonus Virbius* (1638), sig E4.
Oates, Mary I., and William J. Baumol. 'On the Economics of the Theatre in Renaissance London', *Swedish Journal of Economics* 74 (1972): 136–61.
Pritchard, Alan. 'Puritans and the Blackfriar's theatre: The cases of Mistresses Duck and Drake', *Shakespeare Quarterly* 45 (1994): 92–5.
Randolph, *Poems, with the Muses Looking Glass* (1638).
Rogers, Rebecca, and Kathleen McLuskie. 'Who invested in the Early Modern Theatre?', *Research Opportunities in Renaissance Drama* 41 (2002): 29–61.
C.J. Sisson, *The Lost Plays of Shakespeare's Age*, Cambridge University Press, 1936.
Wetherill, Lorna. 'The Meaning of consumer behaviour in late seventeenth and early eighteenth century England', in John Brewer and Roy Porter, eds. *Consumption and the World of Goods*. London: Routledge, 1993: 206–27.
Wickham, Glynne, Herbert Berry, and William Ingram, eds. *English Professional Theatre, 1530–1660*. Cambridge; New York: Cambridge University Press, 2000.

11
The Delusion of Critique: Subjunctive Space, Transversality, and the Conceit of Deceit in *Hamlet*

Anthony Kubiak & Bryan Reynolds

In their recent essay, ' "A little touch of Harry in a night": Translucency and Projective Transversality in the Sexual and National Politics of *Henry V*,' Donald Hedrick and Bryan Reynolds argue that Shakespeare's Princess Catherine potentially undermines King Henry's fantasized domination of her during sex by occupying antithetically the conceptual–emotional spacetime of Catherine's blindness by 'winking' (5.2.262). In other words, Henry's fantasy of Catherine closing her eyes during sex that he shares with Burgundy ('Yet they do wink and yield, as love is blind and enforces' [5.2.259]) so that he can enter her from behind ('and so I shall catch the fly, your cousin [Catherine], in the latter end, and she must be blind too' [5.2.270–1]), inadvertently makes room for Catherine, in her imagination, to 'disappear' and thereby deceive Henry. As Hedrick and Reynolds put it,

> Sex-without-seeing, from the perspective of this [Henry's] fantasy, indicates a trajectory of male and national domination. But a transversal reading suggests a different possibility altogether – a key to the scene, if not to the entire play: by closing one's eyes, one "disappears" the other, or even transforms the other into someone else. Instead of transversality as a becoming-other of one's own subjectivity, becoming what you are not, transversality might be now thought of in terms of transforming the other outside himself or herself, a projective transversality or "Renaissance other-fashioning." What we are suggesting is that transversality and translucency may act as mechanisms with an entirely different outcome or purpose for Catherine than for Henry in his performance of himself.
>
> (*Performing Transversally* 175)

'Disappearing' in *Hamlet*, however, is an enterprise of an entirely different character. Unlike in *Henry V*, where winking reveals irony and empowers, in *Hamlet* a wink in the face of the play's deceptions can be fatal. One cannot 'disappear' what one cannot know, except for those doing the plotting successfully in what Anthony Kubiak has termed the 'Hamletic guise.' In fact, in the play, the retributive violence that participates in various 'disappearings' is also presented in Hamletic guise; that is to say, vengeance is *plotted* like the play itself (or any play for that matter) through the machinations of fabrication and deceit, such as feigned madness, the secret taint of the swords, the hidden poisoning of drink. By *Hamlet*'s final act, deceit and vengeance meld into the same; deceit becomes the cause of violence, and violence the agency of deceit.

Behind all deceit, particularly in *Hamlet*, according to the Hamletic model we are proffering here, is the envenomed, plotting character of thought, played out in what transversal theory refers to as 'subjunctive space,' the hypothetical space of both 'as ifs' and 'what ifs' operative in between 'subjective territory' (the conceptual–emotional–physical range from which a given subject perceives and experiences) and 'transversal territory' (the nonsubjectified, transforming space through which people journey when they defy or surpass the boundaries of their subjective territory).[1] The profound relationship between fabrication and 'subjunctive movement' implies a necessity in the organic patterns of thinking that gives rise to emplottedness, deceit, and violence – a kind of murderous Kantian *a priori*. It is as if in some overarching trajectory of natural history, beyond the pale of mere species evolution or accountable spacetime, the primal/primate mind has framed and indeed authored itself as tragedy. To contextualize this idea, we follow Reynolds's understanding of tragedy:

> Several factors determine the extent to which an action or event [such as thinking or a thought] is a tragedy. First of all, as with any performance (defined here as a self-consciously presented expression for an intended audience),[2] how the event is framed needs be taken into consideration. Framing refers to the aesthetic, social, cultural, political, ideological, and historical context established for the performance, whether it takes place in a stage-play or during a sports game or at a particular venue, like in a courtroom, university classroom, chapel, theater, or a pub. The sociopolitical conductors that work to instill our biases and predilections shape our relationship to that context and thus to what is expected to happen there. In most cases, when the framing is less apparent and less understood, the potential for a tragedy-producing performance is greater. In other words, the more sudden and unexpected the injuring action, the more tragic potential it has. But framing also has to do with investment. The degree to which the audience invests itself in the damaging event and its victims emotionally, conceptually, physically, financially – in terms of

spacetime, energy, and emotion – directly affects the potential for tragedy; the greater the investment, the greater the potential for loss, the greater the potential for tragedy.

(*Performing Transversally* 13)

Hence, framed within this rather tragic view of humanity's investiture in itself as a high-risk endeavor combined with the idea of a 'deceitful imperative' is what could be construed as a 'natural' emergence, a conception of tragedy that moves outside of the realm of literary form, convention, or genre, and comes to represent the structure of thought 'comings-to-be' through the biosocial necessity of deceit. This 'comings-to-be' of thought is, moreover, 'framed' in/by mind – the thinking that 'makes it so.' Yet this 'frame of mind' must always remain unseen, unknowable. The 'frame of mind' that turns something into theater is precisely the 'language game' (following Wittgenstein), or the Unconscious (following Freud) that can never be seen in mind – the unseen and unseeable proscenium.

In this formulation, deceit best precipitates success when least expected, especially if misleading or injuring people – physically and psychically – is, in part, the measure of efficacy (we must, of course, remember that the other measure of its efficacy is how much harmony and stability is retained in the social unit through the uses of deceit). When the subject, in this case human thought, loses control during processes of 'becomings-other' and becomes more of/or something else than anticipated and/or desired, comings-to-be are occurring. According to transversal theory, becomings-other are active engagements, usually self-inaugurated and pursued intentionally, whereas comings-to-be, however spurred by becomings, are generated by the energies, ideas, people, societies, and so on to which the subject aspires, is lured toward, or encounters accidentally. Empathy and assimilation are no longer self-consciously accomplished. Instead, they happen unwittingly and unconsciously through ideological, emotional, and/or physiological adaptation and change. Transversal theory refers to the dynamics that cause and are caused by the linked processes of comings-to-be and becomings as 'pressurized belongings.'[3] For a subject to become a member of an alternative group, to incorporate the qualities of a different subjective territory and/or to operate within a foreign official territory, assimilation and expulsion must occur at the expense of aspects of these destinations. The transformed subject causes overflow, expansion, or reconfiguration such that not all of the extant elements can remain or remain the same if the system is to maintain equilibrium.

The point here, however, relates to the selection by humans, however inadvertently, of the specific play, *Hamlet*, as the bellwether play of lies, subjunctivity, and pressurized belongings. Although over-critiqued and palimpsested throughout literary history, *Hamlet* remains framed as The Play in the Euro-American history of performance. It is the play of the world's most celebrated poet, Shakespeare, that is most invested in by dominant sociopolitical conductors (familial, educational, juridical, and governmental structures) of the state machinery (the amalgamation of the conductors that work to foster a cohesive society) of all Western societies because, we would argue, it deceives deceit itself. In effect, *Hamlet* creates a window through which people can become and come-to-be, among other things, Hamletic. *Hamlet* thus exemplifies what transversal theory calls 'deceit conceits,' which are clever schemes involving artifice and fiction performed in order to fracture, transform, and/or expand the conceptual and/or emotional range of an individual or individuals, which is to say, a targeted subjective territory or subjective territories, such as those occupied by many of *Hamlet*'s audiences throughout history. These are audiences who have engaged, to some degree, in the particular 'articulatory space' – a discursive, multidimensional conceptual-emotional interface – that Donald Hedrick and Bryan Reynolds have termed 'Shakespace,'[4] and the sometimes subset, sometimes superset, but nevertheless always related, 'Hamletspace.' Simply put, Shakespeare's play, *Hamlet*, is brilliantly, strategically transversal.

Else and or? Spaces of subjunctivity

Indeed, in Shakespeare's Elsinore, the setting for the action of *Hamlet*, the manipulations, deceits, ironies, and performances – the subjunctive and transversal movements – are multifarious. The character Hamlet pretends madness so that he might uncover the secret of his father's murder (recalling Henry's pretending in *1 Henry IV* to be genuine member of Falstaff's gang only to become the secret of his own success). But the madness is no mere pretense, or rather, the pretense is itself pretended: 'I am but mad north-north-west: when the wind is southerly I know a hawk from a handsaw' (2.2.374–5). His social performance, in other words, is an amalgam of remembering (to act mad) and forgetting (that he is acting), then remembering again (that he is forgetting), *ad infinitum*. Here remembering (to act), and forgetting (that one is acting) are both equally indispensable functions of consciousness, that is, regardless of the subject's subjective territory, certain performances must occur for the subject to be aware of anything, much less itself, operating anywhere in spacetime. Remembering and forgetting are not successes or failures of consciousness, but consciousness in action, performed, sustained.

This is why, in our view, theater is appropriate as a model for understanding consciousness; consciousness depends on theatricality, the continual framing, unframing, and reframing of performances, such as of remembering and of forgetting that one is acting in a particular spacetime; and theater, structurally, reflects consciousness, with its multiple framings and vistas of experience. Theater, then, the communal product of humans, and not the 'Cartesian theater' often imagined as central to the organization of an individual's brain, is phenomena of interactive liveness, sentience, and awareness more apt to understanding consciousness than, say, computer models, such as Stephen Blaha's 'classical probabilistic account,'[5] or Daniel Dennett's 'multiple drafts model,' neither of which consider phenomena of reactive and communicative reciprocity among the brain and entities beyond its own material limits.

Getting back to *Hamlet*, Claudius the killer, remembering and forgetting, reveals himself concealing his crime: 'My words fly up, my thoughts remain below: / Words without thoughts never to heaven go' (3.3.98–9). Aware of, if nothing else, the inappropriateness of Hamlet's performance, Gertrude conceals her complicity (or seeming complicity, if any) by castigating Hamlet in his grief, 'Why seems it so particular with thee?' (1.2.74). She launches her query as if death, indeed regicide and fratricide, had not come to Elsinore, and she thus enjoys still untainted the office of queen, or at least must appear so, having forgot the loss of her husband, and remembering that she has a new one, while all along she remembers to act the role of queen, and forgets any grief that might distract her from this performance. The Machiavellian tricksters Rosencrantz and Guildenstern, subjected to Hamlet's counter machinations, are themselves tricked to death, while Ophelia is humiliated and confounded by Hamlet's seeming and seamy accusations of infidelity; she is thereby pushed into an all-consuming transversality.[6] Hamlet sets up the play within the play by which he will 'catch the conscience of the king,' and the play within *that* play, a dumb show, that doubly inscribes the murderous deed (presumably) done. Theater frames consciousness by which the theatrical world of the play is exposed, made cognizant. A fun house of mirrors that can be outlined, as Herbert Blau has shown, like this: Hamlet sets into motion – precipitating movements among the audience that are recollective, subjunctive, and/or transversal – by means of the play (both large and small) a theatrical panopticon of universal surveillance – Claudius watching the play, Gertrude watching Claudius watch the play, Hamlet watching Gertrude watching Claudius watch the play, Ophelia watching Hamlet, *ad infinitum, ad nauseum*: all speculations and meanings drowned in the concentric wash of the watching.[7] All the while, we, the audience, watch, and are watched, and so on (by the theater's security, our peers, other audience members, the state machinery ...).

Yet these are the more obvious manifestations or symptoms of deceit, the possibility of deceit (the performative deceit) being the immediate cause for the compulsion for surveillance, for the insecurity, uncertainty, and mistrust that deceit breeds. *Hamlet*'s theater is woven of lies given over to our scrutiny, and lies concealed (as we will see later in one of Hamlet's more famous soliloquies). In seducing us with the obvious lie, Shakespeare slips the deeper deceit in the backdoor, so to speak. Thus, while we congratulate ourselves for our perspicacity, we are blindsided by Hamlet who lies to our faces. Finally, there are those lies that exist in a kind of liminal space: Hamlet feigns madness, but then sees ghosts no one else can see, or Hamlet leads Polonius to see whales and weasels where there are none, then leads Horatio to imagine the king/no-king illusively 'frighted with false fire' (3.2.260). We come to suspect that deceit, employed here with purpose as deceit conceit, is more than a human instrumentality; it is an agent of action in the play (personified in Claudius, Hamlet, Rosencrantz, etc.), more than a social or political strategy: *it is an initial state of mind that needs resistance*. Yet whatever honesty does appear is merely honesty grafted onto lies, lies becoming the bedrock of perception (causing another king, Oedipus, to rake out his eyes), and truth nothing but a hallucinatory touchstone grounding the inevitability of deceit. Hence, the play's deceit conceits are, in salvo, a *tour de force* in projective transversality, which is to say that they powerfully promote transversal movements in all subjective territories exposed to the play, even those of the characters within it. Deceit, as the play's ethos, is, in other words, not a perversion of human conduct, but its first principle. We are born to deceit, *Hamlet* suggests, and we must learn the strategies of truth-telling, or rather, we must *unlearn* the Darwinian impulse to lie. Here, we would suggest, transversality would also appear in the extraordinary perversity of truth-telling, resisting the genetic predisposition for deceit.

To be sure, an effect of the many forms and degrees of deceit conceits perpetrated within and by *Hamlet* is to make us – as we are made to move transversally – suspect that there is something radically amiss 'in this distracted globe' (1.5.97), in the The Globe itself, within and beyond the worlds of the play, and in that special space of phantoms that gives the stage its birth: the brain. Brain and stage become one not through the manifestation of the true, the beautiful, the tragic, the imaginary, the artistic, but through the very architectures of deceit, and perhaps no demonstration of deceit in the play is as calculating and nefarious as this:

> Now I am alone.
> O, what a rogue and peasant slave am I!
> Is it not monstrous that this player here
> But in a fiction, in a dream of passion,
> Could force his soul so to his own conceit
> That from her working all his visage wann'd,
> Tears in his eyes, distraction in's aspect,
> A broken voice, and his whole function suiting
> With forms to his conceit? and all for nothing!
>
> (2.2.543–51)

In this aside, the most direct invocation to a Coleridgean 'willing suspension of disbelief,' there seems to be a contract or trust between actor and audience that runs against the grain of the obvious: it operates in violation of 'ocular proof' – so elusive in *Othello* (3.3.366). The actor is, after all, standing on stage, his fellow actors waiting in the wings, cueing on his words, in a theater filled with spectators, all eyes on him. And what is presumed to be an introspective recitative expression must be heard in the back rows: the aside, in other words, like the fourth wall or proscenium in modern theater, is a convention, a lie universally recognized and accepted, and so necessarily invisible and forgotten.

But in this case, the convention is complicated beyond its normal 'confessional' mode. The Beckettian 'all for nothing,' an emotional Black Monday in the collapse of psychic economy, gives us pause, thinking back through the speech in memory: 'Is it not monstrous that this player here ... '. But wait. Which player where? Is Hamlet indicating the recently departed First Player (who is certainly not *here*, but rather *there*, in memory), or himself – and a player twice removed, an equity actor (Derek Jacobi in the canniest of performances, staring with barely concealed mirth at the camera), an actor playing an actor playing the prince of Elsinore feigning madness? Here, in a very real sense, the issue of performativity reaches a kind of conceptual and perceptual crisis: Which is the fiction, who is dreaming the dream of passion, or better, who most obviously telling the lie? The First player, Shakespeare, Hamlet, or Jacobi? Who, and for what purpose? 'For Hecuba!' of course (echoes of Hecate, that devil, patron saint of actors), but then, 'What's Hecuba to him, or he to Hecuba, / That he should weep for her?' (2.2.552–5). Where is the psychic investment? What are the expectations? Where the risk? Who, exactly, is in danger of being found out? Where is the surprise? How, exactly, is Judith Butler's idea of interpellation, the performative, running here? And then the *coup du théâtre*, the lying double bind:

> What would he do,
> Had he the motive and the cue for passion
> That I have? He would drown the stage with tears
> And cleave the general ear with horrid speech,
> Make mad the guilty and appal the free,
> Confound the ignorant, and amaze indeed
> The very faculties of eyes and ears.
> Yet I,
> A dull and muddy-mettled rascal, peak,
> Like John-a-dreams, unpregnant of my cause,
> And can say nothing.
>
> (2.2.559–64)

'What would he do ... . say nothing.' Why, he would do what he (who?) is doing – act. For there is no Hamlet, and never has been – that is certainly one point of the play over time – only 'this player here,' the very knot and configuration of performative deceit, a deceit conceit plainly revealed, but hidden. The deceit conceit exploits the audience's desire for a 'willing suspension of disbelief' and the seeming impossibility of it (both characteristics of Western theater), revealing an audience 'taken' by the con: the grifter gets the mark to willfully give up his money (like the prospect of Catherine being taken from behind), and then the mark's consciousness, upon recognition, is momentarily paused – the surprise: 'I've been taken' – the world has changed. But for whom? For the mark, perhaps, but certainly for the con-man/contra-man, who remains largely unconcerned with the mark's recognition of being-conned. It is of no consequence to the con-man whether the mark ever finds out. It is the game that gives pleasure – the play. And so the traditional anthem – a Hamlet 'unable to act,' a 'John-a-dreams, unpregnant of my cause' – is itself a bald lie: that is all Hamlet can do – he acts. He is most himself, or rather most what he is, when designating himself at the outset, 'this player here … ' (as Macbeth would have us believe, 'That struts and frets his hour upon the stage. … Signifying nothing' [*Macbeth*, 5.5.25–8]). Hamlet tells us to our faces that he, like the first actor, *is* merely acting his passions, just 'pretending,' and we still do not get it because we trust him at his word, believe in his world. We are, Hamlet (or Shakespeare, or Jacobi, or someone …) tells us to our faces, fools.

'What a rogue and peasant slave am I' (*Hamlet* 2.2.544), certainly, but also in the canny way the play surreptitiously begins over and over again, creating a *mise en abîme* of suspicion, skewed perception, and self-delusion: the opening line, 'Who's there?'; Hamlet speaking to the ghost; the play within the play; the final scene, in which Horatio (echoing oration, 'Flights of angels … ' [5.2.366]) gives the order:

> that these bodies
> High on a stage be placed to the view,
> And let me speak to th'yet unknowing world
> How these things came about. So shall you hear
> Of carnal, bloody, and unnatural acts,
> Of accidental judgements, casual slaughter,
> Of deaths put on by cunning and forc'd cause.
>
> (5.2.382–8)

He becomes the freak show barker, the porn show pimp, the stage manager ready to mount the whole bloody business one more time, right from the beginning, creating a new frame, fusing deceit and its strange attractor, repetition ('What, has this thing appeared again tonight?' [1.1.24]), into something like a genome project for theater's yet unformed history – the playing of roles whose scripts lie concealed within the fury of concealment itself, a performativity that is in reality a theater whose promptbooks and castings have been archived in the cultural unconscious, engendered in an interpellative moment that both expands and recedes hopelessly around us: 'Who's there?', but also the turning back, 'Nay, answer me, stand and unfold yourself' (1.1.1–2). And finally, the seeming end to it all in the invocation of the interpellation itself, 'Long live the king!' (1.1.3). But which king is being hailed: the living king or the king dead?

The pith and marrow of our attribute

What is the nature of this maddening interpellative moment? In her book, *Bodies That Matter*, Butler claims that 'in Althusser's notion of interpellation, it is the police who initiate the call' that establishes subjectivity (121). However, it is not only the police in Althusser's essay that initiate the interpellation, but also God, a stranger on the street, and a friend knocking at the door. It is in fact the latter that the old con-man Althusser mentions first, giving a much less authoritarian face to the process of individuation that Butler invokes, encouraging doubt about, say, one's friends, implying that our world is not as it appears, or, rather, that interpellation is not simply the result of cultural authoritarianism, but of something cellular, genetic, primal. This is no mere quibble. Butler's misreading of Althusserian misreadings is indicative of a series of misapprehensions both large and small that are in the end suggestive of critical theory's general misapprehension of apprehension itself, characterized by Butler's failure to understand the theater of her own discourse.

When Althusser introduces his critical notion of interpellation or 'hailing,' he gives the example of a knock on the door, followed by our question, 'Who's there?' (Again, the Hamletic impasse). The friend, still unseen and unknown answers, 'It's me.' We open the door, and discover, indeed, that it is 'her.' Both she and we are constituted through reciprocal acknowledgement of presence. Similarly, out on the street someone yells, 'Hey, you!' and 'nine times out of ten,' according to Althusser, the 'correct person' responds and turns around (173–5). Putting aside the problematic question of where Althusser's 'nine times out of ten' statistic comes from, his claim that this hailing or interpellation works not out of a sense of guilt – such that one says, 'I turn because I know I have done something for which I might be apprehended' – but rather because the turning toward the voice, or the response, 'It's me!,' constitute 'me' as a subject, and so in some way one comes to recognize that interpellative constitution as the means, the only means, by which one comes to exist within a society governed by 'Ideological and Repressive State apparatuses' – what transversal theory refers to as state machinery.[8] The uses in either case of the universal/personal pronouns you/me underscores Althusser's recognition, out of Jacques Lacan, that it is in the pronomial that one is constituted, not as a self with a particular name, but as a subject (of a sentence), therefore constituted in a sentence. Yet one is not necessarily sentenced to subjectivity in this process. One can resist, or even turn the interpellation into aggression: 'Nay, answer me. Stand and unfold yourself' (*Hamlet* 1.1.2).

But apart from the possibility of resistance, there is also in the Althusserian interpellative moment, actually central to it, a misapprehension (*méconnaissance*) – an 'otherness' to recognition that enforces its power. One might say: 'When I am called, I turn because it really is me; I have not been misrecognized. At the same time, I turn to assure myself – hence the common response of pointing to oneself and asking the silently mouthed, "Me? Really?" ' Misrecognition, the surprise, the transversal movement, or its possibility, thus informs the allure of recognition and one's responses to it. Or so Althusser suggests, and Butler reiterates. Butler's contribution to the schema is to suggest that interpellation is not (as Althusser suggests, she claims) unilateral. When one is constituted as an 'I,' there immediately arises the possibility, as we have mentioned, that one will resist the interpellation (as Catherine may 'disappear' Henry).[9]

While both Althusser and Butler are careful to point out that this process of interpellation does not work in the simple, linear, sequential way described, that the interpellative process is an 'always-already,' to quote Althusser, a construction or 'performative' (to use Butler's misappropriation of Austin) that begins literally before we are born (the giving of a name in utero), both Althusser and Butler miss a crucial point: this process of interpellation cannot exist but for theater. Indeed, even though Butler, in her later work, has grudgingly admitted to theatrical resonances in her theory, she is adamant that the interpellative moment, the moment of performativity, is largely beyond our control, and so not, as she supposes theater to be, subject to rehearsal, but is rather reiterative, merely repetition. However, this is impossible, given that events can never be exactly repeated. She is not aware that her subjective territory, like all subjective territories, although scripted and revised in response to changes in sociopolitical conductors, state machinery, official territory, and other forces, needs to be rehearsed, adapted, and produced over and over again to be convincingly affirmed. This requires preparation, practice, interaction, and amendment in negotiation with audiences, and not just reiteration and exclusion, as Butler would have us believe, even if this were possible. To be sure, Butler does not know the secret: that transversal power can be mutually channeled through theater to endow the subject with agency to rehearse, adapt, and produce, and thereby dismiss Butler's own misuse of Austin's term 'performative,' to show it to be an untruth that Butler espouses. Austin's point is that language most often does something (it acts) rather than signifies something and therefore its efficacy can be seen, experienced, and measured.

Butler is not aware that consciousness occupies 'theaterspace,' works like theater, and vice versa. And even Althusser, for all of his invocation to theatrical metaphor in his discussion of the state apparatus, declines the theatrical consciousness suggested in the interpellated moment: 'Hey, you!,' re-echoing of course the Hamletic preamble, spoken by Barnardo, that sets into motion a veritable torrent of interpellation that *fails* again and again throughout the play, exposing a theater at the heart of the interpellative moment, at the moment of performativity that is predicated on the necessary failure of interpellation, a theater at the heart of performativity that has been performance, to be sure, theater, all along.

When Butler misreads this theater as the societal stage – and the stage in its most perverse form, as deceit, robotics, and evacuation – that ensures the failure of all constitutive acts, the outcome of such failure is, ultimately, not liberation (even the restricted liberation of mimicry she imagines), but rather alienation, insanity, poverty, abjection, death. The *absence* of the constituting authoritative interpellation – of framing – does not usher in possibilities for resistance, empowerment, and transformation, but rather the dissolution of identity, selves, and agency – both personal and political. Such attempts in critical theory to reduce authoritative conductors to repressive apparatuses or to negate them, not only fail, but also unproductively oversimplify what are usually complex situations: for all of their repressive tactics and modalities, authorities are often positively experienced across history as organizing mechanisms in the interest of identity formations, state power, and society, and so operate out of necessity – absolutely neither 'good' nor 'evil' – and thus simultaneously supply us with worlds and refuse us entry to other worlds. It is, in fact, the doubleness of authority – in the sense of its Janus-faced ability to deceive and affirm – that constitutes subjects and preconditions tragedy. It is for this reason that theater as a reconfiguring mechanism (a framed, rehearsed, developed, interactive performance praxis) can be a powerful sociopolitical conductor of transversal power self-consciously deployed in order to change the parameters that oblige us to certain authorities, and allow us to change the authorities themselves.

Earth, yield me roots

> For each true word, a blister; and each false
> Be as cauterizing to the root o' th' tongue,
> Consuming it with speaking!
> (Shakespeare, *Timon of Athens* 5.1.131–3)

In line with a research methodology of transversal poetics commonly referred to as the 'investigative-expansive mode,' we would like our discussion to follow a lead. The investigative-expansive mode requires that the subject matter under investigation be divided up into variables that are then partitioned and examined in relation to other influences, both abstract and empirical, beyond the immediate vicinity. A chief objective of this expansive approach is to contextualize historically, ideologically, and critically both the subject matter and the analysis itself within local and greater milieu.

Mobile and vine-like, the investigative – expansive mode resists anything resembling predetermination or circumscription. Instead, it calls for continuous analytical maneuverings and reparameterizations in response to unexpected, even sudden, emergences of glitches, quagmires, and new information as it deduces, trail blazes, follows off-beat leads, and takes tangential excursions. The present analysis encourages us to take just such a tangential foray into a related area of inquiry, primatology, as a means by which to achieve a more expansive perspective on how we are coming to understand deceit and its relationships to theater, consciousness, and transversal power.

Among other things, so far we have seen that the multifarious (or nefarious) nature of deceit is perhaps it's most salient and maddening quality. The forms of deceit are so many and so varied, so seamlessly graded from one type to another, that it is difficult to determine just what the lie is, what constitutes it; and a deceit conceit is typically only recognizable in its revealed achievements, floundering, or failings *vis-à-vis* a designated subjective territory. Still, it may be safe to say that among the many activities that have been seen as consummately human, lying has remained within the realm of the purely social, the performed, and thus the purely human. But do other animals deceive? Of course some animals engage in mimicry (the false coral snake). Some feign injury to protect young (the killdeer). Some play dead to escape harm (the opposum). But do other, non-human animals lie on purpose; or more precisely, do animals know that they deceive; *do animals have a theory of mind*?

This remains an important question because lying has for most of our philosophical history been seen as quintessentially social, quintessentially problematic, and quintessentially a constructed, human activity. The epistemology of lying (philosophy), the ethics of lying (philosophy and theology), the analysis of lying (criminology), the uses of lying (psychology), and, finally, the hermeneutics of lying (psychoanalysis), have all been studied as primarily human behavior. Indeed, Lacan himself asked the question, 'Can animals lie?' and answered "No."[10] And if animals cannot lie, they certainly cannot create illusions, delude others, employ fictions, or construct *mise-en-scènes*. Animals cannot, in effect, translate behaviors from one domain to another through the operations of an unconscious to produce fictive scenes, illusions, theaters. They cannot, that is, *unless they are primates* and primates of a certain level of intelligence. Primates lie, and, moreover, primates do not merely deceive using a theatricalized intelligence, intelligence in primates (and thus in humans) *is* deception. Put differently, intelligence is the combined awareness of deception's possibility and the capacity to imagine and generate creative representations.

This, then, is a true story,[11] a dumb show, not particularly subtle or ingenious, but one accompanied by, as Artaud says of the Theater of Cruelty, 'cries, groans, apparitions, surprises, theatrical tricks ... a kind of unique language halfway between gesture and thought' (245; 242). A baboon, known as

ML in the literary account, digs in the earth, trying to discover 'one poor root.'[12] A young member of the baboon troupe approaches and watches. He is known in the literature as PA. For PA time passes, but PA keeps watch, always keeps watch, yet no one else is there, no one else sees them. ML digs roots, PA watches, and watches to make certain others are not watching. When the root is nearly uncovered, young PA begins to scream. Hair-raising, inconsolable terror. This is what really happened, but here the story is at the same time not true – there is no danger near. No one is attacking him. It is just PA and the other baboon, ML. The troupe's alpha male, JG, hears the cry and appears over the crest of the hill. He shows raw fury, running and striking the digging baboon, who runs a short distance away, and waits for him to disappear over the crest of the hill again. When he is gone, ML resumes digging. PA, the child baboon, watches.

Now here the true story continues, that is also not true: when the root is fully unearthed, the child, PA, again begins to scream. Again, hair-raising terror. But again there is no danger. Again, no one is attacking him. Again, the protective male, JG, appears over the crest of the hill showing bared teeth. This time he runs at the digging ML and chases her away, over the crest of a different hill, and then leaves. The child-baboon, PA, now alone, picks up the cherished and much-planned-for root and begins to eat. He is, perhaps, amused, even delighted at the sensation that tickles the back of his mind. A faint sensation. Deception? Perversity? The perversity of subversion, perhaps. Or perhaps the more disturbing (for us) perversity of the non-perverse: that in the lie (though the story is true) the young baboon is following the very stage directions of a theatricalized, Darwinian mind that simply does not understand its own ... strangeness.

PA has over time used similar subterfuge. Screaming, crying, calling for help, a guardian running to help him, driving others away from food they have discovered – a scheme enabling him to eat it in their stead. Once, twice, five times – a simian conman. And there are countless other scenarios, other actors in the troupe: different deceptions and subterfuges, some so intricate and multilayered that it is at first hard to believe they have been planned and played-out by mere juveniles and primate juveniles at that. In fact, the observations have so intrigued and puzzled primatologists, that, beginning in the late 1980s, a new theory of intelligence (and by extension, we would argue, consciousness) arose; this theory is called 'Machiavellian Intelligence.' Contrary to earlier assumptions – that intelligence developed in primates and subsequently in humans as a result of technical need; that being slower, weaker, lacking claws and individual killing power, primates and humans were selected for an intelligence that allowed for planning, communication, and social cooperation, and thus survival as a group – this new approach argues that intelligence was in fact selected because it allowed for the use of deception within the social sphere, and consequently enabled survival and prosperity of the individual within the group.

According to observations in the field, primatologists began to realize that primate groups, especially the more intelligent and social species (chimpanzees, bonobos, baboons), rarely utilized the sophisticated intelligence with which they were endowed for solving the logistical and 'technological' problems of hunting, group-defense, or food-gathering that supposedly gave rise to higher and higher levels of intelligence. In a follow-up volume to their first book, *Machiavellian Intelligence*, Andrew Whiten and Richard Byrne explain the issue in a succinct preface:

> How can the intelligence of monkeys and apes, and the huge brain expansion that marked human evolution, be explained? In 1988, *Machiavellian Intelligence* was the first book to assemble the early evidence suggesting a new answer: that the evolution of intellect was primarily driven by selection for manipulative, social expertise within groups where the most challenging problem faced by individuals was dealing with their companions.[13]

If Whiten and Byrne are correct (and the issues are controversial), the potential ramifications of this re-definition are enormous and cut across a huge range of post-humanist disciplines: primatology, of course, but studies of human development as well. These include psychology and philosophy, but also the history of consciousness, as well as studies of social behavior, ethnic and gender theory, performance theory, more precisely, and theater theory, primarily. If Whiten and Byrne's ideas hold merit, we might need to re-think central issues in psychoanalysis, Marxism, and critical theory in general: is deception, for example, and thus performance/theater, merely a constructed behavior – is it, in other words, something 'grafted on,' even unconsciously, to operational intelligence, or is intelligence 'always already' deception? Might the perception of deception, an understanding of its etiology, be the highest, most sophisticated form of deception? Are the patterns, plans, outcomes of deception – self or otherwise – ideological? If so, is intelligence possible without ideology? Can, in other words, Marxist analysis claim the ideological high-ground if all analysis itself is predicated upon deception – strategic deceptions from the illusory 'as ifs' of subjunctive space, to the densely argued discourses of propaganda?

While present modes of critical theory might presuppose a certain cynicism permeating the hegemonic forces of late capitalism, while they might, indeed, agree that deception is the rule in capital and not the exception, critical theory would almost to the person claim dispensation from the desperation of the Machiavellian double-bind, a double-bind that goes back at least as far as David Hume: that is, how can we know the truth of what we think? If deceptions, or the more creative 'as ifs' and 'what ifs' of subjunctivity, are the very *substance* and substrate of thought, if 'the problem of representation' is not merely that it slips, or misses its object, but purposely leads us astray in a kind of perpetual gaming that is the very mechanism of our survival, then is not the rational, even in its guise as poststructural skepticism, which is to say, critical theory, nothing more than 'always already' self-parody? As a discipline, critical theory, we think, would, predominantly, say no. Conveniently, this is because the gaming and illusions of thought and culture can be re-apprehended, re-deconstructed, the fantasy can be recast, 'consciousness raised' again, ideological misperceptions corrected, if only partially, or 'contingently.' For example, in her book, *Simians, Cyborgs, and Women*, and again in *Primate Visions*, Donna Haraway describes, in the work of primatologists, something like the humanization of primate groups, or more precisely, the projection of ideologies of gender onto those groups. As she puts it, 'Scientific debate about monkeys, apes, and humans, that is, about primates, is a social process of producing stories, important stories that constitute public meanings' (81). She continues:

> We find the themes of modern America reflected in detail in the bodies and lives of animals. We polish an animal mirror to look for ourselves.... . The science of non-human primates, primatology, may be a source of insight or a source of illusion. The issue rests on our skill in the construction of mirrors. (21)

While following the now unquestioned Foucaultian assertion that knowledge is constructed not discovered, even empirical, scientific knowledge, Haraway forages blindly before the subterfuge of her own intellect, an intellect that, in the terms of Machiavellian Intelligence, is born neither through a need to construct or discover, nor through a need to master an environment through technique, but rather, through the need for deceit, machination (cybernetic or otherwise), and self-delusion. Both primate and human intelligence came into being – underwent comings-to-be – because it was naturally selected for its ability to produce deceptive behavior. By extension, we are referring to the lies and subterfuges, that, along with cooperative behavior, constitute social and cultural life (subterfuge cannot work, after all, unless there is trust and cooperation seemingly ahead of it). This predicament, as evidenced in Haraway's conclusions, suggests a rather profound and disturbing possibility that even the primatologists often miss: human intellect is not merely prone to dissembling, dissembling is no mere weakness within human character and mind, no aberration or 'subversive' activity, dissembling and deceit are, again, what constitute mind – a mind constructed, as we have said, in the subjunctive modes of 'as if' and 'what if,' in the interstices between subjective and transversal territories.

Against the accusation that such a view is overly cynical, we should remind ourselves that what is remarkable are not the sins of a species so determined, but the apparent altruism that seems to outweigh the self-interest (we have, after all, survived this long). To be sure, Machiavellian theorists would argue that self-interest, in the final analysis, is necessary to social survival at both the individual and group level: this aspect of intelligence is what allows the physically weaker (though perhaps smarter and more creative) members of the group to survive and thrive. In fact, this Machiavellian aspect of intelligence, contra Machiavelli himself, serves the purposes of the weaker individual far more than it serves the interests of the prince, or president, who everyone, in the political scheme of things, suspects is lying. And if, as Haraway might argue, the primatologists are merely seeing their own nefarious scientific practices in the actions of primates, although this is doubtful given the secretly filmed, non-edited simian sequences demonstrating deceit the primatologists provide as evidence, the idea of this projection merely begs the question all over again: Why would critical intelligence fail so easily and obviously unless in some sense consciousness wanted to be deceived – wanted to be lied to even when it knows it is being lied to (picture Derek Jacobi delivering Hamlet's 'what a rogue and peasant slave am I' speech). In other words, if primatologists are projecting their own deceit onto innocent apes, what does that say about the deep structure of mind, the unconscious itself?

Critical theory, especially in its more political modalities, still seems to believe itself capable of discovering the secret ideologies of capitalism, the substrate of sexism, or the representational malaise of gender itself, while believing its own agendas to be relatively transparent. Theater, we would submit, or at least the theater that is the very embodiment of the Machiavellian mind, is not so sure. Theater, the very subjunctive location of deception, subterfuge, and creativity at polymorphous and multifarious levels, because of its ability to willfully move transversally, has always known the lying truth of the Machiavellian mind, while critical theory, in its affirmation of the possibilities of intellectual liberation, however slight, gained through endless analyses (often in bad faith) of 'dominant culture,' has for the most part willingly suspended disbelief in its own secret agendas and self-delusional scams. It is through the transversal power of theater, perhaps in collaboration with the critical theory that – while playing its own games – elucidates theater's opportunities, that worlds can be changed. This can happen through the transposition of deceit in theater, through deceit conceits that work simultaneously to project transversally deceit-as-other outside of subjective and official territories and to reconfigure subjunctively deceit-as-becomings. As both the mind it reflects and the praxis it performs, theater can expand our understanding and experience of deceit to include unlimited, positive potentialities in the worlds it ingeniously creates. But this, perhaps, may be impossible, if consciousness' first impulse is indeed to deceive: whereas we might believe we are working for enlightenment and liberation, we may be, unbeknownst to us, seeking our own desecrations and death. What do you tell yourself?

Notes

1. For more on 'subjunctive space' see Bryan Reynolds, 'Transversal Performance: Shakespace, the September 11 Attacks, and the Critical Future' in his *Performing Transversally: Reimagining Shakespeare and the Critical Future* (New York: Palgrave Macmillan, 2003): 1–28. For detailed discussion on 'subjective territory' and 'transversal territory' beyond coverage in this book, see Bryan Reynolds: 'The Devil's House, "or worse": Transversal Power and Antitheatrical Discourse in Early Modern England' (*Theatre Journal* 49.2 [1997]: 143–67); *Becoming Criminal: Transversal Performance and Cultural Dissidence in Early Modern England* (Baltimore: John Hopkins University Press, 2002), 1–22; and *Performing Transversally: Reimagining Shakespeare and the Critical Future* (New York: Palgrave Macmillan, 2003), 1–28.
2. But we need to ask, of course, if this is in fact how 'performance' or the performative is currently understood. Rather, out of Butler et al., performance seems precisely that mode of 'doing' that *lacks* self-consciousness. 'Performance,' as the term is currently employed, seems to mean little more than 'doing.' See in this regard Jon McKenzie, *Perform or Else: From Discipline to Performance* (New York: Routledge Press, 2001).
3. The term 'pressurized belongings' was coined by Glenn Odom and Bryan Reynolds in their essay, 'Becomings Roman/Comings-to-be Villain: Pressurized Belongings and the Coding of Ethnicity, Religion, and Nationality in Shakespeare's *Titus Andronicus*,' which is forthcoming in Bryan Reynolds, *Transversal Enterprises in the Drama of Shakespeare and His Contemporaries: Fugitive Explorations* (London: Palgrave Macmillan).
4. On Shakespace, see Donald Hedrick and Bryan Reynolds, 'Shakespace and Transversal Power,' in Hedrick and Reynolds, eds., *Shakespeare Without Class*: 3–50; and for more on articulatory spaces, see Reynolds, *Performing Transversally*: 1–28.
5. See Stephen Blaha, *Cosmos and Consciousness: Quantum Computers, Super Strings, Programming, Egypt, Quarks, Mind Body Problem, and Turing Machines* (Auburn, New Hampshire: Pingree-Hill Publishing, 2002) and Daniel Dennett, *Consciousness Explained* (Boston: Little, Brown and Company, 1991).
6. See Jacques Lacan, 'Desire and the Interpretation of Desire in *Hamlet*,' *Literature and Psychoanalysis: The Question of Reading: Otherwise*, ed. Shoshana Felman (Baltimore: Johns Hopkins University Press, 1982).
7. Herbert Blau, *The Dubious Spectacle: Extremities of Theater, 1976–2000* (Minneapolis: University of Minnesota Press, 2002): 107.
8. Reynolds coined the term state machinery for a society's governmental assembly of conductors as a corrective to the political philosophy of Althusser. With state machinery, a term that simultaneously connotes singularity and plurality, he adapted Althusser's conception of what he calls the 'Repressive State Apparatus,' which includes the governmental mechanisms, such as the military and the police, that strive to control our bodies, and fused it with his subsidiary 'Ideological State Apparatuses,' the inculcating mechanisms that strive to control our thoughts and emotions. Reynolds emphasizes that a society's drive for governmental coherence is always motivated by assorted conductors of state-oriented organizational power that are at different times and to varying degrees always both repressive and ideological. This is a sociopower dynamic in which various conductors work, sometimes individually and sometimes in conjunction with other conductors, to substantiate their own positions of power within the sociopolitical field. Hence, use of the term state machinery should make explicit the multifarious and discursive nature of state power, and thus prevent the misperception of the sociopower

dynamic as the result of a conspiracy led by a monolithic state. This is not to say, however, that conspiracies do not occur and take the form of state factions. On the contrary, this must be the case for the more complex machinery to run. See Reynolds, *Becoming Criminal*, 1–22.
9. The very process that constitutes a 'me,' therefore, is the means through which an 'I' can challenge that constitution. Dick Hebdige perhaps says it best when discussing the punk movements of the seventies: the reason for the piercing, provocatively torn clothing and scarification of punk teenagers living within the surveillances of the British police and social service agencies was designed to 'make being looked at an aggressive act.' The quote is from a talk Dick Hebdige gave at the University of Wisconsin in 1985 at the Center for 20th Century Studies.
10. See, for example, Lacan's discussion of signification in the process of analysis in *Ecrits: A Selection*, translated by Bruce Fink (New York: Norton, 2002), 88–90.
11. Perhaps this is the central concern of this essay, the very assertion 'this is a true story': what, exactly, does truth amount to in fiction, in narrative, in theater? How can we believe anything, even our capacity to lie, given that deceit is the ground condition of consciousness? Even more disturbing, how can you (the reader) believe what you are reading at this very moment? What are *your* (whose?) secret agendas, self-delusions, con-games? How can you, finally, even believe in the presence of deceit, if deceit is the condition of consciousness? What, in other words, we see in the primates' lies and deceits is being recapitulated at this very moment, in this very essay. What are we not telling you? What are we leaving out of the story? What theoretical niceties are we invoking, not to elucidate, but to, in essence, cover-up what we do not want you (or ourselves) to know or think about? Paranoia, or simply fear, of 'being on the outside, being politically misaligned, not gettng tenure ... '.
12. The following baboon story is taken from Richard Byrne and Andrew Whiten's Machiavellian Intelligence: Social Expertise and the Evolution of Intellect in Monkey, Apes, and Humans (Oxford: Clarendon Press, 1988) chapter 15.
13. Byrne and Whiten, *Machiavellian Intelligence*: front material.

Works cited

Althusser, Louis. 'Ideology and the State.' In *Lenin and Philosophy*. New York: Monthly Review Press, 1971.

Artaud, Antonin. 'The Theater of Cruelty: First Manifesto.' In *Antonin Artaud: Selected Writing*. Ed. and introduction Susan Sontag. New York: Farrar, Straus and Giroux, 1976.

Blaha, Stephen. *Cosmos and Consciousness: Quantum Computers, Super Strings, Programming, Egypt, Quarks, Mind Body Problem, and Turing Machines*. Auburn, New Hampshire: Pingree-Hill Publishing, 2002.

Blau, Herbert. *The Dubious Spectacle: Extremities of Theater, 1976–2000*. Minneapolis: University of Minnesota Press, 2002.

Byrne, Richard and Andrew Whiten. 'Tactical deception of familiar individuals in baboons.' In *Machiavellian Intelligence: Social Expertise and the Evolution of Intellect in Monkeys, Apes, and Humans*. Edited by Richard Byrne and Andrew Whiten. Oxford: Clarendon Press, 1988.

Butler, Judith. *Bodies That Matter: On the Discursive Limits of 'Sex.'* New York: Routledge: New York, 1993.

Dennett, Daniel. *Consciousness* Explained. Boston: Little, Brown and Company, 1991.
Haraway, Donna. *Primate Visions: Gender, Race, and Nature in the World of Modern Science*. New York: Routledge, 1989.
Hedrick, Donald and Bryan Reynolds. ' "A little touch of Harry in the Night": Translucency and Projective Transversality in the Sexual and National Politics *of Henry V*,' in Bryan Reynolds, *Performing Transversally: Reimagining Shakespeare and the Critical Future*. Palgrave Macmillan: New York, 2003: 171–88.
——. 'Shakespace and Transversal Power,' in Hedrick and Reynolds, Ed., *Shakespeare Without Class: Misappropriations of Cultural Capital* (New York: Palgrave Macmillan, 2000): 3–50.
——. *Machiavellian Intelligence II: Extensions and Evaluations*. Edited by Andrew Whiten and Richard Byrne. Cambridge: Cambridge University Press, 1997.
Reynolds, Bryan. *Performing Transversally: Reimagining Shakespeare and the Critical Future*. Palgrave Macmillan: New York, 2003.
——. *Simians, Cyborgs, and Women*. New York: Routledge, 1991.
Shakespeare, William. *King Henry V*, Ed. Andrew Gurr. Cambridge and New York: Cambridge University Press, 1992.
——. *Macbeth*. Ed. Kenneth Muir. London: Methuen, 1951.
——. *Hamlet*. The Arden Shakespeare. Ed. Harold Jenkins. New York: Routledge, 1989, 1990.
——. *Timon of Athens*. The Arden Shakespeare. Ed. H. J. Oliver. New York. Methuen, 1959.

Index

academic professionalism, 1, 6–11, 139, 141, 154, 204, 222
affective presence, 11, 15, 16n11
Alleyn, Edward, 35–6, 45, 53–4, 61, 66–7, 69n14, 76, 85–6, 91, 201
Althusser, Louis, 223n8; *see also* interpellation
antitheatricalism, 21–4, 26–9, 174–5, 200–1, 204, 216–17
Aristotle, 70n36, 77, 92n7, 121, 155n21, 174, 180n58
Artaud, Antonin, 218
articulatory spaces, 7, 210
Austin, J.L., *see* performative
authority, 15, 21–4, 38, 41, 44, 66, 97, 132–3, 142–4, 147–8, 152, 215–17; *see also* bifold authority
self-authorization, 24, 116

Bakhtin, Mikhail, 92n8, 139–40, 146, 153, 164
Beaumont, Francis, and John Fletcher, *Knight of the Burning Pestle*, 195–7
becoming(s), 10, 12–13, 16n13, 207–9; *see also* comings-to-be
bifold authority, 12, 42, 78–9, 92n9, 116, 127, 217; *see also* doubleness
Bloom, Harold, 1, 77
Brecht, Bertolt, 8, 59, 144–5, 153
Burbage, Richard, 53–4, 69n18
Butler, Judith, 213–17

Caesar Augustus, 36
Caesar, Julius, 35–6, 39, 43, 45, 75, 109–10
Calvin, John, 25, 29, 31n10, 32n18, 33n26, 33n29, 33n35
Cary, Elizabeth, *Tragedy of Maryam*, 87
Castle of Perseverance, 59–60
Catholics and Catholicism, 9, 19–27, 31n13, 33n27, 167–8, 178–9n36, 179n37, 202
Chapman, George, 101–2
The Widow's Tears, 101
Eastward Ho!, *see* Jonson, Ben

Chettle, Henry, 69n4
and Thomas Dekker, *Troilus and Cressida*, 54, 56, 69n4
and Anthony Munday, *The Downfall of Robert, Earl of Huntington*, 103
codes of performance, 47–8, 79–80, 83, 111, 116, 130, 132–3, 135, 213; *see also* performance styles, theatrical wonder
comings-to-be, 10, 209, 221; *see also* becoming(s)
contrariety, 12, 78–9, 86, 125–6, 134; *see also* doubleness
Coventry Corpus Christi cycle, 87–8
The Coxcomb, 196
Cratylism, 115, 121, 125
cultural materialism, 6, 8–9, 79, 139; *see also* materialism, new historicism
Curtis, Richard, *The Skinhead Hamlet*, 130, 136–7
The Custom of the Country, 196
cycle drama, *see* Coventry Corpus Christi cycle, medieval drama

Day, John, *Isle of Gulls*, 195
deceit conceits, 210, 212–14, 218–19
deceitful imperative, 209
De Certeau, Michel, 39, 47, 79
decorum, 54, 96–8, 102–7, 126, 161–2, 171
Dekker, Thomas, 69n4, 174, 195–9
If This be not a Good Play, the Devil is in It, 199
Satiromastix, 84–5
and Webster, John, *Westward Ho!*, 200–1
Troilus and Cressida, *see* Chettle, Henry
Deleuze, Gilles, 12, 16n13; *see also* Guattari, Félix
Derrida, Jacques, 12, 16n12, 49n20, 139, 141–3, 150–2, 154
Descartes, René, 161, 171, 210–11
doubleness, 12, 42, 67, 152–3, 172, 217; *see also* bifold authority; contrariety

Edwardes, Richard, *Damon and Pythias*, 56
Elizabeth I, 55
Elvis (Presley), 82
emergent activity, 11, 152
emergent community, 11, 13
emergent property, 11, 13, 16n10

Ford, John, 197–8
Foucault, Michel, 47, 141, 144, 150–2, 154–5n21, 167, 221
Freud, Sigmund, 67, 209
Freudian, 122, *see also* psychoanalysis

Garber, Marjorie, 38–9, 47
Gascoigne, George, 97, 111n8
  Supposes, 97
  and Francis Kinwelmershe, *Jocasta*, 97
Globe, the (Shakespeare's company's theater), 43, 48, 75, 134, 212
Goffe, Thomas, *The Careless Shepherdess*, 186–92, 194, 196
Greenblatt, Stephen, 1, 31n7, 76, 79, 128n19, 141
Greene, Robert, 83–5, 92n16, 95–6, 99–100, 103
  Alphonsus, King of Aragon, 83–6, 92n16
  Friar Bacon and Friar Bungay, 99
  George a Greene, Pinner of Wakefield, 99
  James IV, 99
  Orlando Furioso, 85
  and Thomas Lodge, *A Looking Glass for London and England*, 99
Guattari, Félix, *see* Deleuze, Gilles

Habington, William, *Queen of Aragon*, 192–3
Halimpsest, *see* principle of translucency
Haraway, Donna, 221–2
Harris, Jonathan Gil, 6–7, 166
Hawkes, David, 15n5, 200, 203
Hedrick, Donald, 7, 79–80, 207, 210
Hegel, Georg Wilhelm Friedrich, 12, 16n13, 88–91, 147
Heidegger, Martin, 149–50, 155–6n21, 156n22
  'world-picturing' system, 95–9, 111n1, 149–50, 168–9
Herod and Antipater, 87
history, 8, 11, 13, 37–42, 76–7, 80, 89–90, 126, 139, 147, 154n3; *see also* Hegel, Georg Wilhelm Friedrich

Horne, Kenneth, *see* 'Round the Horne'
Howard, Jean, 50n35

image, 3, 14–15, 19–26, 38, 65–6, 124–5; *see also* Heidegger, 'world-picturing' system
icon, 1–2, 14–15, 168
iconoclasm, 8, 20–2
idols and idolatry, 19–26, 28, 31n13, 32n21, 33n31
imaginary, the, 8–12, 20, 38, 116–17, 119, 122–4, 151, 180n45, 212
imagination, 75, 122, 141, 151, 167, 179n40, 207–8
impersonation, *see* personation
interpellation, 79, 213, 215–17
intertheatricality, 75–80, 83, 85–6, 88, 90–1
investigative–expansive mode (i.e. mode), 8, 217–18

James VI and I, 35–9, 41, 44–8, 166, 196–7
Jameson, Frederic, 116, 128n6, 145
Jonson, Ben, 35–7, 44, 47, 85, 101, 112n17, 116, 174, 180n57, 193–4, 196, 198–9, 202–4
  The Alchemist, 202
  Bartholomew Fair, 193–4, 196, 198, 202
  George Chapman, and John Marston, *Eastward Ho!*, 101

Kubiak, Anthony, 7, 208
Kyd, Thomas, *The Spanish Tragedy*, 99
  Soliman and Perseda, 83, 92n14, 92n16

Lacan, Jacques, 180n45, 215, 218, 224n10
locus/platea, 42–4, 45–6, 77–8, 80, 89, 140, 153, 172
Lodge, Thomas, 99–100, 103
  A Looking Glass for London and England, *see* Greene, Robert
Lupton, Julia Reinhard, 20–1, 27, 31n7
Luther, Martin, 28–9, 32n21, 168, 178–9n36, 179n37; *see also* Protestantism; Reformation
Lyly, John, 56, 80, 97, 100–1
  Mother Bombie, 62–3
  The Woman in the Moon, 100

228   *Index*

magic, 12, 20–3, 25–8, 31, 32n25, 174,
Machiavelli, Niccolo, 192, 211, 220–2
    'Machiavellian Intelligence', 219–21
Marlowe, Christopher, 15, 76, 84, 88,
    92n16, 95, 98–100, 103, 112n11, 172
    Tamburlaine 1 and *2*, 84, 86, 98–9, 172
    Jew of Malta, 99, 196
    Doctor Faustus, 99
Marston, John, 101–4
    The Dutch Courtesan, 101
    Parasitaster, or the Fawn, 102
    Histriomastix, 172
    Eastward Ho!, *see* Jonson, Ben
Marx, Karl, 9, 77, 89, 143
    Marxism, 6, 8–9, 139–45, 148, 151,
    154, 220; *see also* materialism
materialism, 7, 77, 95, 139, 152
medieval drama, 20, 47, 50, 59–60,
    76–80, 86–8, 97, 143–4; *see also*
    codes of performance; individual
    play titles
Medwall, Henry, *Nature*, 97
Middleton, Thomas, *A Game at Chess*,
    202
    and William Rowley, *The Changeling*,
    189
mimesis, 9, 39, 57–61, 65–6, 68, 79,
    126–7, 140–5, 149, 151–4, 170–2,
    188, 212–14; *see also* presentation/
    representation
moral play, *see* medieval drama
Munday, Anthony, 175
    *The Downfall of Robert, Earl of
    Huntington*, *see* Chettle, Henry
    Fedele and Fortuno, 97
mystery play, *see* medieval drama

name(s), 39, 47, 92n10, 115, 117–21,
    123, 135; *see also* Cratylism;
    nominalism
new historicism, 8–9, 79, 149; *see also*
    cultural materialism
new histrionicism, 79, *see also* virtuosity,
    actors'
Nietzsche, Friedrich, 12, 144, 169
nominalism, 118–21
Northampton *Abraham and Isaac*, 59

Occidental/Oriental palimpsest, 76–7, 90
official territory, 11

Paul, 21–5, 27–30, 178–9n36
Peele, George, 95, 83, 85–6, 92n15, 95,
    100, 103, 112n12
    Battle of Alcazar, 56, 67, 69n14, 83,
    85–6, 92n18
performance styles, 19–21, 25–7,
    41–4, 58–61, 76, 80–1, 87–9,
    95–9, 111, 116, 120, 134–5,
    140, 142–4, 171–3; *see also* codes of
    performance; mimesis
performative, 126, 127n2, 146, 153,
    211–17, 223n2
personation, 59–60, 63, 68, 153;
    see also presentation/
    representation
Petrarchism, 115–25
platea, *see* locus/ platea
Plato, 121, 151–2; *see also* Cratylism
popular culture, 3–4, 6, 35, 76–9, 83–4,
    130, 132–7, 140, 152–3, 173,
    189–90, 201–4
presentation/ representation, 38, 59,
    63–6, 68, 77–8, 95, 105–6, 116,
    126–7, 152–2, 169–70; *see also*
    mimesis; personation
Preston, Thomas, *Cambyses*, 78, 80–2,
    92n14
principle of translucency, 75–9, 81, 89,
    172, 207; *see also* codes of
    performance
projective transversality, 10, 79,
    207, 212
Protestantism, *see* Reformation
psychoanalysis, 122, 179n40, 180n45,
    218, 220; *see also* Freud, Sigmund;
    Lacan, Jacques

The Rare Triumphs of Love and Fortune,
    96–9
Reformation, 9, 20–31, 31n13, 32n21,
    67, 148–9, 167–8, 178–9n36,
    203–4
rematerialization, 9–13
Return from Parnassus, 102
Reynolds, Bryan, 7, 15n6, 16n7, 16n8,
    79–80, 207–8, 210
Rome, 35–48, 110–11
'Round the Horne' (BBC radio program),
    8, 130–6
Rowley, William, 197–8

Sackville, Thomas, and Norton,
  Gorboduc, 97
Saussure, Ferdinand, 12, 15, 124, 152
Scarry, Elaine, 162
Second Maiden's Tragedy, 87
semiotics, 9, 12, 15n3, 77, 79–80, 121–7, 135, 137–8, 142–9, 153–4; *see also* codes of performance; Cratylism, nominalism, Saussure, Ferdinand
sexuality, 8–9, 54–6, 61–6, 70n36, 127n2, 130–5, 137, 164–5, 207–9, 220–2
Shakespeare, William, *passim*
  Anthony and Cleopatra, 53, 68
  All's Well That Ends Well, 55, 131
  As You Like It, 53–5, 57, 62, 67–8, 103, 130–2
  Hamlet, 7–8, 12–13, 55, 57, 59, 69n18, 86–7, 89, 96, 108–11, 153, 164, 170–1, 175, 207–19, 222
  1 Henry IV, 76, 80–2, 85–6, 88, 92n17, 108–9, 136, 197, 210
  2 Henry IV, 63, 75–6, 80, 82–3, 85–6, 88–9, 92n17
  Henry V, 79–80, 87–8, 207–8, 216
  2 Henry VI, 162
  3 Henry VI, 174–5
  Henry VIII, 20, 55, 112n12
  Julius Caesar, 37, 39–48, 57, 110–11
  King John, 57–63, 66–7
  King Lear, 108, 173
  Love's Labours Lost, 62–3
  Macbeth, 61–3, 81, 173, 214
  Measure for Measure, 55, 108, 171
  The Merchant of Venice, 85, 108
  The Merry Wives of Windsor, 63, 87
  A Midsummer Night's Dream, 55–6, 78–9, 85, 151
  Much Ado About Nothing, 30, 55, 131
  Othello, 30, 54, 57, 61–2, 108, 170–1, 175, 212,
  Richard II, 167, 202
  Richard III, 55
  Romeo and Juliet, 15, 53, 57, 68, 115–27
  The Taming of the Shrew, 81, 87, 96, 105–8
  The Tempest, 27, 29
  Timon of Athens, 217
  Troilus and Cressida, 67, 69n4, 92n9
  Twelfth Night, 30, 128n20, 171
  Two Gentlemen of Verona, 62, 120–1, 131
  The Winter's Tale, 19–31, 61, 63–5, 67–8, 173
Shakespace, 7–8, 10–12, 15n6, 116n7, 210
Sidney, Philip, 96, 128n15, 174
sociopolitical conductors, 10, 208, 210, 216–17
Soliman and Perseda, see Kyd, Thomas
Stallybrass, Peter, 6, 155–6n21, 164–5
state machinery, 210–11, 215–16, 223n8
subject, identity-formation, 12, 67, 99, 118–20, 122, 141–2, 147–52, 162–7, 215–16; *see also* subjective territory
subjectification, *see* subjective territory
subjective territory, 13, 209, 216
subjunctive space, 13, 208, 220–2
subjunctivity, 220

Tamar Cam, 61, 85
theatrical wonder, *see* wonder, theatrical
theater space, 35–48, 75, 153, 173, 216; *see also* Globe, the
theological wonder, *see* wonder, theological
translucent effect, *see* principle of translucency
transversal theory, 91, 77–9, 209–10; *see also* Reynolds, Bryan; Shakespace; state machinery; subjective territory
transversal poetics, 9–10
transversal territory, 208
The Two Merry Milkmaids, 199–200

Udall, Nicholas, 62
  Roister Doister, 56–7

virtuosity, actors', 68, 76–8, 86, 108–10, 196, 213–14

A Warning for Fair Women, 174, 195
Webster, John, 197–9
  The White Devil, 199
  Westward Ho!, 200–1, *see* Dekker, Thomas
Weimann, Robert, 21, 41, 59, 63, 68, 77–80, 86, 91, 95, 139–56, 172–3; *see also* bifold authority; *locus/ platea*

Weimann, Robert – *continued*
   Authority and Representation in Early Modern Discourse, 9–10, 21, 95, 111n1, 147–51, 176n2
   Author's Pen and Actor's Voice, 12, 15n1, 42, 47, 50n35, 59, 68, 78–9, 86, 127n4, 140, 145, 149, 151–4, 172, 180n47,
   Prologues to Shakespeare's Theatre, 10–11, 115–16, 127n4, 151, 153
   Shakespeare and the Popular Tradition in Theater, 6, 8, 42, 77–8, 139–40, 143, 155n6
   Structure and Society in Literary History, 140–3

Whetstone, George, *Promos and Cassandra*, 97
The Whore New Vamp'd, 198
Williams, Kenneth, 136; *see also* 'Round the Horne'
Williams, Raymond, 11, 178n32; *see also* emergent property
Wilson, Robert, *The Three Ladies of London*, 97, 99
   The Three Lords and Three Ladies of London, 99–100
wonder
   theatrical, 19–20, 24–5, 27, 30
   theological, 19–25